CONCEPTS AND CHALLENGES IN

Life Science

Annotated Teacher's Edition
Revised Third Edition

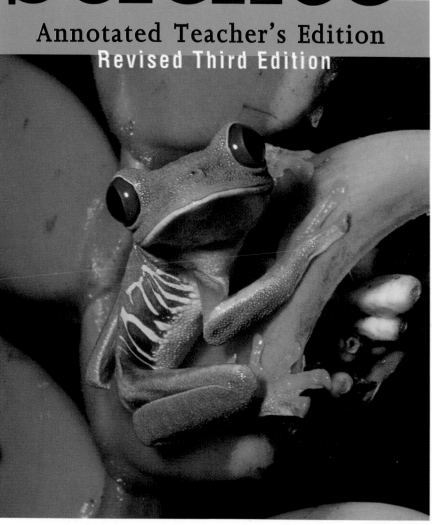

Leonard Bernstein • Martin Schachter • Alan Winkler • Stanley Wolfe

STANLEY WOLFE
Project Coordinator

Globe Fearon Educational Publisher
A Division of Simon & Schuster
Upper Saddle River, New Jersey

AUTHORS
Leonard Bernstein
Martin Schachter
Alan Winkler
Stanley Wolfe
  Project Coordinator

TEACHING THE COVER

Background: Avocado leaf *(Eduardo Garcia, FPG)*
The leaf is a food-making factory. Leaf structure is
adapted for transportation of raw materials needed for
and products produced by photosynthesis. A network of
veins in the leaf surface conduct the exchange of oxygen
and carbon dioxide with the surrounding air. Cells in the
leaf interior are loaded with chloroplasts. The chloroplasts
contain the pigment chlorophyll, which imparts the green
color to the leaf. To help your students learn more about
leaves, see pages 150–153. For more information, visit
this web site on the internet:
http://www.mbgnet.mobot.org/MBGnet

Inset: Red-eyed tree frog *(G. Bradley and J. Ireland)*
This nocturnal amphibian lives in trees in moist tropical
forests of Central and South America. The tips of its toes
are enlarged to form adhesive pads, which help it climb
on and cling to the moist surfaces of leaves and twigs. To
help your students learn more about amphibians, see
page 198. For information about this frog, visit this web
site on the internet:
*http://eagle.online.discovery.com/DCO/doc/1012/world/nature/
    frog/treefrogs1.html*

Printed in the United States of America
  2 3 4 5 6 7 8 9 10   01 00 99 98

ISBN 0-835-92244-8

Globe Fearon Educational Publisher
A Division of Simon & Schuster
Upper Saddle River, New Jersey

Contents

CONCEPTS AND CHALLENGES IN LIFE SCIENCE PROGRAM

Student's Edition

Annotated Teacher's Edition

Teacher's Resource Book including

Lesson Review Worksheets
TechTerm Review Worksheets
Enrichment Worksheets
Evaluation Package
Foreign Language Supplement—Spanish

Laboratory Program, Student Edition

Laboratory Program, Annotated Teacher's Edition

CONCEPTS AND CHALLENGES

In Life, Earth, and Physical Science

Revised Third Edition

As we move into the 21st century, educators agree that teaching science successfully requires special tools. The essentials include a strategy for teaching that maximizes the potential for learning success and maintains a high level of interest and motivation in the classroom.

Concepts and Challenges in Life, Earth, and Physical Science translates this strategy into a practical teaching and learning tool. Students often wonder how science relates to their daily lives. *Concepts and Challenges* addresses this issue by emphasizing everyday experiences to show students that science is all around them.

Over the past decade, almost one million *Concepts and Challenges* textbooks have been used in classrooms throughout the nation. The Revised Third Edition continues to maximize your students' potential for learning success. Experience *Concepts and Challenges* and help your students relate to science while they develop their problem-solving skills, expand their vocabulary, and strengthen their critical-thinking skills.

A wealth of resources to introduce your students to a wide range of science topics.

Life Science

Covering a broad spectrum of topics, this text provides a fascinating introduction to the myriad life forms that inhabit our world. Students will also learn about the many variables that affect life: The diseases that afflict different organisms... the effect of ecology on plants and animals... how various life forms adapt to changes.

Unit Topics: Scientific Methods and Skills • Needs of Living Things • Ecology • Cells, Tissues and Organs • Classification • Simple Organisms • Plants • Plant Structure and Function • Animals Without Backbones • Animals With Backbones • Nutrition and Digestion • Support and Movement • Transport • Respiration and Excretion • Regulation and Behavior • Health and Disease • Reproduction and Development • Heredity and Genetics • Change Through Time

Earth Science

From our own world to the outer reaches of space, the text teaches all about the earth, and also explores other heavenly bodies of the universe. Students will gain insights into the various characteristics that make the earth unique in the solar system, and learn how the objects and phenomena of the universe that they study affect the way we live on our planet.

Unit Topics: Scientific Skills and Methods • Studying the Earth • Minerals • Rocks and How They Form • Wearing Down the Earth • Agents of Erosion • Building up the Earth • Plate Tectonics • The Rock Record • The Hydrosphere • The Atmosphere • Weather • Climate • Natural Resources • Exploring Space • The Solar System • Motions of the Earth • Stars

Physical Science

The principles, theories, and assumptions that guide our understanding of the world and universe are explored in this text. Physics, chemistry, and mathematics are just some of the major topics that help students comprehend the processes that shape every aspect of the universe. They'll learn what causes reflections in a mirror... the nature of matter... how machines work... and more.

Unit Topics: Scientific Methods and Skills • Force • Energy and Work • Motion • Machines • Heat • Waves • Sound • Light • Electricity • Magnetism • Matter • Density • Atoms • Compounds and Mixtures • Chemical Formulas • Chemical Reactions • Metals • Solutions • Suspensions • Acids, Bases, and Salts

THE STUDENT EDITION

This, the Revised Third Edition of a time-tested class-room favorite, continues the features that have made the *Concepts and Challenges in Science* approach to science instruction successful.

The key to the *Concepts and Challenges* approach is student books designed to help students who are reading below grade level to grasp science concepts. Manageable two-page lessons present each topic with a "concept" and a "challenge." The concept, on the left-hand page, is presented in short, manageable paragraphs. The challenge, on the right-hand page, measures understanding with comprehension checks, applications, and engaging activities.

Other features include:

- Learning objectives to define the goal of the lesson
- TechTerms vocabulary to enhance understanding of scientific terminology
- Gradual introduction of new concepts to build understanding
- Frequent questions to reinforce understanding
- Engaging activities to develop interdisciplinary, critical-thinking, problem-solving, and collaborative-learning skills
- Colorful illustrations and photographs to bring concepts to life
- Unit Reviews to provide additional avenues for assessment and application

The real-world emphasis of this program helps students connect content to their daily life as they learn about scientists, science careers, and the practical applications of science.

6-4 What are algae?

Objective ▶ Identify and describe different kinds of algae.

TechTerms

- **chlorophyll** (KLAWR-uh-fil): green pigment used by some organisms to make food
- **plankton** (PLANK-tun): organisms that float at the water's surface

Algae Algae are classified in the protist king-dom. All algae contain **chlorophyll** (KLAWR-uh-fil). Chlorophyll is a green pigment found in plant cells and algae. Plants and algae use chlorophyll to make food. The food-making process is called photosynthesis (foht-uh-SIN-thuh-sis).

▶ **Compare:** How are algae and plants alike?

One-Celled Algae Some kinds of algae are made up of only one cell. Most one-celled algae live in a watery environment. They float on the surface of the water. Algae make up **plankton** (PLANK-tun). Plankton are all the tiny plants and animals that float on the surface of the oceans and lakes.

Although all algae have chlorophyll, all kinds of algae are not green. Fire algae are one-celled algae that are red in color. Golden-brown algae can have a color ranging from yellowish-green to golden-brown. These differences in color are due to other pigments, or colorings, in the algae.

▶ **Identify:** What is plankton?

Euglena The euglena is a unicellular, or one-celled, algae. It is both plantlike and animallike. Like all algae, the euglena contains chlorophyll. It uses the chlorophyll to make food from sunlight. When light is not available, the euglena also can take in food. A structure in the euglena called the eyespot can detect light. The euglena uses its eyespot to find light in the water. The euglena moves to the light by beating the flagellum that extends from its body.

Flagellum
Eyespot
Vacuole
Chloroplast with chlorophyll
Nucleus

▶ **Explain:** How is the euglena animal

Many-Celled Algae Some kinds of al made up of many cells. These are the multi algae. Pigments in multicellular algae m them a green, red, or brown coloring. Mo algae live in fresh water.

Red and brown algae live in the ocean. algae often are called seaweed or kelp. algae are the largest and most complex algae. If you have visited a beach, you ma seen brown algae washed up along the sh

▶ **Infer:** Why are all types of algae not

SCIENTIFIC METHODS AND SKILLS

UNIT 1

CONTENTS

STUDY HINT As you read each lesson in Unit 1, write the lesson title and lesson objectives on a sheet of paper. After you complete each lesson, write the sentence or sentences that answer each objective.

The convenient Unit Opener page gives students a quick preview of concepts to be covered. The Study Hint provides helpful tips for more effective learning.

---

used b

▶ **plankton** (PLANK-tun): organisms that float at the water's surface

Algae Algae are classified in the protist king-dom. All algae contain **chlorophyll** (KLAWR-uh-fil). Chlorophyll is a green pigment found in plant cells and algae. Plants and algae use chlorophyll to make food. The food-making process is called photosynthesis (foht-uh-SIN-thuh-sis).

▶ **Compare:** How are algae and plants alike?

One-Celled Algae Some kinds of algae are made up of only one cell. Most one-celled algae live in a watery environment. They float on the surface of the water. Algae make up **plankton** (PLANK-tun). Plankton are all the tiny plants and animals that float on the surface of the oceans and lakes.

Although all algae have chlorophyll, all kind

Only one idea is introduced in each short paragraph, an effec-tive learning approach for the reluctant reader plus phonetic spellings of new or complex terms to aid in pronunciation.

LESSON SUMMARY

- All algae contain chloroph own food by photosynthes
- Some kinds of algae are o
- All algae are not green, b phyll.
- The euglena is a single-c both plantlike and animal
- Some algae are multicellu
- Red and brown algae are

CHECK *Complete the following.*

make the

Lesson Summaries, at the beginning of each "challenges" page reinforce concepts learned by providing an encapsulated review of key ideas.

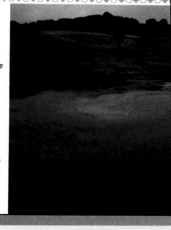

ON SUMMARY

...l algae contain chlorophyll and make their
...wn food by photosynthesis.

...me kinds of algae are one-celled.

...l algae are not green, but still have chloro-
hyll.

...he euglena is a single-celled algae that is
...oth plantlike and animallike.

...me algae are multicellular.

...d and brown algae are multicellular algae.

...K *Complete the following.*

...lgae _____ make their own food.

...ants and algae both contain the green
...gment _____ .

...he euglena uses its _____ to detect light.

...re algae are _____ in color.

...he largest kind of algae is _____ .

...Y *Complete the following.*

...ompare: How is the Euglena similar to the
...rypanosome?

7. Suppose you needed to obtain a water sample that contained both algae and protozoans. Where would you go to obtain the sample?

Skill Builder.................

▲ *Organizing* When you organize information, you put the information into some kind of order. A table is one way to organize information. Make a table with the following headings: "Type of Algae" and "Product." Use library references to determine the kinds of algae used to make the following products: toothpaste, marshmallows, ice cream, detergent, cheese, and silver polish.

SCIENCE CONNECTION ◇◆◇◆◇◆◇◆◇◆◇◆◇◆◇◆◇◆◇◆◇◆◇◆◇◆◇◆◇◆◇◆◇◆
ALGAL BLOOMS

Algae make their own food by photosynthesis. For photosynthesis to occur, three things must be present -- chlorophyll, sunlight, and carbon dioxide. However, algae also must have water and other nutrients, such as nitrogen and phosphorous, to carry out their life processes. When all of these elements are present, algae can reproduce quickly and in large numbers. A sudden, large growth of algae is called an algal bloom.

Algal blooms often occur when wastes containing phosphates are dumped into ponds or lakes. Phosphates are commonly found in detergents. When an algal bloom occurs, algae can be seen living at the surface of a lake or pond in great numbers. However, an algal bloom can be a problem for organisms that live in the lake or pond. As the algae die, they are broken down by bacteria. The bacteria use oxygen from the water when they break down the algae. If the bacteria use too much oxygen, fishes and other organisms living in the water do not have enough oxygen to carry out their life processes. As a result, the organisms may die.

make their own food by photosynthesis. For
...osynthesis to occur, three things must be present --
...ophyll, sunlight, and carbon dioxide. However, algae also
... have water and other nutrients, such as nitrogen and
...phorous, to carry out their life processes. When all of these
...ents are present, algae can reproduce quickly and in large
...ers. A sudden, large growth of algae is called an algal
...n.

...lgal blooms often occur when wastes containing
...hates are dumped into ponds or lakes. Phosphates are
...nonly found in detergents. When an algal bloom occurs,
... can be seen living at the surface of a lake or pond in
... numbers. However, an algal bloom can be a problem for
...nisms that live in the lake or pond. As the algae die, they
...roken down by bacteria. The bacteria use oxygen from the
... when they break down the algae. If the bacteria use too
... oxygen, fishes and other organisms living in the water do
...ave enough oxygen to carry out their life processes. As a
..., the organisms may die.

123

Lesson Features include:
- *Science Connection Activities*
- *People in Science*
- *Leisure Activities*
- *Technology and Society*
- *Looking Back in Science*
- *Careers in Science*

Designed to motivate students to learn with thought-provoking facts, interesting insights and exercises that make science fun.

golden-br... ...ese differences in color are ... to other pigments, or colorings, in the algae.

▶ *Identify:* What is plankton?

Euglena The euglena is a unicellular, or one-celled, algae. It is both plantlike and animallike. Like all algae, the euglena contains chlorophyll. It uses the chlorophyll to make food from sunlight. When light is not available, the euglena also can take in food. A structure in the euglena called the eyespot can detect light. The euglena uses its eyespot to find light in the water. The euglena moves to the light by beating the flagellum that extends from its body.

122

Red and brown algae live in the ocean. Brown algae often are called seaweed or kelp. Brown algae are the largest and most complex kind of algae. If you have visited a beach, you may have seen brown algae washed up along the shoreline.

▶ *Infer:* Why are all types of algae not green?

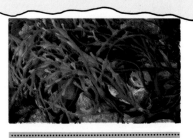

Skill Builder.................

▲ *Organizing* When you organize information, you put the information into some kind of order. A table is one way to organize information. Make a table with the following headings: "Type of Algae" and "Product." Use library references to determine the kinds of algae used to make the following products: toothpaste, marshmallows, ice cream, detergent, cheese, and silver polish.

A wide variety of Challenge Features provide exercises designed to help students develop thinking and learning skills and helps to relate science to their daily lives: Skill Builders, Ideas in Action, Designing an Experiment, Infosearch, Health and Safety Tip, and State the Problem.

Frequent questions, interwoven throughout the lesson reinforce understanding and give students immediate insights into the relationship of scientific principles.

▶ Red and brown algae are multicellular algae.

CHECK *Complete the following.*

1. Algae _____ make their own food.
2. Plants and algae both contain the green pigment _____ .
3. The euglena uses its _____ to detect light.
4. Fire algae are _____ in color.
5. The largest kind of algae is _____ .

APPLY *Complete the following.*

6. **Compare:** How is the Euglena similar to the trypanosome?

The two-part lesson review encourages students to think about what they've learned, and helps them grasp abstract concepts by having them apply what they know to hypothetical situations.

STUDENT BOOK UNIT REVIEW

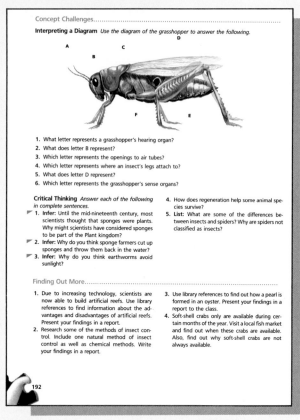

Concept Challenges..............

Interpreting a Diagram *Use the diagram of the grasshopper to answer the following.*

1. What letter represents a grasshopper's hearing organ?
2. What does letter B represent?
3. Which letter represents the openings to air tubes?
4. Which letter represents where an insect's legs attach to?
5. What does letter D represent?
6. Which letter represents the grasshopper's sense organs?

Critical Thinking *Answer each of the following in complete sentences.*
1. **Infer:** Until the mid-nineteenth century, most scientists thought that sponges were plants. Why might scientists have considered sponges to be part of the Plant kingdom?
2. **Infer:** Why do you think sponge farmers cut up sponges and throw them back in the water?
3. **Infer:** Why do you think earthworms avoid sunlight?

4. How does regeneration help some animal species survive?
5. **List:** What are some of the differences between insects and spiders? Why are spiders not classified as insects?

Finding Out More..............

1. Due to increasing technology, scientists are now able to build artificial reefs. Use library references to find information about the advantages and disadvantages of artificial reefs. Present your findings in a report.
2. Research some of the methods of insect control. Include one natural method of insect control as well as chemical methods. Write your findings in a report.

3. Use library references to find out how a pearl is formed in an oyster. Present your findings in a report to the class.
4. Soft-shell crabs only are available during certain months of the year. Visit a local fish market and find out when these crabs are available. Also, find out why soft-shell crabs are not always available.

192

Concept Challenges develop critical thinking skills. Additional activities motivate students to use visuals and conduct research in learning activities outside of the classroom.

Content Challenges reinforce concepts and help students practice science skills. A wide range and variety of questions hold student interest.

Reading Critically encourages the practice of interdisciplinary skills and measures concept understanding. Page numbers in parentheses help students find sections they may want to re-read.

At the end of every unit, a comprehensive Unit Review provides complete reinforcement of all key concepts learned in the lessons that made up that unit. Students will find a wealth of valuable resources to help them retain the information they've studied. These include tips to help students sharpen their study skills...a review of the "Tech Terms" learned in each lesson...additional questions to measure concept and content knowledge and retention...and numerous activities that promote independent learning and critical thinking. In addition, these exercises build confidence by letting students see for themselves how well they're progressing.

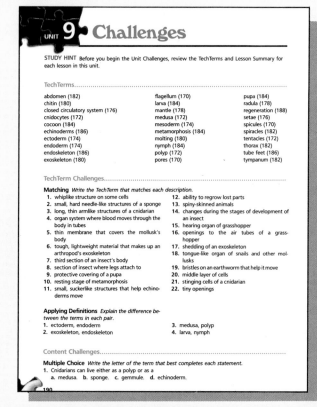

UNIT 9 Challenges

STUDY HINT Before you begin the Unit Challenges, review the TechTerms and Lesson Summary for each lesson in this unit.

TechTerms..............

abdomen (182)	flagellum (170)	pupa (184)
chitin (180)	larva (184)	radula (178)
closed circulatory system (176)	mantle (178)	regeneration (188)
cnidocytes (172)	medusa (172)	setae (176)
cocoon (184)	mesoderm (174)	spicules (170)
echinoderms (186)	metamorphosis (184)	spiracles (182)
ectoderm (174)	molting (180)	tentacles (172)
endoderm (174)	nymph (184)	thorax (182)
endoskeleton (186)	polyp (172)	tube feet (186)
exoskeleton (180)	pores (170)	tympanum (182)

TechTerm Challenges..............

Matching *Write the TechTerm that matches each description.*
1. whiplike structure on some cells
2. small, hard needle-like structures of a sponge
3. long, thin armlike structures of a cnidarian
4. organ system where blood moves through the body in tubes
5. thin membrane that covers the mollusk's body
6. tough, lightweight material that makes up an arthropod's exoskeleton
7. third section of an insect's body
8. section of insect where legs attach to
9. protective covering of a pupa
10. resting stage of metamorphosis
11. small, suckerlike structures that help echinoderms move

12. ability to regrow lost parts
13. spiny-skinned animals
14. changes during the stages of development of an insect
15. hearing organ of grasshopper
16. openings to the air tubes of a grasshopper
17. shedding of an exoskeleton
18. tongue-like organ of snails and other mollusks
19. bristles on an earthworm that help it move
20. middle layer of cells
21. stinging cells of a cnidarian
22. tiny openings

Applying Definitions *Explain the difference between the terms in each pair.*
1. ectoderm, endoderm
2. exoskeleton, endoskeleton

3. medusa, polyp
4. larva, nymph

Content Challenges..............

Multiple Choice *Write the letter of the term that best completes each statement.*
1. Cnidarians can live either as a polyp or as a
   a. medusa. b. sponge. c. gemmule. d. echinoderm.

190

TEACHER'S ANCILLARY MATERIALS

The **Teacher's Resource Book** is a complete package of teaching aids, conveniently organized in an easy-to-use binder. If you have ESL students, you'll appreciate the Spanish supplement. And all worksheets, reviews and testing material—more than 300 pages—are cross-referenced to Student Book lessons. All teaching aids are in reproducible Blackline Master format.

Vocabulary Practice activities designed to make learning more fun.

The Enrichment Worksheet to help develop critical thinking skills, while motivating them to explore concepts further.

A Lesson Review Worksheet provides a variety of review exercises and reinforces key concepts.

The Annotated Teacher's Edition provides complete Student Book text along with on-page annotations. It also contains other vaulable information, including:

- A correlation chart
- Teaching Tips
- Suggestions for cooperative learning activities

- A Materials List
- Supplies and address lists for equipment and materials

LABORATORY PROGRAM

*H*ands-on activities and experiments for students are central to the *Concepts and Challenges in Science* Laboratory Program. Fun and interesting, these formal laboratories enable students to see a wide range of basic scientific processes firsthand. Each Laboratory Program:

- Correlates to activities in the Student Edition to synthesize the lesson concept and help students see it in action.
- Gives students an opportunity to practice the Scientific Method and enhance their critical thinking skills.
- Encourages the use of science process skills as an aid to comprehension.
- Enhances comprehension with numerous drawings, tables, charts, and graphs.

With every experiment students perform, they'll gain not only understanding, but the *confidence* that builds learning success.

Name _____ Class _____ Date _____

Laboratory Challenge 25

How do insects develop?

Insects go through several stages of development as they mature. The changes that take place are called metamorphosis. Metamorphosis may be complete or incomplete. In incomplete metamorphosis, the insect that comes out of a hatched egg looks like a small version of the adult. It is called a nymph. Grasshoppers and roaches are insects that undergo incomplete metamorphosis.

In complete metamorphosis, the insect that comes out of the hatched egg is a larva. The larva usually does not look anything like the adult. For example, a caterpillar is the larva of the butterfly. A larva grows rapidly for a while, and then begins a resting stage in which it is called a pupa. Following this resting stage, the adult insect emerges. In this Challenge, you will observe the metamorphosis of the mealworm, which is the larva of the tenebrio beetle.

Skills: observing, identifying

Materials

magnifying lens   petri dish
mealworm culture   forceps

Procedure

1. OBSERVE: Examine a mealworm culture in a petri dish. Use the magnifying lens to get a better look. Do you see any eggs? What do they look like? Write your observations in Table 1.

2. Examine some of the larvae. Use forceps to handle them. What do they look like? Write your observations in Table 1.

3. As mealworms grow, they shed their old skins. Can you find any empty skins in the culture? Record your observations in Table 1.

4. Find a mealworm in the pupal stage. Does the pupa seem active or inactive? How does it look compared to the larvae? Write your observations in Table 1.

5. Examine an adult tenebrio beetle with your magnifying lens. Look for ways in which it is different from its larva. Notice its color, number of legs, level of activity, and other features. Write your observations in Table 1.

Name _____ Class _____ Date _____

Observations

Table 1   Observing a Mealworm Culture

Item	Present? (Y or N)	Observations
eggs		
larvae		
skins		
pupa		
adult beetles		

Conclusions

1. What is metamorphosis? _____

2. What happens during incomplete metamorphosis? _____

3. What happens during complete metamorphosis? _____

4. IDENTIFY: Does the tenebrio beetle undergo complete or incomplete metamorphosis? _____

A question identifies the problem that's being explored.

Easily obtainable materials used in the experiment are clearly listed. The skills that students will use are also listed.

Step-by-step procedures, and diagrams are provided as a learning aid.

Ample space is provided for recording observations.

A series of simple questions to strengthen observation skills, and the ability to reach logical conclusions are included.

The Annotated Teacher's Edition of the Laboratory Program provides an overview of the laboratory activities and advice on teaching students reading below grade-level. Features include:

- A section on Reading Skills and laboratory procedures
- Using Laboratory Skills Worksheets
- Teaching Tips
- Suggestions for cooperative learning
- activities
- Guidelines for Safety
- Materials List
- A comprehensive Skills Matrix
- Supplies and address lists for equipment and materials

SKILLS DEVELOPMENT IN LIFE SCIENCE

In recent years, science curricula and pedagogy have shifted in order to make science more immediate and relevant for students. Prior to the late 1980s, science teaching was based largely on memorization of vocabulary terms, facts, concepts, and principles. Mastery was evaluated on a student's ability to recall isolated facts. Today, science curricula stress relationships among the facts, concepts, and principles within each branch of science and among the different branches of science. Students are encouraged to apply reading, writing, and study skills to the study of science. Instruction focuses on teaching the methods, processes, and skills of science and on promoting cooperative learning and critical thinking.

Concepts and Challenges has been developed with these new directions in mind. The Revised Third Edition is a readable, relevant, lively textbook. The writing style is highly motivating, interesting, and challenging without being overwhelming.

Science Process Skills and Methods

The implementation of science process skills and methods is a unique and important feature of *Concepts and Challenges*.

* Nine key process skills—organizing, classifying, measuring, observing, inferring, predicting, analyzing, modeling, and hypothesizing—are highlighted and integrated with the presentation of content and with assessments. Process skills are identified with a label, a symbol, and a definition as they appear throughout the text.

* Lesson 1–2 is devoted to explaining the nine highlighted skills in the text in an interesting, readable format. Two additional skills—communicating and researching—are introduced.

* Lesson 1–3 is devoted to explaining scientific methods.

* Lesson 1–4 is devoted to experimental design such as recognizing variables, using controls, and communicating information via a written laboratory report.

* Lessons 1–5 through 1–6 stress measuring while using several other skills throughout each lesson.

Study Skills

To help students study science more successfully, effective study skills are introduced and modeled throughout the text.

* Study Hints on each unit opener page present six important study strategies for approaching the unit content.

* Students are given a study reminder before each Unit Review.

* Lesson Summary statements help students recap important information in each lesson.

* To help students develop good study skills, you may want to suggest that they follow one or more of these procedures:

1. **Previewing** Ask students to read the title and objective of each lesson and to review the TechTerms, their phonetic respellings, where applicable, and their definitions.

2. **Note Taking** Each lesson is divided into several short sections made up of one or two paragraphs. Each paragraph has a topic sentence. Encourage students to write the topic sentences for each paragraph.

3. **Rereading** Encourage students to reread short sections if they cannot answer the question at the end of the section.

4. **Observing and Analyzing** Encourage students to make use of the graphics on each page to help them understand a concept.

5. **Questioning** Encourage students to write questions about the content as they read the lesson.

6. **Answering Questions** Writing often reinforces learning. Have students write answers to in-text questions and assessment questions. Have students discuss their written responses in small groups or as a class.

Comprehension and Reading Skills

The presentation of content, the writing style, and the overall format of a text play a major role in reading comprehension. *Concepts and Challenges* has been developed with student comprehension in mind.

* Two-page, self-contained lessons allow students to concentrate on a complete concept in a manageable amount of text.

* Illustrations support content and help build understanding.

* Each lesson has a consistent design.

1. Each **lesson title**, presented as a question, provides a clear aim for the day's lesson.

2. Clearly stated **objectives** provide students with learning goals.

3. The new vocabulary, **TechTerms**, is introduced prior to reading the lesson.

4. Paragraphs that support **one main idea** help students focus and build to the overall lesson concept.

5. Follow-up **questions** after each short section of text reinforce learning. Students can find the answers by rereading a short passage.

Frequent Review

Each short section in a lesson is followed by a question. Questions stress reading comprehension and skills development. Reading comprehension questions have answers explicitly stated in the reading. If students are unable to answer the question, they should be able to find the answer by rereading the passage.

Skills questions are more challenging but can be answered by rereading a passage or by using the graphics on the page. The gratification of answering these questions successfully reinforces learning and acts as motivation to read each short section carefully.

Vocabulary

The study of science requires a working knowledge of words and terms that may be unfamiliar to students. *Concepts and Challenges* introduces vocabulary terms only when they are essential to the key concept or principle in each lesson. Lessons generally have between one and four new terms. In this way, students are introduced to important terms and develop a working science vocabulary without the burden of memorizing too many new terms.

Each term is introduced before the lesson under the heading TechTerms. The terms are phonetically respelled and defined. Within the lesson, the science terms are boldfaced, phonetically respelled, and defined in context. Students are thus provided with a preview of terms and a reinforcement of the same terms.

Recognizing that vocabulary skills development is important, vocabulary skills such as using prefixes, suffixes, and root words and identifying word origins are further highlighted and developed in many Skill Builder features. Vocabulary development also is reinforced in the Unit Challenge exercises. Besides evaluating knowledge of vocabulary, these exercises stress word relationships and apply definitions.

Writing Skills

Writing is important to all academic disciplines. The process of writing involves a number of skills, including the ability to collect, analyze, and organize information. *Concepts and Challenges* enhances writing competence by correlating writing activities directly to the text. Students are encouraged to collect, analyze, and organize information. Writing activities are found in the Challenge features: Skill Builder, InfoSearch, Ideas in Action, Health & Safety, State the Problem, and Design an Experiment.

Mathematics Skills

The language of scientists includes mathematics. The program also illustrates the close relationship between science and mathematics. Throughout *Concepts and Challenges*, students are encouraged to apply basic arithmetic skills.

- Opportunities are provided to add, subtract, multiply, and divide with whole numbers and decimals.
- Students are encouraged to use mathematical formulas to solve problems.
- Measurement skills are developed through opportunities for students to use metric rules, calibrated tubes and beakers, and balances.

Critical Thinking Skills

Students are encouraged to use critical thinking skills in the Apply section of each Challenge page. Here students are asked to observe, identify, classify, analyze, infer, model, hypothesize, interpret, explain, sequence, compare, and contrast. Questions are labeled to help students make connections to the skill they will apply. Each Unit Review includes a critical thinking section.

Skills Matrix

A comprehensive matrix of skills and lesson features is provided on pages T-xii–T-xiii. The scope and sequence of the skills used throughout the program can be used as a teaching tool to help to develop and reinforce student application skills.

Additional Classroom Support

To reinforce science learning, consider these other science products from Globe Fearon.

Writing Across The Curriculum:
Writing in Science

Helpful hints for students on mastering writing skills needed in science: Keeping a science journal, taking notes, conducting and recording experiments, writing science reports, and more.

Science & Technology:
A Rich Heritage

An inspirational introduction to the achievements of African American men and women in the fields of science and technology.

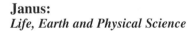

Janus:
Life, Earth and Physical Science

These three hardcover texts parallel the topics and instruction found in *Concepts and Challenges* at a lower reading level. Key features found in *Concepts and Challenges*, such as pre-teaching vocabulary, stating lesson objectives, making real-life connections, and providing frequent opportunities for review and reinforcement, are also found in *Janus Life, Earth & Physical.*

Access to Math:
Whole Numbers & Integers and *Measurement & Geometry*

A fifteen-volume series that targets specific math skills and concepts. Other titles include *Graphing & Interpreting Data, Formulas, Decimals* and *Exponents & Scientific Notation.*

COMPREHENSIVE SKILLS AND FEATURES MATRIX BY LESSON

Category	Skill	1-1	1-2	1-3	1-4	1-5	1-6	1-7	1-8	2-1	2-2	2-3	2-4	2-5	2-6	2-7	3-1	3-2	3-3	3-4	3-5	3-6	3-7	3-8	3-9	3-10	3-11	4-1	4-2
SCIENCE SKILLS	Observe		●			●	●	●				●		●				●				●	●	●					
	Measure		●															●											
	Infer	●	●					●			●	●	●		●	●	●	●	●			●	●	●	●			●	●
	Organize		●		●																								
	Classify	●	●								●		●					●		●		●	●			●			
	Predict		●									●		●						●					●			●	
	Hypothesize		●								●		●			●						●							
	Model		●											●									●						●
	Analyze	●	●		●	●	●					●		●			●					●	●		●				
	Research		●													●	●											●	
	Communicate		●															●											
INTERDISCIPLINARY SKILLS	Define			●	●			●		●		●			●	●	●	●		●	●				●	●	●	●	
	Build Vocabulary	●																				●							●
	Finding Main Ideas																												
	Identify		●							●	●	●	●	●				●	●		●				●		●		
	Locate																												
	Compare				●		●																						
	Contrast													●												●			
	Sequence				●									●									●			●			
	Calculate					●		●																					
CHALLENGE FEATURES	Skill Builder	●		●		●		●	●			●	●		●		●					●	●			●		●	
	InfoSearch											●						●		●	●				●				●
	Ideas in Action		●						●						●										●	●	●		
	Health & Safety														●									●					
	State the Problem								●																	●			
	Design an Experiment			●									●																
LESSON FEATURES	Activity		●			●	●						●												●				●
	Career	●							●									●											
	Technology								●					●							●					●			
	Science Connection			●				●											●	●	●			●					
	Leisure Activity																			●		●			●				
	People in Science				●								●														●	●	
	Looking Back in Science							●						●															

Txii

4-3	4-4	4-5	4-6	4-7	4-8	4-9	5-1	5-2	5-3	5-4	5-5	5-6	6-1	6-2	6-3	6-4	6-5	6-6	7-1	7-2	7-3	7-4	7-5	8-1	8-2	8-3	8-4	8-5	8-6	8-7	8-8	8-9	8-10	9-1	9-2	9-3	9-4	9-5	9-6
	•																	•	•	•		•		•		•	•				•	•		•	•		•		
																								•	•	•													
•	•		•	•	•		•				•		•	•		•		•	•	•	•	•	•	•	•	•			•	•	•			•	•	•	•	•	•
									•							•								•															
							•				•	•		•				•						•	•		•		•	•	•			•			•		•	•
		•																						•		•													
		•								•	•	•						•	•					•	•	•							•	•		•			
•																					•	•	•		•	•	•	•		•									
	•		•					•	•		•		•						•	•	•	•			•	•						•		•			•	•	
					•																•																		
•			•	•	•	•			•		•						•		•		•					•	•			•	•			•				•	•
											•	•									•											•							
		•	•							•	•		•	•	•	•	•		•	•	•		•		•		•		•		•			•		•			•
																						•										•							
•	•			•		•							•		•		•		•		•										•		•						
		•							•	•										•																			
		•	•		•		•		•												•				•														
																						•																	
							•	•		•			•	•		•			•	•		•	•					•	•		•								
•	•			•		•		•	•		•	•		•	•		•		•		•		•						•								•	•	
										•							•		•		•						•		•										
		•		•													•										•		•						•	•		•
	•	•	•				•			•		•		•			•		•		•	•	•						•	•							•		
		•								•																			•										
•			•	•									•																										•
								•					•	•							•					•		•			•					•	•	
																					•						•		•			•							
									•										•																				
								•			•								•																		•		

		9-7	9-8	9-9	9-10	10-1	10-2	10-3	10-4	10-5	10-6	10-7	10-8	11-1	11-2	11-3	11-4	11-5	11-6	11-7	11-8	11-9	11-10	11-11	12-1	12-2	12-3	12-4	12-5
SCIENCE SKILLS	Observe		●				●		●		●			●													●		●
	Measure																												
	Infer		●	●	●	●	●	●	●	●				●	●		●		●	●	●	●		●	●	●	●		●
	Organize												●			●	●												
	Classify	●	●				●			●	●														●				●
	Predict						●	●																					
	Hypothesize								●		●			●				●	●						●		●		
	Model								●		●			●															
	Analyze						●		●			●		●	●	●					●		●						
	Research												●	●							●							●	
	Communicate																												
INTERDISCIPLINARY SKILLS	Define		●		●	●								●		●	●	●	●	●	●	●			●			●	●
	Build Vocabulary			●																									
	Finding Main Ideas																												
	Identify					●	●							●		●	●	●	●	●	●	●							●
	Locate																												
	Compare		●							●	●								●						●				
	Contrast					●	●		●		●	●	●															●	
	Sequence		●						●				●							●	●								
	Calculate																	●											
CHALLENGE FEATURES	Skill Builder		●		●	●				●	●			●	●		●		●		●				●			●	●
	InfoSearch	●					●		●					●			●		●		●					●			
	Ideas in Action																						●						
	Health & Safety								●		●					●			●				●						
	State the Problem				●																								
	Design an Experiment																												
LESSON FEATURES	Activity								●		●			●	●	●		●				●	●				●		
	Career		●		●											●				●									●
	Technology			●		●																	●	●					
	Science Connection	●			●													●	●									●	
	Leisure Activity		●								●																		
	People in Science																												
	Looking Back in Science								●						●							●							

Txiv

12-6	13-1	13-2	13-3	13-4	13-5	14-1	14-2	14-3	14-4	14-5	14-6	14-7	15-1	15-2	15-3	15-4	15-5	15-6	15-7	15-8	15-9	15-10	16-1	16-2	16-3	16-4	16-5	16-6	16-7	16-8	16-9	16-10	17-1	17-2	17-3	17-4	17-5	17-6	17-7

	18-1	18-2	18-3	18-4	18-5	18-6	18-7	18-8	18-9	18-10	18-11	18-12	19-1	19-2	19-3	19-4	19-5	19-6
SCIENCE SKILLS																		
Observe			●		●								●				●	
Measure																	●	
Infer	●	●		●		●		●		●	●	●					●	●
Organize																		
Classify																		
Predict			●	●		●												
Hypothesize			●			●	●		●	●			●		●	●		●
Model											●							
Analyze	●	●						●					●	●				
Research			●													●		
Communicate																		
INTERDISCIPLINARY SKILLS																		
Define	●	●	●	●		●		●	●		●	●	●	●	●			
Build Vocabulary																		●
Finding Main Ideas																		
Identify		●		●			●			●		●						
Locate																		
Compare				●				●		●								
Contrast				●														●
Sequence														●		●		
Calculate							●									●		
CHALLENGE FEATURES																		
Skill Builder			●		●						●		●	●	●			●
InfoSearch	●		●		●		●		●		●	●						
Ideas in Action		●																●
Health & Safety																		
State the Problem							●											
Design an Experiment									●						●			
LESSON FEATURES																		
Activity				●	●			●						●		●		
Career										●								
Technology						●	●				●							
Science Connection									●					●				
Leisure Activity																		
People in Science	●	●																●
Looking Back in Science			●				●							●		●		

MATERIALS LIST
(per 30 students)

Item	Quantity	Lesson	Item	Quantity	Lesson
Acorn nuts, to fit			Nickles	30	18-5
¼″ × 1½″ screws	30	5-4	Oil	1 bottle	4-5
Alcohol, Isopropyl	1 bottle	8-4	Oil, cooking	1 bottle	11-10
Bags, brown paper	30	11-1	Onions	30	8-9
Baking soda	1 box	11-10	Oranges	15	6-6
Balloons	30	9-5	Over-the-counter		
Boxes	30 of each		drugs or		
3 different sizes	size	1-6	medicine labels,	30 of each	
Bread	1 loaf	6-6	3 different kinds	kind	16-8
Calculators	30	16-7	Paper clips	30	12-6
Cardboard	30 pieces	15-2	Paper towels	2 rolls	6-6, 8-4
Celery stalks	30	8-2	Paper, construction		
Clay	1 box	19-1	black	30 sheets	18-4
Clay,	1 box of		blue	60 sheets	11-2, 18-4
3 colors	each color	15-2	brown,		
Clock or watch			11″ × 17″	30 sheets	19-4
with second hand	1	13-2, 15-10	green	30 sheets	18-4
Containers, plastic			green,		
small	30	4-2	11″ × 17″	30 sheets	19-4
with lids	90	6-6	red	60 sheets	11-2, 18-4
Cotton swabs	1 box	15-4	white	30 sheets	18-4
Cups, large plastic	30	4-5	yellow	30 sheets	18-4
Cups, paper			Paper, graph	120 sheets	1-2, 10-8,
large	90	19-1			16-9, 17-6
small	30	8-9	Paper, tracing	30 sheets	18-4
Dishes, small	30	8-8, 10-6	Pennies	30	18-5, 19-1
Drawing compasses	30	4-6	Pens, black felt	30	8-4
Eggs	120	4-5, 10-6	Petroleum jelly	1 jar	19-1
Field guides			Pine cones	30 of each	
plants	30	8-3	3 different types	type	7-4
trees	30	7-4	Pipe cleaners	270	4-6
Flashlights	15	2-3	Plaster of Paris	5 pounds	19-1
Food samples,	30 of each		Plastic bags, small	30	4-2
5 different kinds	kind	11-1	Plastic wrap	1 roll	4-5
Gelatin	30 packages	4-2	Pliers	30	5-4
Glasses, drinking	30	8-2, 8-9,	Potatoes	6	6-6
		15-4	with eyes	15	8-9
Grapes	30	4-2	Scissors	30	8-4, 9-5, 11-1,
Index cards	570	3-7, 15-10			11-2, 11-11,
Ink	1 bottle	8-2			18-4, 19-4
Iodine	1 bottle	8-8	Seeds,	30 of each	
Knives	30	8-2, 8-8, 8-9	5 different kinds	kind	8-8
Leaves,	60 of each		Soil	15 cups	8-9
10 different types	type	7-5, 8-3	Straws, plastic	30	9-5
Lemon juice	1 bottle	15-4	String	3 balls	4-5, 9-5, 11-11
Machine screws,			Table salt	1 container	15-4
¼″ × 1½″	30	5-4	Tape		

Item	Quantity	Lesson	Item	Quantity	Lesson
Magazines and newspapers	30	16-10	cellophane	3 rolls	7-5, 9-5, 15-2
Magnifying glass	30	6-6	masking	2 rolls	11-11, 1
Markers	30	4-6, 18-5	Test tubes, with stoppers	60	11-10
Markers or pencils, 4 colors	30 of each color	15-4	Tonic water	1 bottle	15-4
Measuring spoons	30	11-10	Toothpicks	2 boxes	8-9, 15-2
Medicine droppers	30	8-8, 11-10	Vinegar	1 bottle	4-5
Metric rulers	30	1-5, 1-6, 4-5, 7-4, 8-2, 8-4, 11-11, 15-5	Wire, floral	90 pieces	5-4

UNIT AND LESSON TEACHING STRATEGIES

UNIT 1
SCIENTIFIC METHODS AND SKILLS (p. 13)

Previewing the Unit

Read the titles of the lessons in this unit aloud. Identify terms in the titles with which students are unfamiliar. Write these terms on the chalkboard. Use the Glossary of the text or a dictionary to define the terms as a class. Then have students carry out the task in the Study Hint as they read each lesson.

Bulletin Board Suggestions

1. Assemble a bulletin board entitled *Branches of Life Science.* Have students look for photographs and articles illustrating the main branches of life science. Students can use Table 1 on page 14 as a guide. Discuss with students what each branch of life science entails. If a second bulletin board panel is available, have students devote the bulletin board to the topic of *Biotechnology.* Have students attach articles and photographs that exemplify biotechnology. Discuss with students the branch of life science to which each article or photograph relates.
2. Create a bulletin board entitled *Tools of the Life Scientist.* Cut out photographs and drawings of the tools to which students will be introduced during their study of life science such as meterstick or metric ruler, a balance, a thermometer, a graduated cylinder, a simple microscope, and a compound microscope. Attach the pictures to the bulletin board. Label each tool with its name and its use. You also may wish to label the measuring tools with their metric units.

LESSON 1-1
What is life science? (p. 14)

Teaching Strategies

PREVIEW Before students begin this lesson, have them copy the information in Table 1 into their notebooks. Tell students to leave plenty of space between each entry so that they can add information to their tables. As students read the lesson, have them add careers to their tables. Encourage students to add additional careers to their tables as they continue their study of life science.

DISCUSSION Ask students what they think *science* is. Discuss all student responses. Tell students that people use science to try to understand the world in which they live. Explain that scientists observe what is going on in the world and try to figure out why and how things happen. Point out that because there are so many things to study, many scientists specialize in a particular area of study.

CLASS ACTIVITY Write the term *specialist* on the chalkboard. Elicit from students that a specialist is a person who studies, or works, in only one part of a subject. Ask students to name specialists with which they are familiar. If students have difficulty with this concept, point out a few of the medical specialists with which they are likely to have dealt, such as pediatricians, or dermatologists. Then ask students to name specialists who work in areas other than medicine.

DISCUSSION Ask students how life science affects their lives. Review the topics covered in the text. Use these topics as a springboard to other examples, such as the kinds of clothing people wear and the ways in which food is prepared and stored.

RETEACHING OPTION Bring pieces of a jigsaw puzzle to class. Label each piece with the name of a branch of life science. As you describe each branch of life science, join the pieces of the puzzle together. Emphasize that together the branches make up the field of life science.

Answers to Challenges (p. 15)

Apply

9. ecologist

Skill Builder: Building Vocabulary

doctor: diagnoses and treats illnesses; **physical therapist:** works with patients to strengthen damaged body parts; **physiologist:** studies how the parts of a living thing work; **chiropractor:** works with patients to relieve pain, especially pain related to the spinal column; **horticulturist:** specializes in gardening; **florist:** specializes in the growing and arranging of flowers; **veterinarian:** specializes in the medical care of animals; **marine biologist:** studies or works with living things that live in the ocean; **microbiologist:** studies microscopic living things and their effects on other organisms; **pathologist:** studies the tissues of living things; **ecologist:** studies the interaction between living things and their environments

Teaching Tips for Career in Life Science
Wildlife Biologist

EXTENSION If possible, arrange for a park or forest ranger or an animal conservationist to speak with your class. Ask the person to describe what his or her career entails and the training that is involved within the profession.

COOPERATIVE/COLLABORATIVE LEARNING Have interested students write to the Fish and Wildlife Service of the Department of the Interior to find out about careers in wildlife biology. Have students present their findings to the class.

Questions

1. INFER Why is it important to have laws that regulate hunting and fishing? (Answers will vary. Accept all logical responses.)
2. DEFINE What is "wildlife?" (the natural plants and animals that live in an area)

LESSON 1-2
What are science skills? (p. 16)

Teaching Strategies

PREVIEW Before beginning this lesson, write the title of each section on the chalkboard. Have students copy these titles in their notebooks using an outline format. As students read each section, they should write the topic sentence for each paragraph in the section in their outlines.

DISCUSSION As students read the description of each science skill, ask them to identify examples of how they use the skill in their daily life. Emphasize that these skills are used in all disciplines, not only in science.

CLASS ACTIVITY Have students collect articles from newspapers and magazines about topics related to life science issues. Point out to students that the information in the articles is based upon the research of scientists.

REINFORCEMENT Emphasize to students that observations are made using all of the senses, not just the sense of sight, and that measurements are a way of making observations more exact.

RETEACHING OPTION Students may be able to remember the science process skills more easily if you point out relationships among the skills. For example, classifying is one way to organize information; measurements make observations more concrete by quantifying observations; modeling combines methods of organizing and analyzing information.

COOPERATIVE/COLLABORATIVE LEARNING Have students work in pairs or small groups to answer the Check and Apply Questions.

Answers to Challenges (p. 17)
Ideas in Action

Answers will vary. Accept all logical responses. Likely responses include using a clock or watch to tell time, setting the temperature of an oven or thermostat, measuring the number

of pounds of air pressure in a bicycle tire, using a scale to measure body weight, or using a measuring cup or spoon while cooking a meal.

Teaching Tip for Activity
Organizing Data

Skills: *analyzing, organizing, comparing*

COOPERATIVE/COLLABORATIVE LEARNING Students must work individually at the beginning of this activity and then work in groups of three to carry the activity to completion. Encourage students to carefully analyze the variety of methods used to organize similar sets of data.

Questions

1. Answers will vary. Accept all logical responses.
2. Students should compare their methods of organization.

LESSON 1-3
What is scientific method? (p. 18)

Teaching Strategies

PREVIEW Before beginning this lesson, read the list of TechTerms aloud so students can hear their pronunciations.

DISCUSSION Present scientific method as a step-by-step approach to solving a problem. Have students note that many people use the scientific method in everyday life to help solve problems.

DISCUSSION List the steps of scientific method on the chalkboard. As you describe each step, emphasize that because each problem is different, scientists may use all or part of scientific method in a way that is best suited to a particular problem.

REINFORCEMENT To help reinforce the many skills used in science, have students match the skills and symbols introduced in Lesson 1-2 to the step of scientific method to which each skill relates. Students should recognize that some skills will be used more than once, and that some steps will involve more than one skill.

Answers to Challenges (p. 19)
Skill Builder: Writing a Laboratory Report

Check students' reports for a logical use of the steps of scientific method.

Teaching Tips for Science Connection
Pure and Applied Science

DISCUSSION Be sure students recognize the difference between pure and applied science. You can help to clarify the difference by pointing out the effects of applied science (technology) on students' everyday lives.

INTRASCIENCE CONNECTION Point out to students that technology involves all of the sciences and is not limited to biology. As an example, discuss X-rays. Explain that using X-rays requires knowledge of physical science principles. Then point out how these principles are applied to fields such as medicine and earth science.

Questions

1. APPLY   How is technology a part of your everyday life? (Answers will vary. Accept all logical responses.)
2. RELATE   Television, computers, and medicines all are examples of technological advances. How have these products changed peoples' lives? (Answers will vary. Accept all logical responses.)

LESSON 1-4
What is an experiment? (p. 20)

Teaching Strategies

PREVIEW   Before beginning this lesson, write the title of each section in the lesson on the chalkboard. Have students copy these titles in their notebooks using an outline format. As students read each section, they should write the topic sentence for each paragraph in their notebooks.

DISCUSSION   Explain how to conduct a controlled experiment. Use the figure on page 20, investigating the effect of fertilizer on the growth of a plant, to describe a controlled experiment. Ask the class to explain why the plant on the left is the control.

DISCUSSION   When designing an experiment, scientists look at variables. A variable is anything that can effect the results of an experiment. Have students reread the passage titled *Analyzing an Experiment.* Then have students list all of the variables in this experiment. Elicit from students that a well-designed experiment tests only one variable at a time.

CLASS ACTIVITY   Have students work in small groups to carry out the experiment described on page 20. When each group has concluded the experiment, have students compare their results. Discuss reasons for variations in results as a class.

Answers to Challenges (p. 21)

Apply

6. A control allows scientists to determine how a variable affects the results of an experiment.
7. By changing only one variable, scientists can be sure that any differences between the control and the experimental setup were caused by the variable being tested.
8. Answers will vary. Accept all logical responses.

Designing an Experiment

Check students' experimental designs for logic and accuracy. Be sure students have included a control and are testing only one variable (sunlight) in their experiments. You may wish to have volunteers describe their experiments to the rest of the class.

Teaching Tips for People in Science

Jane Goodall

EXTENSION   Have interested students research the life and work of Jane Goodall. Tell students to present their findings in an oral report. Students will be able to find many interesting articles by Jane Goodall in issues of *National Geographic.*

Questions

1. DEFINE   What is a zoologist? (scientist who studies animals)
2. EXPLAIN   Was the work done by Dr. Leakey and Jane Goodall conducted as a field study or in the laboratory? (as a field study)

LESSON 1-5
What is the metric system? (p. 22)

Teaching Strategies

PREVIEW   Before beginning this lesson, have students review the TechTerms and read the Lesson Summary.

ITERDISCIPLINARY CONNECTION   Discuss some of the units of measurements people used in the past. Tell students that at one time the distance from a king's nose to his hand equaled 1 yard and the length of a king's foot equaled 1 foot. Elicit from students why this system of measurement created problems. (The measuring system changed each time a new king took the throne.) Use this discussion to emphasize the importance of having a standard system of measurement.

CLASS ACTIVITY   Ask students to define an inch, foot, yard, ounce, and pound. Write student responses on the chalkboard. Point out that no simple relationship exists between these units. Perform a sample calculation on the chalkboard, such as changing 1.5 miles into feet. (1 mile = 5280 feet) Then, write the number 1500 mm on the chalkboard. Show students how this number can be changed to centimeters (150) or meters (1.5) simply by moving the decimal point to the left.

REINFORCEMENT   Review the rules for multiplying and dividing by 10,100 and 1000. This will help students convert from one metric unit to another.

EXTENSION   The second is the universal unit of time. The only units common to the metric and English systems are the second and its multiples (minute, hour, day, and so on).

Answers to Challenges (p. 23)

Apply

8. 15000
9. 400

Skill Builder: Sequencing

6 millimeters, 3 centimeters, 40 millimeters, 50 centimeters, 2 hectometers, 6 hectometers, 3 kilometers, 10 kilometers

Teaching Tips for Activity

Measuring Length

Skills: *observing, organizing, sequencing*

COOPERATIVE/COLLABORATIVE LEARNING   Answer the questions as a class.

DEMONSTRATION   Show students a metric ruler. Point out centimeter and millimeter divisions. Demonstrate the proper way to measure using a metric ruler.

Questions

1. 30 cm.
2. 300 mm.
3. the desk
4. the fingernail

LESSON 1-6
How do you measure using the metric system? (p. 24)

Teaching Strategies

CLASS ACTIVITY Introduce the square centimeter and square meter as units of area. Using a meterstick, measure the length and width of your classroom. Then have students calculate the area of the classroom.

DISCUSSION Display a one-liter flask and explain that its volume is equal to 1000 cubic centimeters. Remind students that 1/1000 of a liter is equal to a milliliter and, therefore, 1 milliliter is equal to 1 cubic centimeter.

DEMONSTRATION Show students how to measure the volume of a liquid using a graduated cylinder and the volume of a rectangular solid using the formula: volume = length × width × height.

CLASS ACTIVITY Using Table 1, read out the temperatures of things listed on one of the scales. Have students identify the temperature readings on the other two scales.

CLASS ACTIVITY Distribute one-gram masses to the class. Have students heft these masses. Using only the heft of these masses for comparison, challenge students to estimate the mass (in grams) of books, pencils, and other common objects. Then have students check their estimates using a balance.

Answers to Challenges (p. 25)
Health and Safety Tip

Mercury should be disposed of properly. Because mercury can be absorbed through the skin, a person should wear protective gloves to clean up spilled mercury. The mercury can be cleaned up with paper towels.

Teaching Tips for Activity
Calculating Area and Volume

Skills: *calculating, measuring, organizing*

COOPERATIVE/COLLABORATIVE LEARNING Have students work in pairs.

REINFORCEMENT Review the formulas for calculating area and volume before students begin this activity.

RETEACHING OPTION Tell students that area is recorded in square units because it involves two dimensions (length and width) and volume is recorded in cubic units because it involves three dimensions (length, width, and height).

LESSON 1-7
What is a microscope? (p. 26)

Teaching Strategies

CLASS ACTIVITY Hand out magnifying lenses to students. Have students look at various objects through the lenses and describe what they see. Point out that a lens is a curved piece of glass and that a magnifying lens makes objects look larger.

DISCUSSION Discuss the application of lenses in a microscope. Tell students that a compound microscope has two or more lenses.

INTRASCIENCE CONNECTION Before describing an electron microscope, draw a model of an atom on the chalkboard. Point out the electrons, protons, and neutrons. Identify these different particles as the three main parts of an atom.

ITERDISCIPLINARY CONNECTION After discussing the use of lenses in microscopes, ask students for other examples of tools and instruments that use lenses (eyeglasses, telescopes, cameras, and so on) Discuss with students the functions of the lenses in each of these objects. If possible, display each object in front of the classroom.

EXTENSION You may wish to introduce students to the terms *concave lens* and *convex lens*. If possible, bring examples of each kind of lens to class. Allow students to view objects through the lenses to see how each lens changes the appearance of an object.

Answers to Challenges (p. 27)
Check

1. simple microscope has one lens; compound microscope has two or more lenses
2. curved piece of glass that bends light rays
3. electron microscope
4. television

Apply

5. A compound microscope has a greater magnifying power than a simple microscope.
6. sight

Skill Builder: Making a Simple Microscope

Students should observe that as they move the key, the water acts as a lens and magnifies objects beneath it. Moving the key serves the function of focusing the object being magnified. The drop of water is the lens.

Teaching Tips for Looking Back in Science
Development of the Microscope

RETEACHING OPTION On the chalkboard draw a time line summarizing the information in this feature.

Questions

1. **APPLY** What kind of microscope was used by the ancient Greeks? (simple microscope)
2. **IDENTIFY** Who developed the first compound microscope? (Hans and Zacharias Janssen)

LESSON 1-8
What are the parts of the microscope? (p. 28)

Teaching Strategies

PREVIEW Have students read the Lesson Summary before beginning this lesson.

DISCUSSION Display a compound microscope in front of the classroom. As students read about the parts of the compound microscope, point out each part of the microscope. As you point out each part, review its function.

DEMONSTRATION Demonstrate the proper procedures for the care and handling of a compound microscope. Establish a procedure for the distribution, handling, and storage of microscopes. Stress the importance of caring for a microscope. You may wish to distribute a sheet listing rules for working with a microscope. Discuss why only lens tissue should be used to clean microscope lenses. If microscopes are distributed for class use, demonstrate the proper procedure for carrying the microscope.

EXTENSION Have students view prepared slides using a compound microscope. Discuss with the class the use of stains in prepared microscope slides. Point out that stains make microscopic organisms, cells, and so on, easier to see. Identify iodine and methylene blue as two common laboratory stains.

REINFORCEMENT Distribute outline drawings of the microscope and have the students label the parts. You also may wish to have students describe the function of each part of the microscope.

Answers to Challenges (p. 29)

Apply

7. A compound microscope uses light to produce an image.
8. A fuzzy image leads to inaccurate observations. Answers will vary. Accept all logical responses.
9. Changing the objective lenses makes an image larger or smaller.

Skill Builder: Calculating

a. 50 x **b.** 215 x **c.** 100 x **d.** 200 x **e.** 100 x

Teaching Tips for Technology and Society

Microsurgery

DISCUSSION Discuss how microsurgery benefits society. Relate the development of improved microscopes to improved medical techniques.

Questions

1. RELATE How do you think the ability to perform microsurgery has benefited accident victims? (Accident victims are more likely to survive or retain lost limbs due to microsurgery.)
2. PREDICT How might improved microscopes affect health care in the future. (Answers will vary. Accept all logical responses.)

Answers to Unit Challenges (pp. 30-32)

Understanding the Features: Reading Critically

1. as field studies
2. application of science to everyday situations
3. chimpanzees
4. an anthropologist; fossil-hunter
5. rock crystals, water in glass balls, glass lenses
6. Improved microscopes have led to the ability to perform techniques such as microsurgery.

Critical Thinking

1. An electron microscope uses electrons instead of light to view specimens; electron microscopes have a much greater magnification ability than do light microscopes. Accept all logical responses.
2. Microscopes allow microbiologists to study living things that are too small to see with the unaided eye.
3. The Kelvin scale would be most useful since it begins at absolute zero.
4. Microscopes of today have higher magnifications and better resolution than those of two hundred years ago.

Interpreting a Diagram

1. compound microscope
2. to magnify objects
3. mirror (light)
4. 2
5. 100 X
6. One hand should be under the base the other hand should grasp the arm.
7. stage clips
8. greater than
9. A compound microscope has two lenses; a simple microscope has only one lens.
10. curved piece of glass that bends light and makes an object look either larger or smaller

NEEDS OF LIVING THINGS (p. 33)

Previewing the Unit

Read the titles of the lessons in this unit aloud. Identify terms in the titles with which students are unfamiliar. Write these terms on the chalkboard. Use the Glossary of the text or a dictionary to define the terms as a class. Have students write the terms in their notebooks. Then have students carry out the task in the Study Hint.

Bulletin Board Suggestion

Assemble a bulletin board showing the six characteristics common to all forms of life. Cut out pictures that illustrate cells, adaptations, reproduction, growth, response, and energy use. Attach the pictures to the bulletin board. As you discuss the characteristics of life, have students point to the pictures that illustrate each characteristic.

LESSON 2-1
What are living things? (p. 34)

Teaching Strategies

PREVIEW Have students write the lesson title and objective in their notebooks. As students read the lesson, have them write the sentences from the lesson that meet the objective.

DISCUSSION Write the following heads on the chalkboard: *Living Things* and *Nonliving Things.* Ask students to take turns listing examples of things that belong under each head. Write students' responses on the chalkboard beneath the correct heads. Ask students what all the living things have in common. Discuss student responses. Then list and describe the six characteristics of living things.

DEMONSTRATION Bring a flashlight, a book of matches, and a wind-up or battery-driven toy to class. Demonstrate how each of these objects uses energy. Identify the energy source for each object. Lead students to recognize that nonliving things may have some of the characteristics of living things, but in order to be classified as a living thing, something must have all of the six characteristics of living things.

RETEACHING OPTION Write a list of several different organisms on the chalkboard. Ask students to explain how each organism meets the six characteristics of life.

Answers to Challenges (p. 35)
Apply

8. Grass uses energy from sunlight to make food. The energy is transferred to the cow when it eats the grass.
9. No; living things produce more living things like themselves.
10. Cars and flashlights do not have all of the characteristics of living things. For example, cars and flashlights do not have cells, do not respond to changes in their surroundings, and do not produce more organisms like themselves.

Ideas in Action

Answers will vary. Accept all logical responses.

Teaching Tips for Science Connection
Matter

DISCUSSION Define matter as anything that has mass and volume. Emphasize that everything that exists is either matter or energy.

DISCUSSION On the chalkboard, list the four kinds of organic compounds that are important in the body (carbohydrates, lipids, proteins, nucleic acids). Then discuss the roles of these compounds in the body.

Questions

1. CONTRAST How do elements differ from compounds? (Elements are made up entirely of atoms of the same kind. Compounds are made up of two or more elements that combine chemically).
2. DEFINE What is mass? (the amount of matter an object contains)

LESSON 2-2
What are adaptations? (p. 36)

Teaching Strategies

PREVIEW Before beginning this lesson, have students scan the lesson looking for words with which they are unfamiliar. Have students work in pairs or small groups to define each of the words on their lists.

DISCUSSION Define the environment as everything that surrounds a living thing. Ask students to describe their environment. Be sure students understand that both living and nonliving things make up their environment.

CLASS ACTIVITY Bring in pictures of animals in their natural habitats. Hold up each picture in front of the class. Have students try to identify the features that make each kind of animal adapted to its environment.

DEMONSTRATION If possible, show students an actual cactus plant. Point out the thick stem and the spines. Identify these structures as adaptations that help a cactus survive in the desert.

DEMONSTRATION To demonstrate the importance of a human's thumb, tape the thumbs of two volunteers to the palm of their hands. Ask the students to try to write their names on the chalkboard using the hands with the taped thumbs. Then, provide the students with a shirt that is buttoned down the front. Ask the students to try to unbutton the shirt. Student will observe how the thumb serves as an adaptation for humans.

Answers to Challenges (p. 37)
Check

1. everything that surrounds a living thing
2. air, water, sunlight, rocks, soil
3. any trait of an organism that helps the organism live in its environment
4. dry, desert environment
5. It allows people to use their hands to do many things.
6. air conditioning and heating systems

Apply

7. Answers will vary. Accept all logical responses.

8. Answers will vary. Accept all logical responses.
9. c **10.** d **11.** b **12.** a **13.** e

State the Problem

Students should recognize that a polar bear and a penguin could not survive in a desert environment. These two animals are adapted to cold, snowy environments.

Teaching Tips for Career in Life Science

Ecologist

DISCUSSION Direct students' attention to the photograph illustrating this feature. Ask students what the ecologist in the photograph is doing. (measuring the length of an alligator) Ask students why the ecologist might be interested in finding the length of the alligator. Discuss all student responses.

EXTENSION If possible, arrange for an ecologist from a local university to visit your class. Tell students to prepare questions they would like to ask the ecologist beforehand.

Questions

1. INFER Is the work of an ecologist more likely to involve work in the laboratory or work in the field? (in the field; however, ecologists also may work in laboratories)

LESSON 2-3
What are responses? (p. 38)

Teaching Strategies

PREVIEW Before beginning this lesson, read the list of TechTerms aloud so students can hear their pronunciations.

DISCUSSION Introduce the concept of stimulus and response relationships. Provide students with several examples of how they respond to stimuli in their daily lives. Common examples of stimulus-response relationships include watering of the mouth at the smell of food, answering a ringing telephone, and answering the door when a knock is heard. Have students identify the stimulus and the response in each example. Then tell students plants and other animals also respond to changes in their environments.

CLASS ACTIVITY Place a plant in the classroom with its leaves facing away from the sun. Have students observe the plant for the next week. Students will observe that the leaves of the plant will grow back toward the sun.

EXTENSION You may wish to tell students that plant responses are called tropisms. Some of the stimuli to which plants respond are gravity, light, water, and chemicals.

DISCUSSION Discuss various types of simple responses. Be sure students understand that different organisms may respond in different ways to the same environmental change.

COOPERATIVE/COLLABORATIVE LEARNING Have a volunteer explain the difference between innate and learned behaviors to the rest of the class.

Answers to Challenges (p. 39)

InfoSearch

You may wish to discuss students' questions and answers as a class.

Teaching Tips for Activity

Pupil Responses to Light

Skills: *observing, inferring, hypothesizing, predicting*

COOPERATIVE/COLLABORATIVE LEARNING Students must work in pairs.

Questions

1. The pupil got smaller in size. Increased light caused the pupil to get smaller.
2. a. the light **b.** The pupil gets smaller.
3. a. It got larger. **b.** The pupil got larger to allow more light into the eye.
4. Answers will vary. Accept all logical responses.
5. in total darkness

LESSON 2-4
Where do living things come from? (p. 40)

Teaching Strategies

PREVIEW Before students begin this lesson have them review the objective and read the Lesson Summary.

REINFORCEMENT To help students understand the theory of spontaneous generation, have students look up the definitions of "spontaneous" and "generation" in a dictionary. Tell students to write the definitions. Then tell students to use the meanings of the two words to write the definition of "spontaneous generation" in their own words.

EXTENSION Have interested students research the life of Francesco Redi and write a brief biography of his life.

REINFORCEMENT Review the experiment performed by Redi to disprove spontaneous generation. As you review the experiment, have students identify the variables and the control for the experiment.

Answers to Challenges (p. 41)

Check

1. idea that living things can come from nonliving matter
2. Redi
3. a stage in the life cycle of a fly
4. the meat serves as a food source for the developing offspring
5. the sealed jar

Apply

6. to make sure that any changes that occur during the experiment are caused by the variable being tested
7. that flies do not develop from rotting meat
8. Answers will vary. Accept all logical responses.

Designing an Experiment

Have volunteers describe their experiments to the rest of the class.

Teaching Tips for People in Science
Louis Pasteur

EXTENSION Have interested students research the process of pasteurization. Tell students to present their findings in an oral report.

DEMONSTRATION To help students better understand Pasteur's experiment, demonstrate a similar experiment. Prepare a broth by boiling water with the contents of an instant bouillon packet. Pour the broth into two flasks. Seal one flask immediately and leave the other flask exposed to the air. After a few days, have students observe the broths under a microscope. Students will observe microorganisms growing in the broth that was exposed to air.

Questions

1. APPLY What kinds of products do you think are pasteurized? (Pasteurization is most often used for dairy products.)
2. APPLY How did Pasteur's experiment help to disprove the theory of spontaneous generation? (Pasteur showed that microorganisms carried in the air were responsible for the production of new microorganisms.)

LESSON 2-5
How does life continue on the earth? (p. 42)

Teaching Strategies

PREVIEW Have students scan the lesson for the science process skills symbols. Encourage students to review the definition given on page 16 of their texts for each skill listed.

CLASS ACTIVITY To introduce this lesson, write the following head on the chalkboard: *Reproduction*. From this head, draw arrows to each of the following heads: *Asexual Reproduction, Sexual Reproduction*. From the head *Asexual Reproduction*, draw arrows to each of the following: *Fission, Budding*. Have students copy the chart in their notebooks. Then describe the differences between asexual reproduction and sexual reproduction. Tell students to copy the information in their notebooks under the proper heads.

DEMONSTRATION Demonstrate the difference between fission and budding using a ball of clay. First, roll a ball of clay in your hands. Then, break the ball of clay into two pieces of equal sizes. Tell students that during fission, the parent organism splits in two to produce two offspring (daughter cells) of equal size. Then, put the two pieces of clay together. Again, form a ball with the clay. Gently squeeze a small piece of the clay so a small ball of clay is formed on the side of the large ball. Break the small piece of clay free from the larger ball. Tell students that this demonstration models budding, the process in which a small piece of the parent organism breaks off to form a new organism. Have students observe that the new organism is smaller than the original parent organism.

EXTENSION You may wish to tell students that budding and fission are the most common methods of reproduction for single-celled organisms such as bacteria and yeast. Complex multicellular organisms usually reproduce sexually.

Answers to Challenges (p. 43)
Apply

6. The kind of organism may become extinct.
7. Check students' diagrams. Diagrams should resemble Figure 1 on page 42.
8. fission
9. asexual reproduction
Skill Builder: Researching

Check students' tables. goats: kids; pigs: piglets; giraffes: calves; gorillas: babies; tigers: cubs; deer: fawns; bears: cubs; cows: calves; ducks: ducklings

Teaching Tips for Technology and Society
Cloning

DISCUSSION Tell students that because cloning involves reproduction of an organism from a single cell, it is a form of asexual reproduction.

ENRICHMENT Have interested students research some of the bioethical concern's regarding cloning. Encourage students to present their findings in oral reports.

Questions

1. DESCRIBE Why would people want to clone animals? (to produce organisms with specific traits)
2. DEFINE What is insulin? (a drug used to treat people who can't keep the right amount of sugar in their blood)

LESSON 2-6
What are life processes? (p. 44)

Teaching Strategies

PREVIEW Before students begin the lesson have them review the TechTerms and read the Lesson Summary.

RETEACHING OPTION To introduce this lesson, write the following head on the chalkboard: *Life Processes*. From this head, draw arrows to each of the following heads: *Nutrition, Respiration, Excretion, Transport*. Then point to each heading and describe the life process. Have students copy the information in their notebooks.

REINFORCEMENT Be sure students understand the difference between ingestion and digestion. Emphasize that nutrition is a combination of ingestion and digestion.

DISCUSSION Be sure students understand that plants carry out life processes. Point out that although plants can make their own food, they must take in nutrients in order to carry out their food-making process. Also, stress that plants carry on respiration. Students may tend to think that only animals carry on respiration.

COOPERATIVE/COLLABORATIVE LEARNING Have students quiz each other on the material in this lesson.

Answers to Challenges (p. 45)
Apply

7. If any of the life processes are not carried out, an organism will die.

8. Food is taken into the organism (ingestion) and then broken down into usable forms (digestion). The usable food is transported to cells, where it is combined with oxygen to produce energy (respiration). Waste products formed by respiration and digestion are transported to parts of the organism where they are removed (excretion).

Health and Safety Tip

Check students' charts.

Skill Builder: Researching

$6H_2O + 6CO_2 \rightarrow C_6H_{12}O_6 + 6O_2$
Water plus carbon dioxide yields glucose plus oxygen; photosynthesis is the reverse reaction of respiration.

Teaching Tips for Looking Back in Science
Transport in Humans

EXTENSION Have interested students find out more about the work of William Harvey. Tell students to write their findings in a report.

Question

What tiny blood vessels connect large blood vessels? (capillaries)

LESSON 2-7
What are the needs of organisms? (p. 46)

Teaching Strategies

PREVIEW Before students begin this lesson, have them review the objective and read the Lesson Summary.

DISCUSSION To begin this lesson, ask students what they need to survive. Responses will most likely include food, water, and oxygen. Use students' knowledge as a springboard for a discussion of the needs of all living things.

REINFORCEMENT As students read about each of the needs of organisms, relate each need to the life process to which it is related. For example, food and water are needed for respiration and nutrition. Air is needed for respiration and photosynthesis. A proper temperature is needed for most chemical reactions (respiration, digestion) to occur. Living space provides organisms with the materials they need from their environment as well as shelter and a place to reproduce.

DISCUSSION The concept of homeostasis may be difficult for students to grasp. Tell students that homeostasis is an automatic response of the body that enables organisms to maintain constant internal conditions. Discuss how shivering and perspiring help humans maintain a body temperature of 37 ˚C.

RETEACHING OPTION Ask students what needs of living things are shown in the picture on page 46. Write student responses on the chalkboard. Then review why each of these things is needed by living things.

Answers to Challenges (p. 47)
Apply

6. Shivering and perspiring are ways that the body maintains a constant temperature.
7. Answers may vary. Accept all logical responses.
8. Students may suggest that some organisms die because they cannot meet their needs, while others move to other living spaces. Accept all logical responses.

Ideas in Action

Responses may include drinking, cooking, washing dishes, bathing, swimming, and recreation. Accept all logical responses.

Health and Safety Tip

Botulism bacteria are most commonly found in foods such as canned green beans, peas, and tomatoes.

Teaching Tips For Leisure Activity
Cooking

COOPERATIVE/COLLABORATIVE LEARNING Some of your students may already enjoy cooking as a hobby. Encourage students to bring in their favorite recipes. The recipes can be placed together and photocopied to make a class cookbook.

ENRICHMENT You may wish to have a professional chef speak to the class about a career as a cook. Have the chef discuss the credentials needed to become a chef.

Questions

1. APPLY How is cooking related to life science? (Answers will vary. Accept all logical responses.)
2. LIST What materials do you think you need to begin cooking as a hobby? (Responses may include a stove, pots, pans, food, and utensils. Accept all logical responses.)

Answers to Unit Challenges (pp. 48-50)
Understanding The Features: Reading Critically

1. scientist who studies the relationships between living things and their environments
2. to produce animals with specific traits
3. carbohydrates, lipids, proteins, nucleic acids
4. how transport occurs in the body
5. by performing an experiment with broth, flasks, air, and microorganisms
6. according to similar foods

Interpreting a Diagram

1. the uncovered jars and the jars with the veils
2. jar B
3. jar A
4. the flies could not get into the jar with the lid or the jar with the veil.
5. eggs laid by the flies
6. The experiment showed that flies did not develop from rotting meat.

Critical Thinking

1. A robot does not have all the characteristics of organisms and does not carry out the life processes.
2. Growth is one way in which organisms develop.
3. energy, carbon dioxide, and water
4. Living things compete with each other for living space, food, water, and other needs provided by the environment.
5. because the offspring are made up of cells from both parents

4. robin: predator; worm: prey
5. mouse: prey; cat: predator
6. cheetah: predator; antelope: prey

<table>
<tr><td>UNIT 3
ECOLOGY (p. 51)</td></tr>
</table>

UNIT 3
ECOLOGY (p. 51)

Previewing the Unit

Read the titles of the lessons in this unit aloud. Identify terms in the titles with which students are unfamiliar. Write these terms on the chalkboard. Using the Glossary of the text of a dictionary, define the terms as a class. Have students write the terms and their definitions in their notebooks. Then, have students work in small groups to carry out the task in the Study Hint.

Bulletin Board Suggestions

1. Assemble a bulletin board that shows the six major land biomes. List the names of the land biomes on the bulletin board. Have students find and collect pictures of the plants and animals that inhabit each biome. Attach the pictures under the correct heads.

2. Assemble a bulletin board showing a complex food web. Attach pictures of producers, and first-, second-, and third-level consumers to the bulletin board to make a food web. Add arrows to show the relationships among the organisms.

LESSON 3-1
What is ecology? (p. 52)

Teaching Strategies

PREVIEW Before beginning this lesson, have students review the TechTerms and their definitions and read the Lesson Summary.

REINFORCEMENT Remind students that everything that surrounds a living thing makes up its environment. Then introduce the definition of ecology.

EXTENSION You may wish to introduce the terms *biotic* and *abiotic*. The biotic factors in an environment are the living things. Biotic factors include plants, animals, protists, bacteria, and fungi. Abiotic factors are the nonliving parts of the environment. Ask students to list as many abiotic factors as they can for their classroom environment. Write student responses on the chalkboard.

CLASS ACTIVITY If possible, set up an aquarium in the classroom. Have students identify the living and nonliving things in the aquarium environment. List student responses on the chalkboard under the heads *Living* and *Nonliving*. Be sure that things students cannot see, such as dissolved gases and microorganisms, are included.

DISCUSSION Ask students to list the titles of at least 10 people they interact with in their community. (Responses may include teacher, doctor, cashier, and so on.) Point out that human society has many interactions. Then discuss the interactions that occur in nature. Have students observe Figure 1 on p. 52 and use the interactions on an African plain as an example.

Answers to Challenges (p. 53)
Skill Builder: Classifying

1. lion: predator; zebra: prey
2. fly: prey; frog: predator

Teaching Tips for Career in Life Science
Air Pollution Technician

DISCUSSION Be sure students understand the meaning of the term *pollutants.* Point out that pollutants are harmful substances that enter the environment. Describe some of the substances that cause air pollution such as chemicals and dust and soot. Explain to students that people are the cause of pollution and therefore must be the solution to the problem. Discuss with students methods for reducing the amounts of pollutants in the air.

EXTENSION If possible, arrange for an air pollution technician to speak to your class. Ask the technician to describe a typical working day.

Question

DEFINE What are pollutants? (harmful substances that enter the environment)

LESSON 3-2
What is an ecosystem? (p. 54)

Teaching Strategies

PREVIEW Have students write the lesson title and objective in their notebooks. As students read the lesson, tell them to write down the sentence or sentences that provide the information needed in the objective.

DISCUSSION This lesson introduces three key terms of ecology: *population, community,* and *ecosystem.* Define each of these terms for the class. Be sure students understand that a community is all the populations living in a region, and not the region itself. Point out that there usually are many complex relationships among the populations of a community. Most of these are feeding patterns, but others may involve protection and reproduction. You may wish to describe the pollination of plants by insects as an example of a relationship that is not a feeding relationship in itself, but an outcome of one.

RETEACHING OPTION Hold up a nature scene showing a variety of different kinds of animals. Ask students how many different animal populations are shown. Tell students that all the populations together make up a community. Then point out some of the nonliving parts of the environment in the picture. Ask students what the living and nonliving parts of the environment make up. (ecosystem)

COOPERATIVE/COLLABORATIVE LEARNING Ask a volunteer to describe the four processes that occur in an ecosystem to make it self-supporting.

Answers to Challenges (p. 55)
Apply

6. 2
7. 2
8. The pond is made up of both living and nonliving parts. The organisms in the pond interact with the nonliving parts of the environment and with each other.

InfoSearch

You may wish to discuss students' questions and answers as a class.

Teaching Tips for Science Connection
The *Gaia* Hypothesis

REINFORCEMENT   This feature provides a perfect opportunity to review the meanings of the terms *hypothesis* and *theory*.

DISCUSSION   Not all scientists agree with the *Gaia* Hypothesis. After students read the feature, ask them if they agree or disagree with Lovelock's ideas. Use the question for an open ended discussion of the *Gaia* hypothesis.

Questions

1. HYPOTHESIZE   Why might a small change in the Earth's environment be harmful to living things? (Answers will vary. Accept all logical responses.)
2. IDENTIFY   Who formulated the *Gaia* Hypothesis? (James Lovelock)

LESSON 3-3
What are habitats and niches? (p. 56)

Teaching Strategies

PREVIEW   Before beginning this lesson, read the list of TechTerms aloud so students can hear their pronunciations.

DISCUSSION   To provide motivation for this lesson, ask students what their roles, or jobs, in life are. (They will most likely respond that they are students.) Use the question as a springboard for a discussion of a niche. Point out that all organisms have a role in their communities. Define niche as an organism's role in its habitat.

REINFORCEMENT   Be sure students understand why organisms may have the same habitat but not the same niche. Emphasize that competition among species living in the same place is the reason organisms cannot share the same niche.

Answers to Challenges (p. 57)

Apply

  6. The population most suited to the environment will survive and reproduce. The other population will decrease in size.
  7. No; a rattlesnake is not adapted for life in a cold, Arctic habitat.
  8. air and land
  9. salt water
 10. land
 11. fresh water
 12. salt water, fresh water
 13. fresh water
 14. air and land
 15. land

Skill Builder: Communicating

Answers will vary. Accept all logical responses.

Teaching Tips for Leisure Activity
Nature Photography

DISCUSSION   Have students bring in some of their own nature photographs to display and discuss.

CLASS ACTIVITY   Have students flip through their textbooks to observe some photographs taken by nature photographers. Ask students to choose their favorite photographs in the book.

Questions

1. EXPLAIN   Why should nature photographers learn about the animals they wish to photograph? (Answers will vary. Accept all logical responses.)
2. LIST   What are three great places for photographing plants and animals? (state and national parks, recreation areas, seashores, wildlife preserves)

LESSON 3-4
What are limiting factors? (p. 58)

PREVIEW   Before beginning this lesson, write the title of each section in the lesson on the chalkboard in an outline format. Have students copy these titles in their notebooks. As students read each section, have them write the topic sentence of each paragraph beneath each section title.

DISCUSSION   Introduce this lesson with a discussion of the childhood game *Musical Chairs.* Make an analogy between the number of chairs and limiting factors. Relate the number of people who can sit to an area's carrying capacity.

CLASS ACTIVITY   Have students work in small groups to make graphs showing the relationship between the sizes of animal populations and the sizes of plant populations. Students' graphs should show that as plant populations decrease, animal populations decrease.

INTRASCIENCE CONNECTION   Have students collect soil samples from around their neighborhoods. Have students examine the soil and make a chart listing the following information: overall appearance, kind and size of soil particles, shape of rock particles, presence of organic material. Use the information students organize to determine the type of soil in your area. Point out that type of soil is a limiting factor for plants.

RETEACHING OPTION   Write the following head on the chalkboard: *Limiting Factors.* From this head, draw arrows to each of the following heads: *Plants, Animals.* From the head *Plants,* draw arrows to the following: *Amount of Sunlight, Type of Soil, Temperature, Amount of Water.* From the head *Animals,* draw arrows to the following: *Temperature, Water, Food Supply, Shelter.* Have students copy the charts in their notebooks.

Answers to Challenges (p. 59)

Apply

5. Humans can eat many different kinds of food, can make their own shelters, and can make clothing that helps them to live in different climates.
6. Yes, because humans rely on plant and animal populations to meet their need for food.

InfoSearch

You may wish to discuss students' questions and answers as a class.

Teaching Tips for Science Connection
World Population Growth

EXTENSION   Have students research world population growth for the past 300 years. Tell students to organize their findings in a graph.

Questions

1. What is the total world population today? (about 5 billion)
2. Why can the earth carry a population that is so much larger than it was 20,000 years ago? (improved methods of food production, medical advances)

LESSON 3-5
What cycles take place in nature? (p. 60)

Teaching Strategies

PREVIEW Before beginning this section, have students scan the lesson looking for words with which they are unfamiliar. Have students work in pairs or small groups to define each of the words on their lists.

DISCUSSION Describe the water cycle, the oxygen-carbon dioxide cycle, and the nitrogen cycle. Use the pictures on p. 60 to illustrate your descriptions.

CLASS ACTIVITY Divide the class into small groups. Have students in each group draw pictures of plants, animals, soil, the sun, clouds, and so on. Have students cut out the pictures and assemble them in ways that illustrate the water cycle, the oxygen-carbon dioxide cycle, and the nitrogen cycle. Have students paste the pictures on a posterboard and then add arrows to show the flow of water, oxygen and carbon dioxide, and nitrogen through the environment.

Answers to Challenges (p. 61)

Apply

7. Answers will vary. Accept all logical responses.
8. They supply each other with the gases needed for the life processes.
9. Nitrogen given off by animals is changed into a useable form by nitrogen-fixing bacteria and is then used by other living things. Thus, the nitrogen is recycled through the environment.

InfoSearch

You may wish to discuss students' questions and answers as a class.

Teaching Tips for Science Connection
The Rock Cycle

DEMONSTRATION Bring in examples of an igneous rock, a sedimentary rock, and a metamorphic rock. Display the rocks in front of the classroom. List the three main types of rocks on the chalkboard. Then pass around a sample of each type of rock for students to examine.

Questions

1. CLASSIFY What kind of rock is rock that forms when liquid volcanic rock cooled? (igneous rock)
2. DEFINE What is the rock cycle? (process by which rocks change form)

LESSON 3-6
What are producers and consumers? (p. 62)

Teaching Strategies

PREVIEW Before beginning this lesson, have students scan the lesson for the science process skill symbols. Have students identify each skill used in the lesson. Students should then review the definition given for each skill on page 16 of their text.

DISCUSSION Introduce students to the four major groups of organisms, as classified by the way they get food. Have students provide familiar examples of producers, consumers, scavengers, and decomposers to illustrate these groups.

EXTENSION You may wish to tell students that animals that eat only plants are called herbivores, animals that eat only meat are called carnivores, and animals that eat both plants and animals are called omnivores.

REINFORCEMENT Remind students that algae are plantlike protists. If possible, display a wall chart showing various types of algae. Emphasize the importance of algae as the main producers in lakes and oceans.

Answers to Challenges (p. 63)

Apply

6. Organisms depend upon each other for food.
7. A human is a primary consumer when eating plant products, such as fruits and vegetables. A human is a secondary consumer when eating animal products such as eggs, milk, poultry, and lamb that come from plant-eating animals. A human is a tertiary consumer when eating meats that come from animal-eating animals.
8. consumers

Skill Builder: Building Vocabulary

1. omnivore	5. omnivore
2. carnivore	6. herbivore
3. herbivore	7. carnivore
4. carnivore	8. herbivore

Teaching Tips for Technology and Society
Hydroponics

CLASS ACTIVITY If possible, arrange for your class to visit a place where plants are grown using hydroponics. Possible places include a local university's research laboratory or a botanical garden.

Questions

1. What are the advantages of growing plants using hydroponics? (Plants are protected from harsh weather and from insect and animal pests.)
2. INFER What are two minerals that are put in the special liquid used for hydroponics? (nitrogen, calcium)

LESSON 3-7
What are food chains, webs, and energy pyramids? (p. 64)

Teaching Strategies

PREVIEW Before beginning this lesson, write the title of each section in the lesson on the chalkboard. Have students copy these titles in their notebooks using an outline format. As students read each section, they should write the topic sentence for each paragraph in the section in their notebooks.

DISCUSSION Refer students to the pictures on p. 64 showing a food chain and a food web. Tell students that the major difference between the two models is that the food web shows how a number of food chains are related. Be sure students understand that a food web is a more accurate account of what happens in nature.

CLASS ACTIVITY Have students work in small groups to construct various food chains and food webs. Tell students to label the producers, the primary consumers, the secondary consumers, and the tertiary consumers on their models. Have students illustrate their models with pictures. When all groups are finished, have a representative from each group display and describe the group's models for the rest of the class.

DEMONSTRATION Make a model of an energy pyramid using four different sized boxes, the largest on the bottom and the smallest on the top. Label each of the pyramid levels with appropriate examples. Use the model the explain how energy moves through a food chain.

REINFORCEMENT Be sure students understand that energy is not recycled through the environment. Emphasize that at each level of the energy pyramid, energy is lost. Ask students why they think energy is lost at each level. (Elicit from students that energy is lost as heat during growth, respiration, and other life processes.)

Answers to Challenges (p. 65)

Apply

6. There would be more minnows in the pond because they are at a lower level in the food chain.
7. flower
8. primary consumer
9. Check students' models to make sure that the arrows are pointing in the correct direction.
10. Students' models will vary. Accept all logical organisms. Check students' models for logic and accuracy.

Skill Builder: Modeling

The grass should be at the bottom of the pyramid; the rabbit at the primary consumer level; the snake at the secondary consumer level; and the wolf at the tertiary consumer level.

Teaching Tips for Activity
Modeling Food Chains

Skills: *analyzing, relating concepts, organizing, modeling*

COOPERATIVE/COLLABORATIVE LEARNING Have students compare their food chains with a partner.

Questions

1. Answers will vary. Accept all logical responses.
2. Answers will vary.
3. a. tree, grass, shrub **b.** rabbit, field mouse, snake, owl, elk, cricket, mountain lion, hawk, frog
4. Check students' food webs for logic and accuracy.

LESSON 3-8
What is succession? (p. 66)

Teaching Strategies

PREVIEW Have students read the lesson feature before beginning the lesson. Discuss the concepts presented in the

feature. Ask students how they think this information relates to topics they have already studied or to the lesson they are about to study.

DISCUSSION Introduce students to the process of ecological succession. Explain that environments go through a series of changes in their populations and communities, until a climax community forms.

CLASS ACTIVITY Divide the class into four groups. Have each group draw one of the following communities on a posterboard: open field, shrub land, pine forest, hardwood forest. Then display the students' artwork in sequence to illustrate succession.

EXTENSION Succession can occur when an ecosystem is changed due to fire, wind, farming, and so on. An ecosystem also can change when a new habitat, such as an island is created. Ecological succession also can start in areas that did not previously support live. Have students research how lichens can start ecological succession. Tell students to write their findings in a report.

Answers to Challenges (p. 67)

Apply

5. No, because different organisms live in different places.
6. Faster-growing plants that can live in the burnt soil grow first.
7. A bog is an area with plants and very wet land.
8. pond, bog, meadow, shrub land, pine forest, hardwood forest

Health and Safety Tip

Student responses will vary but may include that matches should be completely extinguished before being disposed of, campfires should be confined to a small area, and a campfire should never be left unattended. Accept all logical responses.

Teaching Tips for Science Connection
Seed Dispersal

CLASS ACTIVITY Bring in an assortment of fruits. Cut the fruits open to expose their seeds, and pass the fruits around the class.

DISCUSSION Discuss how wind, water, and animals play a role in the dispersal of seeds.

Questions

1. ANALYZE Why do you think a fruit does not ripen until its seeds are mature? (to insure survival of the plant; Animals will not eat the fruit until the seeds are ready for dispersal.)
2. DEFINE What is seed dispersal? (movement of seeds away from the parent plant)

LESSON 3-9
What are biomes? (p. 68)

Teaching Strategies

PREVIEW Have students write the lesson title and objective in their notebooks. As students read the lesson, tell them to write down the sentence or sentences that provide the information needed in the objective.

DISCUSSION Refer students to the biome map on p. 68. Have students locate the six major biomes as you describe the plants and animals that are characteristic of each biome.

EXTENSION You may wish to tell students that the tropical rain forests of the world are being cut down at an alarming rate. Point out that the destruction of tropical rain forests leads to the extinction of many species and the loss of valuable resources.

INTRASCIENCE CONNECTION Be sure students understand the difference between weather conditions and climate. Explain that weather is the day-to-day conditions of the atmosphere, such as wind conditions, humidity, and temperature. Climate is the overall weather in an area over a long period of time.

EXTENSION Have interested students research the marine biome which is the largest biome of Earth. Tell students to find out the characteristics of the ocean, estuary, and intertidal zone. Tell students to write their findings in a report.

Answers to Challenges (p. 69)

Apply

5. More kinds of plants are suited to life in the deciduous forest than in the tundra. Therefore, a larger and more diversified animal population can be supported. Accept all logical responses.
6. Deserts receive far less rainfall than tropical rain forests.

InfoSearch

You may wish to discuss students' questions and answers as a class.

Teaching Tips for Leisure Activity

Leaf Peeping

CLASS ACTIVITY If possible, take students on a leaf peeping class trip.

EXTENSION You may wish to identify the New England states on a map of the United States. The New England states are Maine, New Hampshire, Vermont, Massachusetts, Rhode Island, and Connecticut.

Questions

1. Would you like to go leaf peeping? Why or why not? (Answers will vary. Accept all logical responses.)
2. IDENTIFY What are some great places for leaf peeping in the United States? (the New England states)

LESSON 3-10
What are natural resources?
(p. 70)

Teaching Strategies

PREVIEW Before beginning this lesson, have students review the TechTerms and their definitions and read the Lesson Summary.

RETEACHING OPTION Write the following head on the chalkboard: *Natural Resources*. From this head, draw arrows to each of the following heads: *Renewable Resources, Nonrenewable Resources*. Under *Renewable Resources* list air, water, soil, and living things. Under *Nonrenewable Resources* list oil, coal, natural gas, and minerals. Have students copy the charts in their notebooks.

DISCUSSION Discuss conservation. Be sure students understand the necessity of conserving renewable resources, as well as nonrenewable resources.

COOPERATIVE/COLLABORATIVE LEARNING Have one student explain and give examples of renewable resources. Have another student explain and give examples of nonrenewable resources.

Answers to Challenges (p. 71)

Apply

6. Answers will vary. Accept all logical responses.
7. because they take millions of years to form
8. renewable resources: plants, soil, elephant, flies, water, sun; nonrenewable resources: coal, motor oil

Ideas in Action

Answers will vary. Accept all logical responses.

Skill Builder: Classifying

Renewable resources include nutrients, food, oxygen, wood, and fish. Nonrenewable resources include marble, gasoline, charcoal, methane gas, kerosene, and propane gas.

Teaching Tips for Technology and Society

Nuclear Energy

CLASS ACTIVITY Have a class debate about the pros and cons of nuclear energy.

CLASS ACTIVITY Have students collect articles pertaining to nuclear energy from magazines, newspapers, and so on. Read and discuss the articles as a class.

Questions

1. DEFINE What is nuclear energy? (energy released when atoms are split)
2. What is the most common fuel for nuclear energy? (uranium)

LESSON 3-11
What is balance in an ecosystem? (p. 72)

Teaching Strategies

PREVIEW Before beginning this lesson, read the TechTerms aloud so students can hear their pronunciations.

DISCUSSION Write the term *Pollution* on the chalkboard. Discuss what students think of when they hear the word *pollution*. Emphasize that pollution is upsetting the balance of the environment.

EXTENSION Have students find out what measures are being taken to prevent endangered animals from becoming extinct. Tell students to present their findings in an oral report.

Answers to Challenges (p. 73)

State the Problem

Polluted water is flowing into the lake.

Teaching Tips for People in Science

Rachel Carson

EXTENSION   Have students read *Silent Spring* and write a book report.

Question

What were Rachel Carson's two main occupations? (biologist, writer)

Answers to Unit Challenges (pp. 74-76)

Understanding the Features: Reading Critically

1. harmful substances that enter the environment
2. 3.5%
3. Learning the habits of the animals makes it easier to obtain photographs of the animals in their natural habitats. Accept all logical responses.
4. It is getting larger.
5. igneous, sedimentary, metamorphic
6. growing of plants in water instead of soil
7. Seeds are carried to new places where they are more likely to germinate. An area undergoing succession has more space for the seed to grow and develop. Accept all logical responses.
8. the fall
9. energy released when atoms split
10. marine science; Accept all logical answers.

Interpreting a Diagram

1. food web
2. grass
3. rabbit, mice, grasshoppers
4. wolves, owls, snakes, frogs, hawks
5. hawks and snakes
6. the food relationships among organisms
7. Check students' drawings for logic and accuracy.
8. Answers will vary. Accept all logical responses.

Critical Thinking

1. Check students' energy pyramids for logic and accuracy.
2. Both show the movement of energy through an ecosystem.
3. Because the bacteria can make their own food, they are producers.
4. Scavengers feed upon the remains of organisms without breaking down the remains.
5. The remains of dead organisms would pile up.

CELLS, TISSUES, AND ORGANS (p. 77)

Previewing the Unit

Have students work in small groups to carry out the task in the Study Hint. Have students record the words on their lists in a Unit Glossary. Students should include a definition for each word in their glossaries.

Bulletin Board Suggestions

1. Create a bulletin board display entitled *Cells*. Divide the bulletin board into two sections, labeled *Plant Cells* and *Animal Cells*. Beneath each section include a large labeled drawing of each kind of cell. Be sure the drawing illustrates each of the cell parts discussed in Lessons 1 through 4 of this unit. Refer to the bulletin board as you discuss each cell part.
2. Create a Bulletin board display entitled *Human Organ Systems*. Down the left side of the bulletin board, list each of the ten organ systems of the human body. Place cards listing the major organs of each system next to the name of each organ system.

LESSON 4-1
What are cells? (p. 78)

Teaching Strategies

PREVIEW Before students begin this lesson, have them read the objective and review the Lesson Summary.

DISCUSSION To introduce this lesson, build a small house of cards in front of the classroom. Ask students to identify the basic unit of structure of a card house. (a card) Then tell students that the basic unit of structure in living things is the cell. Point out that all living things are made up of one or more cells.

CLASS ACTIVITY Have students observe cork slices with a compound microscope. Tell students to sketch what they see. Then have students compare their drawings with the picture of cork cells on p. 78.

DISCUSSION Write the three parts of the cell theory on the chalkboard and discuss each part. Explain to students that scientists consider these ideas to be a theory because the ideas have been supported by data over time. Be sure students understand each of the ideas that make up the cell theory.

EXTENSION Have interested student find out more about the work of Hooke or van Leeuwenhoek. Tell students to write their findings in a report. Students should recognize that these men were pioneers in scientific studies.

Answers to Challenges (p. 79)
Check

1. an idea that explains something; A theory is supported by data over and over.
2. cell
3. Robert Hooke
4. single-celled organisms
5. other living cells

Apply

6. As microscopes improve, scientists are better able to see the parts of a cell and how they function.
7. Yes; respiration is a life process and cells carry on all life processes.
8. No; cork is made up of dead plant cells. Only living cells can produce new cells.

Ideas in Action

Answers will vary. Accept all logical responses.

Skill Builder: Researching

The organisms seen by van Leeuwenhoek were protozoans. Because protozoans are able to move, van Leeuwenhoek likened them to animals.

Teaching Tips for People in Science
Schleiden and Schwann

DISCUSSION Stress to students that although both Schleiden and Schwann contributed to the cell theory, the two scientists did not work together. Point out the importance of communication among scientists and of how scientific research builds upon past discoveries.

EXTENSION Have interested students research Schwann cells. Tell students to draw and label a Schwann cell and to briefly describe its function.

Questions

1. IDENTIFY   In what branch of life science did Matthias Schleiden work? (botany)
2. RELATE   How did the studies of Schleiden and Schwann contribute to the development of the cell theory? (Both Scientists observed that living things were made up of cells.)

LESSON 4-2
What are the main cell parts?
(p. 80)

Teaching Strategies

PREVIEW Before students begin this lesson, read the list of TechTerms aloud so students can hear their correct pronunciations.

DISCUSSION Draw and label the three main parts of the cell on the chalkboard. Tell students that although the size, shape, and function of cells may differ, almost all cells have a nucleus, cytoplasm, and a cell membrane. Then describe the functions of these three cell parts.

REINFORCEMENT The functions of the nucleus of a cell often are compared to the functions of the brain. Explain to students that the brain controls all of the activities of their bodies. The nucleus controls all of the functions in a cell.

EXTENSION You may wish to tell students that most of the cytoplasm of a cell is made up of water. This is important because most of a cell's activities take place in the cytoplasm and most chemical reactions take place in water.

CLASS ACTIVITY Divide the class into small groups. Distribute three different colors of clay to each group. Have students use the clay to make models showing the three main parts of a cell.

RETEACHING OPTION   Have students begin a table in their notebooks listing cell parts and their functions. Tell students to add to their tables as they learn about other cell parts.

Answers to Challenges (p. 81)

Apply

6. nucleus
7. The functions of the nuclear membrane are the same as those for the cell membrane: support, shape, and the control of materials into and out of the nucleus.
8. Check students' models for logic and accuracy.

Skill Builder: Building Vocabulary

The prefix *cyto-* means "cell." Answers will vary, but definitions should include the term cell.

Teaching Tips for Activity

Modeling a Cell

Skills: *modeling, comparing*

COOPERATIVE/COLLABORATIVE LEARNING Have students work in pairs. Encourage students to compare their models with those of their classmates.

DISCUSSION Place a completed model at the front of the class. Discuss which cell part is represented by each part of the model.

Questions

1. Check students' diagrams.
2. a. cell membrane   **b.** cytoplasm   **c.** nucleus
3. a. gelatin   **b.** Most of a real cell is made up of cytoplasm, which is represented by the gelatin.

LESSON 4-3
What are other cell parts?
(p. 82)

Teaching Strategies

PREVIEW Before beginning this lesson, have students read the Lesson feature.

DISCUSSION Compare a cell to a factory. Relate the machines in a factory to the "machines" in a cell. Point out that each organelle has a special job to do. Then describe the functions of mitochondria, vacuoles, ribosomes, and transport tubes.

DISCUSSION Tell students that the singular form of mitochondria is mitochondrion.

DEMONSTRATION Show students photomicrographs of actual cells. Point out the different organelles in the pictures.

Answers to Challenges (p. 83)

Apply

6. railroad: transport tubes; cabinets: vacuoles; battery: mitochondria; electric company: mitochondria
7. There are more mitochondria in muscle cells. Extra mitochondria are needed to provide the energy muscle cells need to carry out their functions.
8. Check students' diagrams.

InfoSearch

You may wish to discuss students' questions and answers as a class.

Teaching Tips for Technology and Society

Electron Microscopes

DEMONSTRATION To help students understand the differences between SEMs and TEMs, bring in photomicrographs of images produced by each kind of microscope. Challenge students to identify the kind of microscope that produced each image and to explain their choices.

INTRASCIENCE CONNECTION Images produced by a SEM are black and white. Discuss with students the use of computers to colorize these images. Ask students why scientists might want to colorize the images. Discuss all student responses.

Questions

1. ANALYZE   Which kind of electron microscope would be more useful for studying a living cell, an SEM or a TEM? Explain. (a SEM; A TEM kills cells.)
2. CONTRAST   How does an electron microscope differ from a compound microscope? (An electron microscope is larger, more costly, and has a higher magnification than a compound microscope. An electron microscope uses electrons instead of light to form images.)

LESSON 4-4
How do plant and animal cells differ? (p. 84)

Teaching Strategies

PREVIEW Before students begin this lesson, have them review the TechTerms and their definitions and read the Lesson Summary.

REINFORCEMENT Before beginning this lesson, review the basic structure of an animal cell.

DISCUSSION Have students study the diagram of a plant cell shown on p. 84. Ask students how plant and animal cells differ. Encourage students to use their own observations to state the similarities and differences of plant and animal cells.

CLASS ACTIVITY Have students view prepared slides of plant and animal cells under a microscope. Tell students to sketch and label the parts of the cells they observe.

RETEACHING OPTION Prepare a table that lists each of the cell structures students have studied down the left-hand column. Across the top of the table list the following heads: *Plant Cell, Animal Cell.* Have students place a plus sign (+) below the appropriate head if the structure listed is found in a plant cell or an animal cell. If the structure is not found in the cell have students place a minus sign (−) in the column. Tell students to use their tables as study guides.

COOPERATIVE/COLLABORATIVE LEARNING Have students work in pairs to answer the Check and Apply questions.

Answers to Challenges (p. 85)

Check

1. Plants do not need a skeleton because their cell walls provide them with support.
2. The cell wall gives a plant cell shape and support. It also protects the inside of the cell.

3. structures within a plant cell that contain chlorophyll
4. a nonliving material that makes up plant cell walls
5. They are smaller and more numerous.
6. Chlorophyll is used by plants to trap the energy in sunlight to make food.

Apply

7. a. Plant cells and animal cells have a cell membrane, a nucleus, ribosomes, mitochondria, transport tubes, and cytoplasm. **b.** Plant cells have a cell wall and chloroplasts. Plant cells also have fewer and larger vacuoles than do animal cells.
8. a, d, and e
9. Nonliving; wood is made up mostly of cellulose, which is a nonliving material.

InfoSearch

You may wish to discuss students' questions and answers as a class.

Teaching Tips for Activity
Analyzing Cells

Skills: *measuring, analyzing, inferring*

COOPERATIVE/COLLABORATIVE LEARNING   Answer the questions as a class.

Questions

1. nucleus, cell membrane, ribosomes.
2. a. A **b.** B **c.** Plant cells have a cell wall.
3. b. Yes. **c.** It contains chlorophyll.

LESSON 4-5
What is diffusion? (p. 86)

Teaching Strategies

PREVIEW   Before beginning this lesson, have students scan the lesson for the science process skill symbols. Have students identify each skill used in the lesson. Students should then review the definition given for each skill on p.16 of their text.

DEMONSTRATION   To demonstrate diffusion, open a bottle of perfume in the classroom. The molecules of perfume will diffuse throughout the room. Have students raise their hands as they observe the scent of the perfume.

DEMONSTRATION   Place a few drops of ink in a glass filled with water. Ask students why the ink begins to move through the water. (The molecules of ink are moving.) Have students observe that the ink molecules move from areas where they are crowded to areas where they are less crowded until they are evenly distributed. Identify this process as diffusion.

RETEACHING OPTION   Draw an arc representing a cell membrane on the chalkboard. Draw ten Xs and five Os on the inner side of the arc. Draw five Xs and ten Os on the outer side of the arc. Using the idea that a cell membrane will try to keep substances balanced both inside and outside the cell, elicit from students in which direction the Xs will move. (They will move out of the cell until an equal number of Xs appear inside and outside the cell.) Then ask students in

which direction the Os will move. (The Os will move into the cell until an equal number of Os are inside and outside the cell.)

REINFORCEMENT   Be sure students understand the difference between diffusion and osmosis. Point out that osmosis is a special kind of diffusion.

Answers to Challenges (p. 87)
Apply

5. in a glass of fresh water; The concentration of existing molecules in the fresh water is less than that of the salt water, thereby allowing the salt to dissolve more rapidly in the less concentrated solution.
6. The carbon dioxide will move into the cells.
7. The molecules given off by the bread will move through the air by diffusion.

State the Problem

Students should recognize that the arrow in this diagram shows the molecules moving in the wrong direction. The model could be fixed by pointing the arrow in the opposite direction.

Teaching Tips for Activity
Measuring Diffusion in Eggs

Skills: *measuring, observing, calculating*

COOPERATIVE/COLLABORATIVE LEARNING   Have students work in pairs.

Questions

1. a. the vinegar **b.** Answers will vary.
2. The eggs got larger as the volume of the liquid decreased.
3. the vinegar's

LESSON 4-6
How do cells produce new cells? (p. 88)

Teaching Strategies

PREVIEW   Before beginning this lesson, read the list of TechTerms aloud so students can hear their pronunciations.

DISCUSSION   Provide motivation for this lesson by asking students the questions: "How much did you weigh when you were born?"; How much do you weigh now? Ask students to account for the differences in their present weights and their weights at birth. Develop the idea that living things grow because cells reproduce and make more cells. Explain that new cells are produced by the process of cell division.

DISCUSSION   Refer students to the diagram on p. 88 showing cell division in an animal cell. Use the diagram to introduce and explain the process of mitosis.

DEMONSTRATION   Use charts, models, and prepared slides to show students the process of mitosis.

REINFORCEMENT   Be sure students understand the difference between cell division and mitosis. Emphasize that mitosis is division of the nucleus. Cell division includes mitosis, as well as the splitting of the parent cell into two daughter cells.

Answers to Challenges (p. 89)

Check

1. process by which cells reproduce
2. division of the nucleus
3. nucleus
4. Their cells can reproduce and make new cells.
5. The two new cells formed by cell division.
6. cell parts that determine what traits a living thing will have

Apply

7. The same number of chromosomes must go to each new daughter cell.
8. asexual reproduction; It involves only one parent cell.
9. c, a, d, b
10. plant cell division

Health and Safety Tip

The seven warning signs for cancer are: a sore that does not heal, unusual bleeding or discharge, thickening or lump in the breast or elsewhere, continued indigestion or difficulty in swallowing, a nagging cough, obvious change in a wart or mole, change in bowel or bladder habits.

Teaching Tips for Activity

Modeling Cell Division in an Animal Cell

Skills: *modeling, relating*

COOPERATIVE/COLLABORATIVE LEARNING Have students work in pairs.

Questions

1. **a.** large circle: cell; smaller circle: nucleus
   b. chromosomes
2. 4
3. by drawing two more separate cells

LESSON 4-7
Why do cells have different shapes? (p. 90)

Teaching Strategies

PREVIEW Before beginning this lesson, write the title of each section in the lesson on the chalkboard. Have students copy these titles in their notebooks using an outline format. As students read each section, they should write the topic sentence for each paragraph in the section in their notebooks.

DISCUSSION Describe the shapes and functions of nerve cells, muscle cells, blood cells, and guard cells. Lead students to conclude that the shape of a cell is related to its function.

DEMONSTRATION Using a bioscope, project as many slides as possible of different cells. Have students note the size and shape of each cell. Review the function of the various types of cells shown.

Answers to Challenges (p. 91)

Apply

7. A nerve cell is long and thin like a telephone wire. The size and shape of a nerve cell allows it to carry messages from one part of the body to another.

8. Red blood cells do not have a nucleus.

InfoSearch

You may wish to discuss students' questions and answers as a class.

Teaching Tips for Career in Life Science

Cytology Lab Technician

REINFORCEMENT Read the term ''cytology'' aloud so that students can hear its pronunciation.

EXTENSION If possible, arrange for a cytology lab technician to visit your class. Ask the technician to describe a typical workday. Have students prepare questions they would like to ask the technician beforehand.

Questions

1. Where do cytology lab technicians work? (universities and hospitals)
2. DESCRIBE What does a cytology lab technician do on the job? (works with tissue samples, prepares slides of cells, performs tests on cells)

LESSON 4-8
What are tissues? (p. 92)

Teaching Strategies

PREVIEW Before beginning this lesson, read the list of TechTerms aloud so students can hear their pronunciations.

DISCUSSION To provide motivation for this lesson, ask students to name their favorite team sports and their favorite teams. List student responses on the chalkboard. Then hold up action photographs of a baseball or football game. Ask students to point out all the players in the pictures who are on the same team. Ask students how they know which players are on the same team. Elicit the response that players on the same team wear the same uniform. The players work together to try and win the game. Then make an analogy between sports teams and tissues. Point out that a tissue is made up of a group of cells that look alike and work together. Describe the four main kinds of tissue and give students examples of each type.

CLASS ACTIVITY If possible, allow students to examine prepared slides showing the four main kinds of tissues. Tell students to sketch the different tissues in their notebooks. Have students identify individual cells.

RETEACHING OPTION Write the following head on the chalkboard: *Tissues.* From this head, draw arrows to each of the following heads: *Muscle Tissue, Epithelial Tissue, Connective Tissue, Nerve Tissue.* Under *Muscle Tissue* list muscles. Under *Epithelial Tissue* list skin. Under *Connective Tissue* list bone, ligaments, tendons, and blood. Under *Nerve Tissue* list the brain, spinal cord, and nerves. Have students copy the chart in their notebooks.

Answers to Challenges (p. 93)

Apply

7. Muscle tissue makes movement possible; connective tissue holds parts of the body together and supports and protects the body; nerve tissue carries messages.

8. to prevent calcium in the bones from being used by other parts of the body

Health and Safety Tip

Check students' posters. To help prevent brain and spinal cord injuries people should always wear seatbelts, check depths of water before diving, wear helmets when cycling or playing contact sports, and so on.

Teaching Tips for Technology and Society
Cornea Transplants

DEMONSTRATION If available, point out the cornea and other parts of the eye on a model or wall-sized poster of the eye.

Questions

1. DEFINE What is the cornea? (clear, outer layer of the eye)
2. Where was the first eye bank formed? (New York City)

LESSON 4-9
What are organs and organ systems? (p. 94)

Teaching Strategies

PREVIEW Have students write the lesson title and objective in their notebooks. As students read the lesson, tell them to write down the sentence or sentences that provide the information needed in the objective.

DISCUSSION Review the definition of tissue. Elicit that a tissue is a group of similar cells which work together to do a job. Then list several body organs on the chalkboard. Point out that each organ listed consists of several different tissues. Develop the concept that organs are made of different kinds of tissues which work together to do a job. Be sure students realize that plants also have organs.

REINFORCEMENT Challenge the class to list a number of animal organs and to identify the kinds of tissues found in each organ.

CLASS ACTIVITY Refer students to Table 1 on p. 94. Randomly read out the major organs listed. Have students identify the organ systems and their functions.

REINFORCEMENT You may wish to develop flash cards to help students review organ systems. On the front side of index cards, write the names of each organ system. On the other side of the cards, write the major organs that make up each system. Hold up each card in front of the class. Show students the sides listing the major organs. Have students identify the organ system. To vary this activity, show students the names of the organ systems and have students identify the major organs.

Answers to Challenges (p. 95)

Apply

10. b, d, c, e, a
11. muscles and bone tissue, nerve tissue, epithelial tissue, blood

Skill Builder: Researching

Check students' tables. The main functions: epidermis: pre-

vents drying out; ground tissue: stores food and provides support for a plant; vascular tissue: transports food and water throughout a plant; meristem tissue: growth

Teaching Tips for Technology and Society
The Visible Human Project

EXTENSION Ask interested students to visit the website http://www.nlm.nih.gov/research/visible for the project and download the sample images. Show the images to the class and have them identify any body organs they recognize.

Question

DESCRIBE What is the Visible Human Project? (a computer program showing the entire male and female body in three-dimensional detail)

Answers to Unit Challenges (pp. 96–98)
Understanding the Features: Reading Critically

1. a kind of nerve cell
2. A TEM cannot be used to study living things. A scanning electron microscope can be used to study living things.
3. Keeping careful records is important in all scientific research. Accept all logical responses.
4. A damaged cornea is removed from the eye during surgery. The cornea from a donor is then used as a replacement for the damaged cornea.
5. An eye bank worker may keep records, be responsible for shipping organs, or assist in the removal and preparation of transplant organs. Accept all logical responses.
6. The Visible Human can be used to practice medical treatments, to test products, or to train Army medics.

Critical Thinking

1. Answers will vary. Suggested response: cells are too small to be seen without the assistance of a microscope.
2. All living things are made up of one or more cells, cells are the basic units of structure and function in living things, and cells come only from other living cells.
3. mitochondria: produce energy for a cell; ribosomes: make protein; vacuoles: store food and waste; transport tubes: move substances in the cell from one organelle to another
4. Plant cells have cell walls; plant cells contain chlorophyll and chloroplasts; animal cells have many small vacuoles; plant cells usually have one or two very large vacuoles.
5. It is the movement of water through a cell membrane.
6. In animal cells, the cell pulls apart and forms two daughter cells. In plant cells, a new cell wall and cell membrane form down the middle of the cell and form a wall between two new nuclei.

Interpreting a Diagram

1. chloroplast; animal cells contain no chloroplasts
2. transport tubes
3. cytoplasm
4. mitochondria
5. cell wall; animal cells have no cell walls
6. vacuoles
7. ribosomes; They make proteins.

CLASSIFICATION (p. 99)

Previewing the Unit

Read the titles of the lessons in this unit aloud. Identify terms in the titles with which students are unfamiliar. Write these terms on the chalkboard. Using the Glossary of the text or a dictionary, define the terms as a class. Have students write the terms and their definitions in their notebooks. Then, have students work in small groups to carry out the task in the Study Hint.

Bulletin Board Suggestions

1. Assemble a bulletin illustrating the five kingdoms. Divide the bulletin board into five sections. Place one of the following heads at the top of each section: *Monerans, Protists, Fungi, Plants, Animals.* Attach pictures showing representative organisms under the appropriate heads. Use the bulletin board when describing the characteristics of organisms in each kingdom.

2. Assemble a bulletin board entitled *Animals.* Have students find and collect pictures of as many different animals as possible. Tell students to look for pictures of both vertebrates and invertebrates. Make a collage with all the students' pictures.

LESSON 5-1
What is classification? (p. 100)

Teaching Strategies

PREVIEW Before beginning this lesson, have students review the TechTerms and their definitions and read the Lesson Summary.

DISCUSSION Display a variety of grocery store products in front of the classroom, such as a can of soup, apples, a bottle of juice, toothpaste, dog food, and so on. Ask students why they can find products in a grocery store with relative ease. Elicit the response that items in a grocery store are classified, or grouped based upon similarities. Point out that if supermarkets shelves were stacked randomly, it would be very difficult to find anything. Then relate classification in a grocery store to taxonomy. Stress that in order to keep track of living things, scientists have established a classification system for them.

REINFORCEMENT Be sure students understand that taxonomists do not classify organisms based solely on physical appearance. Emphasize that scientists also study chromosome structure, blood proteins, and embryology.

Answers to Challenges (p. 101)

Apply

5. New organisms are discovered and new information becomes available.
6. Answers will vary. Accept all logical responses.
7. Some organisms that look alike may not be related.

Skill Builder: Comparing

In libraries that use the Dewey Decimal System, books are divided into ten major categories and each category is numbered with a call number. In libraries that use the Library of Congress Classification System, books are classified by a set of capital letters and numbers. The first letter indicates a major area of study. The second letter stands for a subclassification. The number represents a specific topic.

Teaching Tips for Activity
Classifying Objects

Skills: *classifying, observing*

COOPERATIVE/COLLABORATIVE LEARNING Answer the questions as a class.

Questions

1. Answers will vary. Accept all logical responses.
2. Answers will vary. Accept all logical responses.
3. Answers will vary. Accept all logical responses.
4. Answers will vary. Accept all logical responses.

LESSON 5-2
How are living things classified? (p. 102)

Teaching Strategies

PREVIEW Before beginning this lesson, read the list of TechTerms aloud so students can hear their pronunciations.

DISCUSSION List the seven major classification groups on the chalkboard starting with kingdom and ending with species. Discuss the stepwise progression from the broadest category of kingdom to the narrowest of species. Emphasize the idea that the kingdom has the largest number of different kinds of organisms and the number of different kinds of organisms decreases as you move from the kingdom level to each of the next levels. Be sure students understand that a species is made up of only one kind of organism.

REINFORCEMENT You may wish to tell students that they can remember the order of the classification groups by remembering the sentence: *Kings play cards on fat green stools.* Point out that the first letter of each word is the first letter for each group.

CLASS ACTIVITY Refer students to Table 1 on p. 102 to observe the classification of four organisms. Ask students a variety of questions based on the table, such as: To what class do humans belong? Then have students identify which organisms are the most closely related (dogs and wolves).

EXTENSION When writing a scientific name, tell students that the genus name begins with a capital letter and both the genus and species name are written in italics or underlined.

Answers to Challenges (p. 103)
Apply

4. four
5. *Homo sapiens*
6. dogs and wolves

InfoSearch

You may wish to discuss students' questions and answers as a class.

Teaching Tips for Looking Back in Science
History of Classification

CLASS ACTIVITY Have students make time lines to summarize the information in this feature.

Questions

1. RELATE   How did exploration affect classification? (Many organisms were discovered as a result of exploration. Scientists recognized the need for an improved system of classification.)
2. HYPOTHESIZE   What problems do you think resulted from Aristotle's classification system? (Answers will vary. Accept all logical responses.)

LESSON 5-3
What are the five kingdoms?
(p. 104)

Teaching Strategies

PREVIEW   Have students write the lesson title and objectives in their notebooks. As students read the lesson, tell them to write down the sentence or sentences that provide the information needed in the objective.

RETEACHING OPTION   Write the following head on the chalkboard: *Five Kingdoms.* From this head, draw arrows to each of the following heads: *Monerans, Protist, Fungi, Plants, Animals.* List sample organisms under each head. Have students copy the chart in their notebooks.

REINFORCEMENT   Emphasize the differences between monerans and protists, and fungi and plants. Be sure students understand that monerans do not have a true nucleus.

DEMONSTRATION   Show students as many interesting pictures as possible of members of the five kingdoms. Hold up each picture. Identify the organism and the kingdom to which it belongs. Have students describe some of its characteristics based on the kingdom.

COOPERATIVE/COLLABORATIVE LEARNING   Have students quiz each other on the material in this section.

Answers to Challenges (p. 105)

Apply

7. Monerans do not have a nucleus or other organelles; Protists do.
8. Fungi and plants are not closely related. Fungi do not have chlorophyll and cannot make their own food.
9. As technology improves, the classification of living things has changed.

Skill Builder: Organizing Information

Check students' tables.

Teaching Tips for People in Science
Robert Whittaker

DISCUSSION   Describe Robert Whittaker's contributions to science. Although he is best-known for the five-kingdom classification system, Whittaker made many other contributions to science.

Questions

1. In what two fields of science did Whittaker work? (ecology and botany)
2. What did Whittaker use to learn how substances move in a food chain? (radioactive tracers)

LESSON 5-4
Are viruses living? (p. 106)

Teaching Strategies

PREVIEW   Before beginning this lesson, have students scan the lesson for the science process skill symbols. Have students identify each skill used in the lesson. Students should then review the definition given for each skill on page 16 of their text.

REINFORCEMENT   Before beginning this lesson, review the six characteristics of living things. This review will help students understand why viruses are not classified as living things.

DISCUSSION   To provide motivation for this lesson, ask students what they think of when they hear the word *Virus.* Most students will correctly identify the term with disease. Use students' knowledge as a springboard for a discussion of the characteristics of viruses. Stress that the main activity of viruses is replication.

CLASS ACTIVITY   Have students work in small groups to make models of viruses. Tell students to label the capsids and nucleic acids on the models.

RETEACHING OPTION   List several viral diseases on the chalkboard such as measles, mumps, chicken pox, yellow fever, polio, AIDS, and influenza. Have students read the names of the diseases aloud. Ask students what each of the diseases has in common with the others. Point out that each disease is caused by a virus.

Answers to Challenges (p. 107)

Apply

7. attachment to the surface of a cell; release of enzymes, which make a hole in the surface of the cell; nucleic acid of the virus enter; the cell; virus takes control and causes the cell to make new viruses
8. A virus does not have cytoplasm or cell parts, does not carry on any life processes, and can only reproduce inside a living cell.
9. Answers will vary. Accept all logical responses.

Ideas in Action

Check students' tables. The viruses that cause measles, the flu, and the common cold are spread through the air. The hepatitis virus is spread by contact with an infected person or eating contaminated foods. Chicken pox is spread by contact with an infected person.

InfoSearch

You may wish to discuss students' questions and answers as a class.

Teaching Tips for Activity
Modeling a Bacteriophage

Skills: *modeling, identifying, applying*

COOPERATIVE/COLLABORATIVE LEARNING   Have students work in pairs.

Questions

1. bacteriophage
2. bacteria
3. capsid

LESSON 5-5
How are plants classified? (p. 108)

Teaching Strategies

PREVIEW Have students read the lesson feature before beginning the lesson. Discuss the concepts presented in the feature. Ask students how they think this information relates to topics they have already studied or to the lesson they are about to study.

CLASS ACTIVITY Have students observe prepared slides of plant cells under a microscope. Tell students to look for the cell wall and chloroplasts.

RETEACHING OPTION Write the following head on the chalkboard: *Plant Divisions.* From this head, draw arrows to each of the following heads: *Tracheophytes, Bryophytes.* Describe the characteristics of each plant division. Be sure students understand that bryophytes do not have transport tissue.

EXTENSION In botany, the term *division* is used instead of phylum.

INTRASCIENCE CONNECTION You may wish to compare the transport tissue of tracheophytes to the blood vessels in animals.

DEMONSTRATION If possible, bring a sample bryophyte, such as a moss to class. Have students note how small bryophyte plants are. Allow students to observe the moss specimens with a hand lens.

Answers to Challenges (p. 109)

Apply

6. Bryophytes do not have transport tissue or true roots, stems, or leaves. Tracheophytes have transport tissue and roots, stems, and leaves.
7. Answers will vary. Accept all logical responses.

InfoSearch

You may wish to discuss students' questions and answers as a class.

Teaching Tips for Career in Life Science
Florist

EXTENSION Hobby and craft stores often give classes in flower arranging. Students who are interested in a career as a florist may benefit from taking a flower arranging class. Tell interested students to contact a local craft store for more information.

Question

What is a florist? (a person who arranges and sells fresh flowers and plants)

LESSON 5-6
How are animals classified?
(p. 110)

Teaching Strategies

PREVIEW Before beginning this section, have students scan the lesson looking for words with which they are unfamiliar.

Have students work in pairs or small groups to define each of the words on their lists.

CLASS ACTIVITY To begin this lesson, tell students to run their hands along their backbones. Ask students if they know what the "bumps" they feel are called (vertebrae). Point out that vertebrae are small bones that make up the backbone. Then, tell students that animals that have backbones are called vertebrates. Explain that vertebrates are one of the two large groups of animals. Then introduce some of the characteristics of both vertebrates and invertebrates.

RETEACHING OPTION Bring in a variety of pictures showing vertebrates and invertebrates. Hold up each picture in front of the class and have students classify each organism as a vertebrate or an invertebrate. Point out the exoskeletons of any invertebrates.

Answers to Challenges (p. 111)
Apply

6. a. e **b.** i **c.** i **d.** i **e.** e **f.** i
7. a. invertebrate **b.** invertebrate **c.** vertebrate **d.** vertebrate
e. invertebrate **f.** invertebrate

Skill Builder: Building Vocabulary

The prefix *endo-* means inside; *exo-* means outside. Answers will vary.

Teaching Tips for Science Connection
Taxonomy Today

DISCUSSION Ask students to compare the way Carolus Linnaeus classified organisms to the way modern-day taxonomists classify organisms. Be sure students understand that modern-day taxonomists still study physical appearances. However, they also study other factors, such as embryology, to establish relationships among organisms.

Questions

1. DEFINE What is embryology? (study of organisms in the early stages of development)
2. LIST What are four things modern-day taxonomists study to classify organisms? (physical appearance, chromosomes, blood proteins, embryology)

Answers to Unit Challenges (pp. 112-114)

Understanding the Features: Reading Critically
1. ecology and botany
2. physical appearance, chromosomes and blood proteins, embryology
3. Carolus Linnaeus
4. Answers will vary. Accept all logical responses.

Critical Thinking
1. Answers will vary. Accept all logical responses.
2. Taxonomy involves studying many aspects of an organism.
3. It is difficult to treat viral infections because they are found inside living cells.
4. multicellular, cells are organized into tissues and organs, cells have cell walls, cells contain chlorophyll
5. Fungi are not green, but were thought to be plants.

Interpreting a Diagram
1. viral reproduction
2. capsid
3. nucleic acid
4. The nucleic acid of the virus is entering a cell.
5. New viruses are leaving the cell.

Previewing the Unit

Read the titles of the lessons in this unit aloud. Identify terms in the titles with which students are unfamiliar. Write these terms on the chalkboard. Using the Glossary of the text or a dictionary, define the terms as a class. Have students write the terms and their definitions in their notebooks. Then, have students work in small groups to carry out the task in the Study Hint.

Bulletin Board Suggestions

1. Assemble a bulletin board showing the importance of bacteria. Attach pictures illustrating bacterial diseases, food spoilage, the nitrogen cycle, products made using bacteria, and so on. Use the bulletin board when teaching Lesson 6-2.
2. Assemble a bulletin board illustrating members of the Kingdoms *Monera, Protista,* and *Fungi.* Divide the bulletin board into three sections. Label each section with one of the following heads: *Monerans, Protists, Fungi.* Attach representative organisms under each head. Be sure to include both a protozoan and algae under protists.

LESSON 6-1
What are bacteria? (p. 116)

Teaching Strategies

PREVIEW Before beginning this lesson, read the list of TechTerms aloud so students can hear their pronunciations.

REINFORCEMENT Remind students that bacteria are members of the Kingdom *Monera.* Have students recall how monerans differ from members of the other four kingdoms. (Monerans do not have a nucleus or cell organelles.)

CLASS ACTIVITY Obtain prepared slides of cocci, spirilla, and bacilli from a biological supply house. Have students view the different types of bacteria under a microscope. Tell students to sketch and label the bacteria they observe.

DISCUSSION Review the process of photosynthesis before describing blue-green bacteria. Then point out that blue-green bacteria are unusual because they carry out photosynthesis.

COOPERATIVE/COLLABORATIVE LEARNING Have volunteers draw the three different shapes of bacteria on the chalkboard. Have other volunteers go to the chalkboard and label the drawings.

Answers to Challenges (p. 117)
Apply

8. No, blue-green bacteria can make their own food.
9. **a.** cocci **b.** cocci **c.** spirilla **d.** bacilli

Skill Builder: Building Vocabulary

Diplo- means two; *staphylo-* means bunches; *strepto-* means chains. diplococci: cocci that form pairs; staphylococci: cocci that grow in grapelike bunches; streptococci: cocci that form chains. Check students' models.

Teaching Tips for Looking Back in Science
Classification of Bacteria

DISCUSSION Describe the progression of classification from two kingdoms to five kingdoms. Emphasize the relationship between the classification of living things and improved technology.

Questions

1. Why were bacteria once classified with the protists? (Bacteria are simple, one-celled organisms.)
2. CONTRAST How are the cells of bacteria different from those of protists, plants, and animals. (Bacteria do not have a nucleus or cell organelles.)

LESSON 6-2
How are bacteria helpful and harmful? (p. 118)

Teaching Strategies

PREVIEW Before beginning this lesson, have students scan the lesson for the science process skill symbols. Have students identify each skill used in the lesson. Students should then review the definition given for each skill on page 16 of their text.

DISCUSSION Bring in an empty milk bottle or carton and display it in front of the classroom. Point out the term "pasteurized" on the bottle. Ask students if they know what the term means. Discuss all student responses. Point out that pasteurization is a process used to kill bacteria growing in milk. Tell students that the term pasteurization is named for the scientist who developed the process, Louis Pasteur. Identify Louis Pasteur as the scientist who started the science of bacteriology.

CLASS ACTIVITY Display photographs or actual samples of butter, buttermilk, cheese, sauerkraut, coffee, and cocoa. Ask students what all of the foods have in common. Write student responses on the chalkboard. When you are satisfied that students have exhausted possible answers, guide students to an understanding that bacteria are used in the production or preparation of all the foods.

REINFORCEMENT Draw the nitrogen cycle on the chalkboard. Remind students that special bacteria in the soil allow plants to use the nitrogen in the atmosphere.

DISCUSSION Write the names of several bacterial diseases on the chalkboard, such as scarlet fever, strep throat, diphtheria, tetanus, and typhoid fever. Challenge the class to state what all of these human diseases have in common. Elicit the response that each of these diseases is caused by a different type of bacteria. Then point out that people are not the only living things affected by bacteria. Describe some plant diseases caused by bacteria, such as blight and rot. Emphasize the economic loss these diseases cause.

EXTENSION Have interested students research the role of bacteria in sewage treatment plants or in producing antibiotics. Tell students to write their findings in a report.

RETEACHING OPTION Students often have many misconceptions concerning bacteria and view bacteria solely as disease-causing organisms. Tell students that of the thousands of known bacteria, only a small number are harmful. Then, describe how bacteria are helpful to people and other organisms.

Answers to Challenges (p. 119)

Apply

6. Bacteria are growing in the can.
7. They stop bacterial growth.
8. Answers will vary. Accept all logical responses.

InfoSearch

You may wish to discuss students' questions and answers as a class.

Teaching Tips for Technology and Society

M.A.P.: Modified Atmosphere Packaging

DISCUSSION Describe how M.A.P. stops food spoilage. Be sure students understand that canning, pickling, and freezing slow down the action of bacteria by impeding the conditions bacteria need to grow. M.A.P. actually prevents airborne bacteria from reaching food.

Question

COMPARE How are the plastic coverings used in M.A.P. similar to a cell membrane? (The plastic coverings and cell membranes only allow certain substances to pass in and out.)

LESSON 6-3
What are protists? (p. 120)

Teaching Strategies

PREVIEW Have students write the lesson title and objective in their notebooks. As students read the lesson, tell them to write down the sentence or sentences that provide the information needed in the objective.

DISCUSSION Discuss the characteristics of protists. Explain that most protists have only one cell, but that some have many cells. Emphasize that many-celled protists do not have tissues or organs.

DISCUSSION Refer students to the diagrams on p. 120 showing an amoeba, a paramecium, and a trypanosome. Have students locate the pseudopods, cilia, and flagella as you describe these structures and how they are used for movement.

REINFORCEMENT Ask if any students have ever been in a rowboat. If so, have the students describe their experiences to the rest of the class. Compare the movement of cilia to a rowboat's oars.

RETEACHING OPTION Write the following head on the chalkboard: *Protists*. From this head, draw arrows to each of the following heads: *Protozoans, Algae, Slime Molds*. Identify protozoans as the animallike protists and algae as the plantlike protists. Have students copy the chart in their notebooks.

Answers to Challenges (p. 121)

Apply

6. protozoans, algae, slime molds
7. Both are used for movement in protists.

InfoSearch

You may wish to discuss students' questions and answers as a class.

Teaching Tips for Activity

Analyzing Movement in Protists

Skills: *classifying, observing, inferring*

COOPERATIVE/COLLABORATIVE LEARNING Answer the questions as a class.

Questions

1. animallike; the protists move.
2. **a.** Anarma **b.** 25
3. in water
4. a microscope; Most protists are microscopic.

LESSON 6-4
What are algae? (p. 122)

Teaching Strategies

PREVIEW Before beginning this lesson, write the title of each section in the lesson on the chalkboard. Have students copy these titles in their notebooks using an outline format. As students read each section, they should write the topic sentence for each paragraph in the section in their notebooks.

DISCUSSION Describe the characteristics of algae. Point out how algae are plantlike. Be sure students understand that all algae contain chlorophyll, although not all algae are green.

EXTENSION You may wish to tell students that the microscopic algae and tiny plants that float on the surface of water are called phytoplankton. The tiny animals are called zooplankton. Together, all of the organisms are called plankton.

CLASS ACTIVITY If possible, take the class on a field trip to observe a stagnant pond. Students will see many different types of algae. Collect samples from the surface of the pond. Have students examine the samples under a microscope when they return to the classroom. Tell students to sketch their observations and identify as many algae as they can.

RETEACHING OPTION Ask students who have been to a beach if they noticed any seaweed washed up along the shoreline. Have students describe the seaweed. Point out that seaweed is one type of multicellular algae. Then describe the other types of algae to the class.

Answers to Challenges (p. 123)

Apply

6. Answers will vary. Accept all logical responses.
7. Answers will vary. Accept all logical responses.

Skill Builder: Organizing

Brown algae are used to make toothpaste and ice cream. Golden-brown algae are used to make detergent, silver polish, and toothpaste. Red algae are used to make ice cream, cheese, and marshmallows.

Teaching Tips for Science Connection
Algal Blooms

DISCUSSION Bring in a detergent with a label stating that the detergent does not contain phosphates. Before students read the feature, ask them if they know what the label means and why it is put on the detergent. Discuss student responses. Then have students read the feature to find out how phosphates may cause an algal bloom.

Questions

1. When do algal blooms often occur? (when wastes containing phosphates are dumped into ponds or lakes)
2. RELATE How does an algal bloom affect the oxygen content of a lake or pond? (Oxygen content decreases.)

LESSON 6-5
What are fungi? (p. 124)

Teaching Strategies

PREVIEW Have students read the lesson feature before beginning the lesson. Discuss the concepts presented in the feature. Ask students how they think this information relates to topics they have already studied or to the lesson they are about to study.

DISCUSSION Discuss the similarities and differences between plants and fungi. Emphasize that the differences led scientists to classify fungi in their own kingdom.

CLASS ACTIVITY If possible, take students on a field trip to observe different kinds of fungi. Have students draw the fungi they observe and use a field guide to identify the group to which each fungus belongs.

CLASS ACTIVITY Grow bread mold as a class. Moisten a piece of bread and place it in a dark, warm place. After a few days, have students check the bread for mold growth. Allow students to use a hand lens to examine the mold.

DEMONSTRATION Bring a mushroom to class. Point out the cap, the stalk, and the gills.

RETEACHING OPTION Write a recipe for making bread on the chalkboard that calls for using yeast. Some students may know that yeast is used to make bread rise. Ask students why they think yeast makes bread rise. Discuss all student responses. Point out that yeasts are one-celled fungi. Tell students that as bread dough is baked, yeast in the dough produces carbon dioxide gas. The gas causes bubbles to form in the bread. As the bubbles form in the bread, the bread rises.

Answers to Challenges (p. 125)

Apply

7. Spores from the parent mushroom are carried away by wind, water, or insects.
8. Answers will vary. Accept all logical responses.
9. A mushroom is not green.

Health and Safety Tip

Answers will vary. Accept all logical responses.

Teaching Tips for Science Connection
Fungicides

CLASS ACTIVITY To help students remember that fungicides are used to kill fungi, have them look up the meaning of the suffix -cide in a dictionary. (-cide: relating to killing) Then, ask students how its meaning relates to its use in the term fungicide.

Question

RELATE Why do you think drying the skin between the toes after bathing reduces your chances of getting athlete's foot? (Fungi grow best in moist places.)

LESSON 6-6
How do yeasts and molds reproduce? (p. 126)

Teaching Strategies

PREVIEW Before beginning this lesson, have students review the TechTerms and their definitions and read the Lesson Summary.

CLASS ACTIVITY Mix a pinch of baker's yeast with 100 mL of warm water and 1/2 teaspoon of sugar. Gently swirl the mixture for 15 minutes. Then have students make slides of the yeast solution. Have students add a drop of crystal violet to stain the slides. Tell students to observe the yeast cells under the microscope. Have students sketch the yeast cells and look for budding cells.

DISCUSSION Describe sporulation in bread molds. Use the diagram on p. 126 to illustrate your description.

COOPERATIVE/COLLABORATIVE LEARNING Have one student describe the process of budding to the rest of the class. Have another student describe sporulation.

Answers to Challenges (p. 127)
Check

1. one
2. yeasts
3. thousands
4. attached to the parent cell
5. It produces many more offsprings.

Apply

6. Both mushrooms and molds produce spores.
7. Answers will vary. Accept all logical responses.

InfoSearch

You may wish to discuss students' questions and answers as a class.

Teaching Tips for Activity
Growing Mold

Skills: *observing, inferring, hypothesizing*

COOPERATIVE/COLLABORATIVE LEARNING Have students work in pairs.

Questions

1. Answers will vary. Accept all logical responses.
2. **a.** Answers will vary. Accept all logical responses.
b. Answers will vary. Accept all logical responses.
3. They are different types of molds.
4. moisture, darkness, a food source
5. Answers will vary. Accept all logical responses.

Answers to Unit Challenges (pp. 128-130)

Understanding the Features: Reading Critically

1. ponds and lake into which wastes containing phosphates are dumped
2. chemical preparation used to prevent or cure diseases caused by fungi
3. because they were simple, one-celled organisms
4. a method of keeping fresh foods from spoiling based on controlling the food's environment

Interpreting a Diagram

1. cap
2. gills
3. to produce spores
4. stalk
5. rhizoids
6. anchor the mushroom; absorb nutrients

Critical Thinking

1. They take away one or more of the conditions needed for bacterial growth.
2. They do not have tissues or organs.
3. Fungi grow in soil, have cell walls, and most are multicellular. Fungi do not have chloroplasts or chlorophyll.
4. Nitrogen-fixing bacteria in the soil change nitrogen into compounds that can be used. Animals get nitrogen compounds by eating plants. Animals use the compounds to make proteins.
5. dark, warm, moist places

Previewing the Unit

Read the titles of the lessons in this unit aloud. Identify terms in the titles with which students are unfamiliar. Write these terms on the chalkboard. Using the Glossary of the text or a dictionary, define the terms as a class. Have students write the terms and their definitions in their notebooks. Then, have students carry out the task in the Study Hint.

Bulletin Board Suggestions

1. Assemble a bulletin board illustrating the importance of plants. Attach pictures showing products that are made from or derived from plants, such as food products, medicines, lumber, clothing, and so on.
2. Divide the bulletin board into two sections. Label each section with one of the following heads: *Gymnosperms, Angiosperms.* Have students look for and collect pictures of different seed plants. Tell students to label each picture. Attach all the pictures under the appropriate heads to make a collage.

LESSON 7-1
Why are plants important?
(p. 132)

Teaching Strategies

PREVIEW Before beginning this lesson, have students scan the lesson for the science process skill symbols. Have students identify each skill used in the lesson. Students should then review the definition given for each skill on page 16 of their text.

DISCUSSION Begin this lesson by asking students why plants are important. Discuss all student responses. Elicit from students that plants are used for food and to make many useful products, such as paper. Point out that plants also are used to make drugs and medicines.

RETEACHING OPTION Bring in a variety of products made from plant parts and display them in front of the classroom. Products may include paper, rubber, wood, plastics, string, cotton, and linen. Ask students what all the products have in common. Point out that they are all obtained from plants.

CLASS ACTIVITY If possible, arrange for your class to visit a botanical garden. Ask a tour guide to point out and describe some of the plants commonly used by people to make useful products.

Answers to Challenges (p. 133)

Ideas in Action

You may wish to have students list the plants on the chalkboard.

Teaching Tips for People in Science
George Washington Carver

EXTENSION You may wish to explain how legumes help revive soil from which minerals have been depleted. Nitrogen-fixing bacteria live in nodules on the roots of legumes. The bacteria change nitrogen gas from the atmosphere into nitrogen compounds that plants can use.

Questions

1. INFER What is crop rotation? (planting legumes one season and plants such as cotton in the same field the next year)
2. LIST What are three uses for peanuts? (Answers will vary. Accept all logical responses.)

LESSON 7-2
What are spore plants? (p. 134)

Teaching Strategies

PREVIEW Before beginning this lesson, read the list of TechTerms aloud so students can hear their pronunciations.

REINFORCEMENT Before beginning this lesson, remind students that botanists have divided plants into two main divisions, bryophytes and tracheophytes. Ask students on what the two divisions are based. (how water and dissolved minerals are moved throughout a plant)

CLASS ACTIVITY Bring some samples of moss to class. Have students observe the moss specimens with a hand lens. Tell students to note the short main stalk, the flat, green leaflike structures growing around it, and the rhizoids. Tell students to also look for spore cases.

EXTENSION Have interested students research the use of peat moss in gardens and as a fuel source. Tell students to write their findings in a report.

DEMONSTRATION If possible, bring a liverwort and a hornwort to class and point out the various structures on each plant.

RETEACHING OPTION Write the following head on the chalkboard: *Bryophytes.* From this head, draw arrows to each of the following heads: *Mosses, Liverworts, Hornworts.* Then describe the characteristics of bryophytes. Have students copy the information in their notebooks.

Answers to Challenges (p. 135)
Apply

6. Bryophytes need water for reproduction.
7. Rhizoids grow down into the soil and anchor a plant. They also take in water and dissolved minerals.

Teaching Tips for Looking Back in Science
Scouring Rushes

REINFORCEMENT Be sure students understand that horsetails are spore plants, but not bryophytes. Horsetails were among the first tracheophytes to appear on the earth.

Questions

1. Why would horsetails be good for cleaning pots? (The rough surface of horsetails can remove dirt.)
2. COMPARE   How do modern horsetails compare to ancient horsetails? (They are smaller.)

LESSON 7-3
What are ferns? (p. 136)

Teaching Strategies

PREVIEW   Have students write the lesson title and objective in their notebooks. As students read the lesson, tell them to write down the sentence or sentences that provide the information needed in the objective.

DEMONSTRATION   Hold up a fern in front of the classroom. Point out the fronds, the rhizomes, and the spore cases.

DISCUSSION   Discuss the similarities and differences between ferns and bryophytes. Point out that both ferns and bryophytes reproduce by spores. Then, tell students that unlike bryophytes, ferns have true roots, stems, and leaves. Ask students to state in which plant division ferns are classified. (tracheophytes)

EXTENSION   Have interested students research the life cycle of a fern, which involves alteration of generations. Tell students to write their findings in a report. Have students include a diagram showing the life cycle of a fern.

COOPERATIVE/COLLABORATIVE LEARNING   Have students work in pairs to answer the Check and Apply questions.

Answers to Challenges (p. 137)

Apply

5. Check students' drawings
6. frond; It is the leaf of a fern.

InfoSearch

You may wish to discuss students' questions and answers as a class.

Skill Builder: Researching

Lignite is called brown coal. Bituminous coal is called soft coal. Anthracite is the hardest kind of coal.

Teaching Tips for Leisure Activity
Indoor Gardening

CLASS ACTIVITY   Have students set up a terrarium suitable for the growth of ferns in the classroom. Assign two students to take care of the terrarium each week.

Questions

1. Why are ferns common house plants? (Ferns are attractive and easy to take care of.)
2. LIST   What are the growth requirements of ferns? (light, peat-filled soil, water, moist air, indirect light)

LESSON 7-4
What are gymnosperms? (p. 138)

Teaching Strategies

PREVIEW   Before beginning this lesson, write the title of each section in the lesson on the chalkboard. Have students copy these titles in their notebooks using an outline format. As students read each section, they should write the topic sentence for each paragraph in the section in their notebooks.

DISCUSSION   Obtain colorful pictures of gymnosperms, such as sequoias, red woods, spruces, firs, ginkgoes, and cycads. While displaying the pictures to the class, point out that all of the plants produce seeds as opposed to having spores.

CLASS ACTIVITY   If possible, have students examine the cones of several different conifers. Tell students to note the size and shape of the cones. Students may be able to shake some pollen from a fresh pollen cone. If so, have students examine the pollen with a hand lens.

DEMONSTRATION   Try to obtain mature pinecones. Boil the cones and remove the seeds. Have students examine the seeds.

DISCUSSION   Discuss the economic significance of gymnosperms. Point out that they are used as a source of lumber, fuel, and many other products.

Answers to Challenges (p. 139)
Apply

7. Check students' models.
8. A; It has needles.

Ideas in Action

Check students' tables. Answers will vary.

Teaching Tips for Activity
Observing Pine Cones

Skills: *comparing, contrasting, measuring*

COOPERATIVE/COLLABORATIVE LEARNING   Answer the questions as a class.

LESSON 7-5
What are angiosperms? (p. 140)

Teaching Strategies

DISCUSSION   Provide motivation for this lesson by asking students to name as many flowering plants as they can. List student responses on the chalkboard. Students will most likely name plants with noticeable flowers. Add to the list examples, such as carrots, oak trees, corn, eggplants, palm trees, grass, and so on. Emphasize that all of these plants are angiosperms. Point out that angiosperms are the dominant plants today.

REINFORCEMENT   Try to dispel the idea that fruits can be only like apples and oranges. Give the example of an acorn, which is the fruit of an oak tree.

DISCUSSION Distinguish between monocots and dicots, stressing that cotyledons store food for the developing plant in the seed.

CLASS ACTIVITY Have students bring some leaves to class. Have them observe the venation of the leaves to determine if the plants are monocots or dicots.

Answers to Challenges (p. 141)

Apply

7. Check students' models. The monocot should have petals in groups of three and parallel veins. The dicot should have petals in groups of four or five and branched veins.

Skill Builder: Using Prefixes

Mono- means one; *di-* means two. Monocots have one cotyledon. Dicots have two cotyledons. A monorail is a transportation system with one rail. A monosyllable is a one syllable word.

Teaching Tips for Activity

Classifying Monocots and Dicots

Skills: *modeling, classifying*

COOPERATIVE/COLLABORATIVE LEARNING Have students work in pairs.

Answers to Unit Challenges (pp. 142-144)

Understanding the Features: Reading Critically

1. cheese substitutes, paper, face cream, soap, ink, dyes
2. by growing legume plants in the soil
3. silica
4. Answers will vary. Accept all logical responses.
5. A fern grows best in dark, moist places.

Critical Thinking

1. Answers will vary. Accept all logical responses.
2. Both are spore plants.
3. cone
4. A monocot has flowers with petals arranged in groups of three. A dicot has flowers with petals arranged in groups of four or five. The veins in the leaves of monocots are parallel. The veins in the leaves of dicots are branched.
5. Answers will vary. Accept all logical responses.

Interpreting a Diagram

1. cotyledons
2. Corn; it has a single cotyledon.
3. Bean; it has two cotyledons.
4. within the seeds
5. seed coat

PLANT STRUCTURE AND FUNCTION (p. 145)

Previewing the Unit

Before students begin this unit, have them read the objectives and Lesson Summary for each lesson in the unit. Then, have students work in pairs to carry out the task in the Study Hint. As you read each lesson, have student volunteers read their descriptions of how the information in the lesson applies to their daily lives.

Bulletin Board Suggestion

Assemble a working bulletin board on plants to use while teaching this unit. Attach a diagram of a plant with perfect flowers to the bulletin board. Label the structures of a plant as they are introduced to students. Labeled structures should include the roots, the stem, the leaves, and the male and female parts of the flower.

LESSON 8-1
What are roots? (p. 146)

Teaching Strategies

PREVIEW Before you begin the lesson, read the TechTerms aloud so students can hear their pronunciations.

DEMONSTRATION To introduce this lesson, bring a potted plant to class. Pull the plant out of the pot in front of the class. Have students observe the plant's roots. Identify the kind of root system the plant has. Point out the root hairs extending from the root and describe their function. Then repot the plant.

DISCUSSION Refer students to the diagrams on p. 146 showing a cross section and a longitudinal section of roots. Have students locate the three layers of roots as you describe a root's structure. Tell students to observe the root cap as you discuss its protective function.

CLASS ACTIVITY If possible, have students observe prepared slides of root tips under a microscope to see the different cells found in a root.

INTRASCIENCE CONNECTION Ask students if they have ever noticed cracked or uplifted sidewalks in areas near trees. Have students discuss what they think caused the cracking and uplifting. Point out that it was caused by the action of tree roots. Root action is one cause of mechanical weathering.

RETEACHING OPTION Emphasize the fact that plants have organs. Identify roots as a plant organ. List the functions of roots on the chalkboard: **1.** anchorage **2.** absorption **3.** food storage. Point out that roots also conduct absorbed materials up to the stem, which is another plant organ.

Answers to Challenges (p. 147)
Apply

6. 606 km. It is most likely more than the area of the classroom.
7. Difficult; the many roots that make up the root system would tend to hold the plant firmly in the soil.

8. taproot: a, b; fibrous roots: c

Skill Builder: Organizing Information
Check students' tables.

Teaching Tips for Science Connection
Specialized Roots

REINFORCEMENT Write the following head on the chalkboard: *Specialized Roots*. From this head, draw arrows to each of the following heads: *Aerial Roots, Prop Roots, Aquatic Roots*. Then describe the functions of these specialized roots. Have students copy the information in their notebooks under the proper heads.

Questions

1. What are three plants that have aerial roots? (orchids, bald cypress, English ivy)
2. What is the function of prop roots? (They help support a plant.)

LESSON 8-2
What are stems? (p. 148)

Teaching Strategies

PREVIEW Before you begin the lesson, have students read the TechTerms and their definitions and review the Lesson Summary.

DEMONSTRATION A few hours before class begins, obtain two large beakers and two stalks of celery. Cut several centimeters from the bottom of the celery. Fill one beaker halfway with water and place a celery stalk in it. Fill the other beaker halfway with water and add several drops of food coloring to the water. Place the other stalk of celery in the beaker. When class begins, place the two beakers in front of the classroom. Students will observe that water has been conducted through the stalk. Tell students that water is transported up from the roots by tubes called xylem. Identify transport as one function of stems. Then ask students to state another function of stems. (support)

DISCUSSION Describe the two kinds of stems. Note that plants with woody stems usually live for more than two years, whereas plants with herbaceous stems usually live for only one or two years.

COOPERATIVE/COLLABORATIVE LEARNING Have students work in pairs to answer the Check and Apply questions.

Answers to Challenges (p. 149)
Apply

5. roots, xylem, leaves
6. The weight of the plant would cause the stem to bend and break.
7. herbaceous: a, c, e; woody: b, d, f

InfoSearch

You may wish to discuss students' questions and answers as a class.

Teaching Tips for Activity
Transport in Plants

Skills: *measuring, predicting, organizing data*

SAFETY TIP Caution students to be careful when using a knife.

COOPERATIVE/COLLABORATIVE LEARNING Have students work in pairs.

Questions

1. The ink rose through the celery.
2. Answers will vary.
3. transport

Answers may vary. Accept all logical responses.
2. Answers will vary depending upon the leaves chosen.
3. Answers will vary depending upon the leaves chosen.
4. Students should see two basic vein patterns, parallel and branched.

Lesson 8-4
What is photosynthesis? (p. 152)

Teaching Strategies

PREVIEW Before students begin this lesson, have them review the TechTerms and read the Lesson Summary.

REINFORCEMENT Review the role of plants as producers. Remind students that plants are able to make their own food by the process of photosynthesis. Point out that the food plants make is sugar.

DISCUSSION Write the chemical equation for photosynthesis on the chalkboard: $CO_2 + H_2O \xrightarrow{energy} C_6H_{12}O_6 + O_2$. Point to and identify each substance involved in the reaction. Develop the concept that carbon dioxide and water are the materials needed for photosynthesis and that oxygen is a waste product of photosynthesis. Explain that the oxygen produced by photosynthesis is used by both plants and animals to carry on respiration. Ask students where plants get the energy to carry on photosynthesis. (sunlight)

EXTENSION Have interested students use library references to find out more about accessory pigments, such as carotenoids and phycobilins. Tell students to write their findings in a report.

LESSON 8-3
What are leaves? (p. 150)

Teaching Strategies

PREVIEW Before beginning this lesson, read the TechTerms aloud so students can hear their pronunciations.

DEMONSTRATION Bring a leaf to class. Point out the stalk, the blade, and the veins in the leaf as you describe these structures. Be sure students understand that the veins are made up of xylem and phloem.

DISCUSSION Distinguish between simple and compound leaves. If possible, show some examples of each.

DISCUSSION Refer students to the diagram on p. 150 showing the structure of a leaf. Discuss, in turn, the epidermis, the stomates, and the mesophyll.

CLASS ACTIVITY Divide the class into small groups and distribute different colored clay to each group. Have students use the clay to make models of a leaf. Tell students to use the diagram on p. 150 as a guide.

Answers to Challenges (p. 151)

Apply

5. The epidermis of the leaf protects the leaf. The skin protects the parts of the body.
6. The stomata would be closed on a hot day to prevent the plant from losing too much water.
7. because the many plants in the forest are giving off carbon dioxide and water
8. simple leaf
9. compound leaf
10. simple leaf

Health and Safety Tip

All three plants have compound leaves. Check students' drawings for accuracy.

Teaching Tips for Activity
Classifying Leaves

Skills: *modeling, analyzing, measuring, classifying*

SAFETY TIP Caution students not to touch the leaves of poison ivy, poison oak, or poison sumac.

COOPERATIVE/COLLABORATIVE LEARNING Have students work in pairs.

Questions

1. Pictures in a field guide can be compared to the leaf specimens gathered and used as a means of identification.

Answers to Challenges (p. 153)

Apply

5. B
6. Water enters the leaf through C.
7. No; it does not have chloroplasts.

Skill Builder: Building Vocabulary

Photo- means light; *synthesis* means to put together; *chlor-* means green; *-plast* means structure or body: *-phyll* means leaf. Chlorophyll is a green (chlor-) pigment found in leaves (-phyll); chloroplast is a green (chlor-) structure (-plast) inside plant cells. Photosynthesis is a process in which plants use sunlight (photo-) and other raw materials to put together (synthesis) food.

Teaching Tips for Activity
Separating "Plant Pigments"

Skills: *observing, predicting, modeling*

COOPERATIVE/COLLABORATIVE LEARNING Have students work in pairs.

Questions

1. It began to separate into different colors.
2. Students should detect at least three colors; however depending upon the ink used, more colors may be evident.
3. plant pigments
4. The plant pigment would separate into its component colors.

LESSON 8-5
What are flowers? (p. 154)

Teaching Strategies

PREVIEW Before you begin this lesson, read the TechTerms aloud so students can hear their pronunciations.

DISCUSSION To provide motivation for this lesson, ask students what their favorite flowers are and why. List student responses on the chalkboard. Point out that people appreciate flowers for their beauty and fragrance. Then develop the concept that flowers are the organs of sexual reproduction in plants.

DEMONSTRATION Bring actual flowers to class, including a perfect flower and an imperfect flower. Point out and describe the sepals, the petals, the pistils, and the stamens.

REINFORCEMENT Draw a perfect flower on the chalkboard. Have students come up to the chalkboard and label the parts of the flower.

COOPERATIVE/COLLABORATIVE LEARNING Have a volunteer explain the difference between a perfect flower and an imperfect flower for the rest of the class.

Answers to Challenges (p. 155)
Apply

5. Students' models should resemble the diagram of a flower on p. 154.
6. a. perfect **b.** perfect **c.** imperfect

Skill Builder: Classifying

A pistillate flower has a pistil, but no stamens. A staminate flower has stamens, but no pistil. Pistillate and staminate flowers are imperfect flowers. The flower shown in C is a pistillate.

Teaching Tips for Leisure Activity
Gardening

DISCUSSION Have any students who enjoy gardening describe their hobby to the rest of the class.

CLASS ACTIVITY If possible, have students grow and maintain a garden on the school grounds.

Questions

1. Why do people like to garden? (to beautify their homes; to have fresh cut flowers; to raise their own fruits and vegetables)
2. ANALYZE Why do you think gardening is good exercise? (Answers will vary. Accept all logical responses.)

identify each skill used in the lesson. Students should then review the definition given for each skill on page 16 of their text.

DISCUSSION To provide motivation for this lesson, ask students if they, their friends, or members of their families suffer from hay fever. Ask students if they know what causes hay fever. As a hint, refer to the pollen count given during certain months of the year. Elicit from students that pollen is responsible for hay fever. Define pollen grains as the male reproductive cells in plants.

REINFORCEMENT Be sure students understand the difference between fertilization and pollination. Students often confuse the two terms.

DISCUSSION Ask students to describe some instances of pollination that they have observed in nature, such as bees pollinating flowers. Guide students to understand that for pollination to take place, pollen must move from the stamen to the pistil. Tell students that wind, birds, and insects are important agents of pollination. Then ask students to suggest the importance of color and odor in flowers. Discuss all student responses. Point out that these features are ways of making flowers attractive to insects.

COOPERATIVE/COLLABORATIVE LEARNING Have a volunteer explain the difference between self-pollination and cross-pollination for the rest of the class.

Answers to Challenges (p. 157)
Apply

6. An insect carries pollen from one flower to another in its mouth or on its body when it feeds upon the flowers.
7. flat open flowers; Flat open flowers would be more easily pollinated than tall closed flowers.

Health and Safety Tip

Check students' posters.

Teaching Tips for Science Connection
Mutualism

EXTENSION Have interested students find out about other relationships among organisms such as commensalism and parasitism. Tell students to define these terms in a report and to give examples of each.

Questions

1. DEFINE What is mutualism? (relationship between two living things that is helpful to both living things)
2. How are bees helpful to plants? (Bees help pollinate plants.)

LESSON 8-6
How do flowering plants reproduce? (p. 156)

Teaching Strategies

PREVIEW Before beginning this lesson, have students scan the lesson for the science process skill symbols. Have students

LESSON 8-7
What are seeds and fruits? (p. 158)

Teaching Strategies

PREVIEW Have students write the lesson title and objectives in their notebooks. As students read the lesson, tell them to write down the sentence or sentences that provide the information needed in the objectives.

DISCUSSION Describe the parts of a pistil and the growth of a pollen tube. Use the diagrams on p. 158 to illustrate your descriptions.

DEMONSTRATION Remove as many pollen grains from a flower as you can. Add the grains to a small test tube filled with water and a little sugar. Allow the test tube to stand overnight. The next day prepare microscope slides of the pollen. Have students observe the slides under a microscope to look for growth of pollen tubes.

CLASS ACTIVITY Bring in an assortment of fruits. Cut the fruits open to expose their seeds. Have students explain how the seeds form and to note whether each fruit has one or many seeds.

RETEACHING OPTION Write the following heads on the chalkboard: *Stamen, Pistil.* From the head *Stamen,* draw arrows to each of the following heads: *Filament, Anther.* From the head *Pistil,* draw arrows to each of the following heads: *Stigma, Style, Ovary.* Have students copy the charts in their notebooks.

Answers to Challenges (p. 159)

Apply

5. Check students' drawings.
6. The stickiness of the stigma helps to attract and keep pollen grains on the flower.

Skill Builder: Organizing Information

Students' tables will vary depending upon the fruits selected. Check students' table for logic and accuracy.

Skill Builder: Classifying

a. tomato: fruit; vegetable **b.** beets: vegetable; vegetable **c.** cucumber: fruit; vegetable **d.** carrot: vegetable; vegetable **e.** peach: fruit; fruit **f.** celery: vegetable; vegetable **g.** lettuce: vegetable; vegetable **h.** papaya: fruit; fruit **i.** green pepper: fruit; vegetable

Teaching Tips for Career in Life Science

Greengrocer

EXTENSION Arrange for a greengrocer to visit your class. Ask the greengrocer to describe a typical work day.

Questions

1. What are two things a greengrocer does on the job? (Students should restate two things listed in the feature.)
2. Why should you take science and mathematic courses in high school if you want to become a greengrocer? (Caring for fruits and vegetables requires some knowledge of science. Running a business requires mathematical skills.)

LESSON 8-8
What are the parts of a seed?

(p. 160)

Teaching Strategies

PREVIEW Before beginning this lesson, have students scan the lesson looking for words with which they are unfamiliar. Have students work in pairs or small groups to define each of the words on their lists.

CLASS ACTIVITY Provide motivation for this lesson by distributing dry lima beans to the class. Tell students to note the hard, outer covering of the seed. Discuss the protective function of the seed coat.

CLASS ACTIVITY Distribute lima beans that have been soaked in water overnight to the class. Have students locate the hilum and the small opening near it. Point out that the opening is where the pollen tube entered the ovule.

RETEACHING OPTION If possible, show students time-lapsed pictures of plant germination. Have students describe what is happening in each picture.

Answers to Challenges (p. 161)

Apply

7. sunlight

Ideas in Action

Answers will vary. Accept all logical responses.

Skill Builder: Inferring

a. wind **b.** attachment to animals
c. wind **d.** water **e.** animals

Teaching Tips for Activity

Testing Seeds for Starch

Skills: *observing, measuring, analyzing*

SAFETY TIP Caution students to be careful when using a knife.

COOPERATIVE/COLLABORATIVE LEARNING Have students work in pairs.

Questions

1. a. black **b.** Answers will vary depending upon the kinds of seeds chosen.
2. a. food **b.** energy
3. All of the seeds have seed coats.

LESSON 8-9
How do plants reproduce asexually? (p. 162)

Teaching Strategies

PREVIEW Before beginning this lesson, write the title of each section in the lesson on the chalkboard. Have students copy these titles in their notebooks using an outline format. As students read each section, they should write the topic sentence for each paragraph in the section in their notebooks.

DISCUSSION To begin this lesson, ask students if they think it is possible to grow a plant without seeds. Discuss student responses. Develop the concept that some plants can reproduce by asexual reproduction.

DEMONSTRATION Bring in a potato. Identify the potato as an underground stem called a tuber. Point out the buds, or eyes, of the potato. Tell students that when planted, each eye may grow into a new potato plant.

CLASS ACTIVITY Have students plant the eyes of white potatoes. Tell students to check their potatoes for growth and to report on their results.

DISCUSSION Bring in an onion and display it in front of the classroom. Point out that an onion is a bulb. Define a bulb as an underground stem covered with fleshy leaves. Tell students that a bulb is another organ of vegetative propagation. Then ask students if they know of any other plants that grow from bulbs. (Some students may be familiar with the bulbs of plants such as tulips and daffodils.)

CLASS ACTIVITY Have students use cuttings of plants, such as carrots, turnips, beets, or sweet potatoes, to grow new plants.

Answers to Challenges (p. 163)

Apply

6. a. root **b.** stem **c.** stem

InfoSearch

You may wish to discuss students' questions and answers as a class.

Teaching Tips for Activity

Growing Plants Asexually

Skills: *observing, comparing*

SAFETY TIP Caution students to be careful when using a knife.

COOPERATIVE/COLLABORATIVE LEARNING Have students work in pairs.

EXTENSION You may wish to have students grow plants using other methods of vegetative propagation such as leaf cuttings and stem grafting.

Questions

1. Both the onion and the potato can reproduce through vegetative propagation.
2. Answers may vary, but the onion is more likely to develop roots first.

LESSON 8-10
What are tropisms? (p. 164)

Teaching Strategies

PREVIEW Before you begin this lesson, have students read the TechTerms and review the Lesson Summary.

REINFORCEMENT Review the concept of stimuli and responses. Ask students to give some examples of animals responding to stimuli. Then remind students that response is one of the six characteristics used to classify something as living. Emphasize that plants respond to changes in their environment too. Define tropism as the reaction of a plant to a stimulus.

DEMONSTRATION You can demonstrate the response of a plant toward light by placing a plant near a window that receives sunlight. Place the plant so its leaves and/or flowers are facing in a direction away from the light. Have students observe the plant for the next week. In a few days, students should observe that the plant has changed position so that its leaves and/or flowers are facing toward the sun.

EXTENSION You may wish to introduce the concept of positive and negative tropisms. In a positive tropism, a plant part grows in a direction *toward* the stimulus. In a negative tropism, a plant part grows *away* from the stimulus.

EXTENSION You may wish to introduce the term *auxins*. Auxins are plant hormones. Auxins are responsible for the growth of plants toward or away from stimuli.

Answers to Challenges (p. 165)

Apply

6. For a short time, the plant stems would grow up, away from the pull of gravity. However, the plant would quickly die if not exposed to light because it would be unable to carry on photosynthesis.
7. The roots of the willow tree have grown into the drain causing the clog.

Skill Builder: Building Vocabulary

The prefix *geo-* means earth; *hydro-* means water; and *photo-* means light. When added to the word *tropism*, each of these prefixes identifies the stimulus to which a plant is responding.

Teaching Tips for Science Connection

Carnivorous Plants

DEMONSTRATION Bring in a Venus' flytrap to show the class.

Question

How does a Venus' flytrap digest an insect? (Special chemicals that digest the soft parts of an insect are given off by the leaf.)

Answers to Unit Challenges (pp. 166-168)

Understanding the Features: Reading Critically

1. a relationship between two living things that is helpful to both living things
2. sells fresh fruit and vegetables; buys fruit and vegetables from growers; arranges fruit and vegetables; answers customers' questions
3. Answers will vary. Accept all logical responses.
4. Special chemicals are given off by the leaf.
5. aerial roots, prop roots, aquatic roots

Interpreting a Diagram

1. e
2. b
3. c
4. d
5. c and d
6. perfect; It has both male and female reproductive structures.
7. a
8. f

Critical Thinking

1. It would grow up.
2. The stem would bend and break.
3. Pollination is the transfer of pollen from the stamen to the pistil. Fertilization is the union of male and female reproductive cells.
4. The fruit will normally not be eaten until the seeds are ready for distribution. This helps ensure survival of the species.
5. It helps the root tip move easily through the soil.

ANIMALS WITHOUT BACKBONES (p. 169)

Previewing the Unit

Read the titles of the lessons in this unit aloud. Identify terms in the titles with which students are unfamiliar. Write these terms on the chalkboard. Using the Glossary of the text or a dictionary, define the terms as a class. Have students write the terms and their definitions in their notebooks. Then, have students work in small groups to carry out the task in the Study Hint.

Bulletin Board Suggestions

1. Assemble a bulletin board illustrating the animal phyla introduced in this unit. At the top of the bulletin board write the following head: *Animals Without Backbones.* Underneath the head attach pictures of representative sponges, cnidarians, flatworms, segmented worms, mollusks, echinoderms, and arthropods. Label each picture with the name of the organism and its phylum. Use the bulletin board to show students the wide variety of invertebrates.
2. Assemble a bulletin board illustrating the importance of invertebrates to people. Attach pictures to the bulletin board showing the ways invertebrates are both harmful and helpful to humans. You may wish to include pictures showing natural sponges, pearl jewelry, seafoods. coral reefs, honey, insects pollinating flowers, crop destruction by insects, diseases caused by parasitic invertebrates, and so on.

LESSON 9-1
What are sponges? (p. 170)

Teaching Strategies

PREVIEW Before students read this lesson, have them scan through the lesson looking for the science process skill symbols. Have students identify each skill used in the lesson. Students should then review the definition given for each skill on page 16 of their text.

REINFORCEMENT Before beginning this lesson, remind students that taxonomists divide animals into two large groups, invertebrates and vertebrates. Have students recall that invertebrates are animals without backbones.

DISCUSSION To introduce this lesson, ask students what they think of when they hear the term *sponge.* (Most students probably will think of the synthetic sponges used for cleaning.) Point out that there also are natural sponges and they are the simplest animals in the animal kingdom. Then tell students that sponges were once classified as plants. Ask students if they can figure out why. Discuss all student responses. Point out that unlike most animals, sponges do not move from place to place.

DISCUSSION Describe the structure of the sponge. Refer students to the diagram of a sponge on p. 170. Have students locate the two cell layers, the collar cells and their flagella, the wandering cells, and the spicules as you describe the function of each of these structures.

DISCUSSION Bring a natural sponge to class. Show students the many pores of the sponge.

CLASS ACTIVITY Obtain natural sponges and a variety of synthetic sponges made out of different materials. Divide the class into small groups. Distribute a natural sponge and synthetic sponge to each group. Have students in each group work together to design experiments testing the absorbance capabilities of each kind of sponge. Tell students to present their results in laboratory reports. (Students should observe that a natural sponge absorbs more water than a synthetic sponge.)

DISCUSSION Using the diagram of the sponge on p. 170, trace the path of water into and out of a sponge. Be sure students recognize that water moves through the sponge in only one direction.

Answers to Challenges (p. 171)
Apply

6. As its name implies, a sponge contains many pores.
7. A sponge filters the materials it needs from water to survive.
8. No; the job of the flagella is to keep water moving through the sponge. If no water moves through the sponge, the sponge cannot take in the materials it needs for its life processes.

Ideas In Action

Most synthetic sponges are made from rubber products. The prices for synthetic sponges usually are much less than the prices of natural sponges.

Teaching Tips for Leisure Activity
Snorkeling

COOPERATIVE/COLLABORATIVE LEARNING Have any students who have been snorkeling describe their experiences to the rest of the class.

Questions

1. Would you like to go snorkeling? Why or why not? (Answers will vary.)
2. LIST What equipment do you need to go snorkeling? (fins, a face mask, a snorkel)

LESSON 9-2
What are cnidarians? (p. 172)

Teaching Strategies

PREVIEW Before students begin this lesson, have them read the objective and review the Lesson Summary.

REINFORCEMENT Before beginning this lesson, review the definition of tissues. Ask students what a tissue is. (group of cells that look alike and work together) This review will help students understand the structure of cnidarians because the cells of these animals are organized into tissues.

DISCUSSION Provide motivation for this lesson by asking students to describe any personal experiences they may have had with jellyfish. Students who have spent time at the seashore may already be familiar with the appearance of jellyfish. Point out that jellyfish are one kind of cnidarian.

CLASS ACTIVITY If possible, obtain some hydra from a biological supply company. Place a few hydra in a petri dish and allow students to observe the hydra under a binocular microscope. Tell students to describe their observations of movement and response by the hydra.

EXTENSION Have interested students find out about the Portuguese man-of-war. Tell students to present their findings in an oral report.

REINFORCEMENT Students may be better able to remember the body forms of cnidarians if you tell them that the mouth of a medusa always faces downward and is on the bottom of the cnidarian. In contrast, the mouth of a polyp always faces upward and is at the top of the cnidarian.

RETEACHING OPTION Show students pictures of sea anemones and coral polyps. Ask students if they think the organisms in the pictures are plants or animals. After discussing student responses, point out that the organisms are animals called cnidarians. Then identify jellyfish as cnidarians with which students probably are more familiar.

Answers to Challenges (p. 173)

Check

1. The phylum gets its name from the cnidocytes.
2. All cnidarians live in water.
3. medusa
4. digestive, muscle, nerve, and sensory tissues

Apply

5. a jellyfish
6. Both medusas and polyps have one opening (a mouth), two cell layers, a jellylike layer between the cell layers, and tissues.
7. Cnidarians have cells organized into tissues.

Health and Safety Tip

When a person is stung by a jellyfish, it is important to keep the victim calm and to seek medical attention as soon as possible.

Teaching Tips for Science Connection

Coral Reefs

EXTENSION You may wish to tell students that in the United States, coral reefs are located off the coasts of Florida, Texas, and California.

EXTENSION Have interested students research artificial reefs and their uses. Tell students to write their findings in a report.

Questions

1. LIST What are the three kinds of coral reefs? fringing reef, barrier reef, atoll)
2. Why are coral reefs valuable to marine organisms? (They are important sources of food and shelter.)

LESSON 9-3
What are flatworms and roundworms? (p. 174)

Teaching Strategies

PREVIEW Have students read the lesson feature before beginning the lesson. Discuss the concepts presented in the feature. Ask students how they think this information relates to topics they have already studied or to the lesson they are about to study.

DISCUSSION Write the term *worms* on the chalkboard. Ask students what they think of when they hear the word *worm*. (Most students probably will think of the earthworm.) Point out that there are many other kinds of worms too. Then describe the characteristics of flatworms and roundworms. Stress that flatworms are the simplest animals with bilateral symmetry and roundworms are one of the simplest animals to have a complete digestive system.

CLASS ACTIVITY To help students remember the three cell layers of worms, have students look up the meanings of the prefixes *ecto-*, *endo-*, and *meso-* in a dictionary. (*ecto-*: outer; *endo-*: inner; *meso-*: middle)

DEMONSTRATION If possible, obtain planaria from a biological supply company. Place the worms in petri dishes filled with spring water or distilled water. Have students observe the planaria and note their eyespots.

DISCUSSION Discuss the meaning of the term *parasite*. Point out that both flukes and tapeworms are parasites. Have students locate the hooks and suckers on the diagram of a tapeworm on p. 174. Identify these structures as adaptations for life as a parasite.

RETEACHING OPTION Write the following head on the chalkboard: *Worms*. From this head, draw arrows to each of the following heads: *Flatworms, Roundworms, Segmented Worms*. Under flatworms list planaria, flukes, and tapeworms. Have students copy the chart in their notebooks. Tell students they will learn more about segmented worms in the next lesson.

Answers to Challenges (p. 175)

Apply

6. The flatworms have long, flat, ribbonlike bodies.
7. The parasite takes in nutrients that the host organism needs for growth.

Health and Safety Tip

Pork must be cooked thoroughly to avoid contamination by the *trichina* worm.

Teaching Tips for Science Connection

Pets and Worms

EXTENSION If possible, have a veterinarian visit your class to discuss how pets are treated for worms.

Questions

1. IDENTIFY What are the most dangerous parasites of dogs? (heartworms)
2. How can you help prevent your pet from getting worms? (keep pets on a leash or in a yard; clean its area regularly; feed it a balanced diet; have it checked by a veterinarian)

LESSON 9-4
What are segmented worms? (p. 176)

Teaching Strategies

PREVIEW Before beginning this lesson, have students scan the lesson for the science process skill symbols. Have students identify each skill used in the lesson. Students should then review the definition given for each skill on page 16 of their text.

DISCUSSION Tell students that the third phylum of worms, *Annelida,* includes the worms most familiar to students--earthworms. Ask students to describe an earthworm. Try to elicit that an earthworms' most striking characteristic is its segmentation.

CLASS ACTIVITY Set up a terrarium for earthworms in the classroom. Have students observe the external structure of an earthworm and the way an earthworm burrows in soil.

DISCUSSION Refer students to the diagram of an earthworm on p. 176. Have students observe the diagram as you describe the features and organ systems of an earthworm. Emphasize that earthworms are the simplest animals to have a closed circulatory system.

REINFORCEMENT Have students draw a diagram of an earthworm. Tell students to label its external and internal structures.

RETEACHING OPTION Ask students what happens to earthworms during a heavy rain. Challenge students to explain why so many earthworms can be found on the streets and sidewalks after a heavy rain. List student responses on the chalkboard. Point out that during a heavy rain, earthworms begin to drown as the soil becomes saturated with water. The water prevents earthworms from obtaining enough gases through their skin.

Answers to Challenges (p. 177)

Apply

6. The bodies of annelids are made up of many ringlike sections, or segments.
7. If exposed to direct sunlight, the earthworm would dry out and be unable to carry on respiration through its moist skin. As a result, the earthworm would die.

InfoSearch

You may wish to discuss students' questions and answers as a class.

Teaching Tips for Looking Back in Science
Medical Uses of Leeches

ITERDISCIPLINARY CONNECTION You may wish to tell students that George Washington's death is attributed to the practice of ''bloodletting'' using leeches.

EXTENSION If possible, show students a preserved specimen of a leech.

Question

How are leeches being used in medicine today? (The chemicals given off by leeches are being used to keep blood from clotting, dilate blood vessels, heal damaged tissues, and prevent infection.)

LESSON 9-5
What are mollusks? (p. 178)

Teaching Strategies

PREVIEW Before beginning this section, have students scan the lesson looking for words with which they are unfamiliar. Have students work in pairs or small groups to define each of the words on their lists.

DISCUSSION Provide motivation for this lesson by asking

T38

students if they have ever eaten clams, scallops, oysters, mussels, escargots, or squid. Point out that all of these seafood are animals that belong to the phylum *Mollusca.* Then describe the three major classes of mollusks and the characteristics of each.

EXTENSION You may wish to tell students that mollusks with one shell are called univalves, mollusks with two shells are called bivalves, and mollusks with no shell are called cephalopods.

DISCUSSION Describe the three body parts of mollusks and their organ systems using the clam as an example. Refer students to the diagram of a clam on p. 178 to illustrate your description.

CLASS ACTIVITY If possible, obtain a variety of different kinds of mollusk shells. Allow students to examine the shells closely to see how the shells differ.

CLASS ACTIVITY If your school is located near a shoreline, you may wish to arrange a class trip to the ocean to provide students with an opportunity to collect and observe mollusk shells first-hand.

INTRASCIENCE CONNECTION Describe Newton's third law of motion and relate it to the way cephalopods move. Newton's third law of motion states that for every action there is an equal and opposite reaction.

ITERDISCIPLINARY CONNECTION Have interested students read Jules Verne's *Twenty Thousand Leagues Under the Sea* and write a book report.

Answers to Challenges (p. 179)

Apply

5. The movement of squid and octopuses is an example of an action-reaction relationship. These animals shoot out a stream of water from their bodies. The force of the water causes the body to move in a direction opposite the stream of water.

InfoSearch

You may wish to discuss students' questions and answers as a class.

Teaching Tips for Activity
Modeling Squid Jet Propulsion

Skills: *analyzing, modeling*

SAFETY TIP Caution students to be careful when using scissors.

COOPERATIVE/COLLABORATIVE LEARNING Have students work in pairs.

Questions

1. opposite the direction of its neck
2. The movement caused by the balloon releasing air is the same as the movement that would be caused by the squid releasing water.
3. The squid would move farther and faster.

LESSON 9-6
What are arthropods? (p. 180)

Teaching Strategies

PREVIEW Read the TechTerms aloud so that students can hear their pronunciations.

DISCUSSION Describe the main characteristics of arthropods. Point out that arthropods have a segmented body, jointed legs, an exoskeleton, an open circulatory system, and undergo the process of molting.

REINFORCEMENT To help students visualize an arthropod's exoskeleton, you may wish to compare it to a knight's suit of armor.

EXTENSION The two other classes of arthropods are centipedes and millipedes. Have interested students research the characteristics of these organisms. Tell students to write their findings in a report.

REINFORCEMENT Students often mistakenly refer to spiders, ticks, and scorpions as insects. Be sure students understand that these organisms are arachnids.

RETEACHING OPTION Show students many interesting pictures of arthropods to illustrate the great diversity of this largest group of animals. Try to include pictures which show the many different specialized body parts of arthropods. Have students try to identify the organisms shown and classify them into their proper classes.

Answers to Challenges (p. 181)

Check

1. Chitin is the material that makes up the exoskeleton of arthropods.
2. Arachnids are one class of arthropods.
3. *Arthropoda*
4. Accept any three of the following: exoskeleton, segmented body, jointed legs, open circulatory system, molting.
5. When an arthropod molts, it sheds its exoskeleton and grows a new one.
6. Claws are used for defense and capturing food.

Apply

7. The ants and flies are insects, the lobster is a crustacean, and the spider is an arachnid.
8. Arthropods with wings are able to fly.
9. A grasshopper moves by jumping and flying. Large back legs enable a grasshopper to jump large distances.

Health and Safety Tip

The rash that results from Lyme disease usually forms in the shape of a bull's eye target. Other symptoms of the disease include fever and pain in the joints. The white-tail deer often serves as a carrier for the deer tick that causes Lyme disease.

Teaching Tips for Technology and Society

Uses of Chitin

CLASS ACTIVITY After students read this feature, have them work in pairs to construct charts summarizing the uses of chitin.

Questions

1. Why is chitin especially good as a material for medical uses? (It does not cause allergic reactions in most people.)
2. INFER Why do you think chitin can be used in water filters? (It is waterproof.)

LESSON 9-7
What are insects? (p. 182)

Teaching Strategies

PREVIEW Before beginning this lesson, read the list of

TechTerms aloud so students can hear their pronunciations.

DISCUSSION Ask students what they think of when they hear the word *insect*. Discuss all student responses. Many students probably will think of insects solely in negative terms. Point out that many insects are helpful to people and the environment. Cite pollination by bees as an example. Emphasize that insects are incredibly successful organisms in terms of their number of species and distribution.

RETEACHING OPTION Obtain a wall-sized poster of a grasshopper. Have volunteers locate the grasshopper's three body segments, three pairs of legs, and antennae. Stress that these structures are characteristic of all insects.

EXTENSION Have interested students research beekeeping as a career. Tell students to present their findings in an oral report. Students may obtain information by writing to the New Jersey Beekeepers Association, 157 Five Point Road, Colts Neck, NJ 07722.

Answers to Challenges (p. 183)

Apply

7. There are more insect species than there are other animal species.
8. The fly is larger to show that the number of insect species is greater than the number of all other animal species.

InfoSearch

You may wish to discuss students' questions and answers as a class.

Teaching Tips for Science Connection

Camouflage and Mimicry

CLASS ACTIVITY Before students read this feature, refer them to the photograph on p. 183. Ask students to find the walking stick in the photograph. This activity will demonstrate the adaptation of camouflage.

ITERDISCIPLINARY CONNECTION You may wish to discuss the use of camouflage by people. Many students probably are familiar with *camouflage* as the uniform worn by members of the military. Ask students why they think members of the armed forces wear green and brown uniforms. (to blend into the surroundings)

Question

1. EXPLAIN Why do birds avoid eating the viceroy butterfly? (It looks like the monarch butterfly, which tastes bad to birds.)
2. DEFINE What is camouflage? (ability of an organism to blend in with its surroundings)

LESSON 9-8
How do insects develop? (p. 184)

Teaching Strategies

PREVIEW Before beginning this lesson, have students review the TechTerms and their definitions and read the Lesson Summary.

DISCUSSION Describe the differences between complete and incomplete metamorphosis. Guide students to understand that in complete metamorphosis, an insect undergoes a *complete* change in form. In *incomplete* metamorphosis, the young insect (nymph) closely resembles the adult. A complete change in form does not take place.

CLASS ACTIVITY If possible, show students a sequence of time-lapsed photographs showing the metamorphosis of a butterfly. Arrange the photographs in front of the classroom in random order. Have students put the pictures in the proper sequence and identify each stage of development.

COOPERATIVE/COLLABORATIVE LEARNING Have students quiz each other on the TechTerms for this lesson.

Answers to Challenges (p. 185)

Apply

6. The eggs of insects, like the eggs of birds, contain yolk that the developing embryo uses for food. Accept all logical responses.
7. During the pupa stage the insect does not eat.
8. a, e, d, b, c

Teaching Tips for Career in Life Science
Exterminator

REINFORCEMENT Be sure students understand that an exterminator may kill mice and rats as well as insect pests.

Questions

1. RELATE Why should a person interested in becoming an exterminator take biology and chemistry courses in high school? (Extermination involves living things and often the use of chemicals to destroy them.)
2. INFER Why are termites harmful to people? (Termites destroy property.)

LESSON 9-9
What are echinoderms? (p. 186)

Teaching Strategies

PREVIEW Have students write the lesson title and objectives in their notebooks. As students read the lesson, tell them to write down the sentence or sentences that provide the information needed in the objectives.

DEMONSTRATION If possible, obtain a preserved specimen of a seastar to show to the class. As you discuss each echinoderm characteristic, point to the part of the seastar that exemplifies the characteristic.

DEMONSTRATION Demonstrate the action of tube feet with a medicine dropper. Place the tip of a medicine dropper against the tip of your finger. Squeeze the bulb of the medicine dropper to force all air out of the tube. When you release the bulb, the vacuum formed by the lack of air inside the dropper should cause the dropper to remain attached to your finger. Relate this to the action of a seastar's tube feet.

Answers to Challenges (p. 187)

Apply

7. The sand or mud would not allow the tube feet to form the vacuum needed to grasp a surface.
8. The animals who fed on sea stars would decrease.

Skill Builder: Building Vocabulary

Check students' diagrams.

Teaching Tips for Leisure Activity
Seashore Collections

DISCUSSION Point out to students that seashore collections usually are made up of shells from mollusks, crustaceans, and echinoderms.

CLASS ACTIVITY If possible, arrange for a class trip to a shoreline or an aquarium for students to observe different seashells.

Question

Why should a person avoid collecting live animals on a beach? (Answers will vary. Accept all logical responses.)

LESSON 9-10
What is regeneration? (p. 188)

Teaching Strategies

PREVIEW Before beginning this lesson, write the title of each section in the lesson on the chalkboard. Have students copy these titles in their notebooks using an outline format. As students read each section, they should write the topic sentence for each paragraph in the section in their notebooks.

DEMONSTRATION Obtain a planarian from a biological supply company. Cut the planarian in half using a scalpel. Have students observe that each half eventually regenerates into a new planarian.

REINFORCEMENT Be sure students understand that regeneration of a whole organism is a form of asexual reproduction.

COOPERATIVE/COLLABORATIVE LEARNING Have a volunteer compare the regeneration abilities of a planaria and a human for the rest of the class.

Answers to Challenges (p. 189)

Apply

6. Both methods of asexual reproduction allow a new organism to grow from a part of the parent organism.
7. because a whole new organism is not produced
8. A crab can regrow a lost claw. A seastar can regrow an entire organism.

State the Problem

Students should recognize that new seastars would grow from the parts, and the population of seastars would increase.

Teaching Tips for Technology and Society
Organ Transplants

CLASS ACTIVITY Have students find and collect recent newspaper and magazine articles pertaining to organ transplants. Read and discuss the articles as a class.

Questions

1. What are some organs that can be transplanted? (liver, kidneys, heart, pancreas, lungs)
2. Why is cyclosporine important in organ transplants? (It helps keep the body of the person receiving the organ from rejecting the transplanted organ.)

Answers to Unit Challenges (pp. 190-192)

Understanding the Features: Reading Critically

1. for safety reasons
2. fringing reef, barrier reef, atoll
3. Answers will vary. Accept all logical responses.
4. Chemicals given off by leeches are being used to keep blood from clotting, dilate blood vessels, heal damaged tissue, and prevent infection.
5. A type of thread made from chitin is used for sewing up wounds and incisions.
6. It looks like a monarch butterfly, which birds do not like to eat. Thus, birds also avoid eating the viceroy butterfly.
7. Answers will vary. Accept all logical responses.
8. Answers will vary. Accept all logical responses.
9. liver, kidneys, heart, pancreas, lungs

Interpreting a Diagram

1. F
2. head
3. E
4. C
5. abdomen
6. A

Critical Thinking

1. They do not move.
2. They will regenerate and their population will increase.
3. Sunlight would dry out an earthworm. An earthworm must be moist in order to breathe.
4. Answers will vary. Accept all logical responses.
5. Answers will vary. Accept all logical responses.

UNIT 10
ANIMALS WITH BACKBONES (p. 193)

Previewing the Unit

Before beginning this unit, read the titles of the lessons in the unit aloud. Then, have students work in pairs to carry out the task in the Study Hint.

Bulletin Board Suggestions

1. Create a bulletin board display entitled *Vertebrates*. Tell students to find and collect as many photographs of each vertebrate class discussed in this unit as possible. Attach each photograph to the bulletin board under a heading that identifies the class name. Refer to the bulletin board as you discuss characteristics and examples of the animals in each class.

2. Prepare a bulletin board display entitled *Kinds of Birds*. Divide the bulletin board into five sections. Label each section with one of the following heads: *Swimming Birds, Birds of Prey, Perching Birds, Wading Birds, Nonperching Land Birds*. Attach pictures of representative birds under each head. Have students choose one of the birds included in the bulletin board display on which they would like to do further research. When you are discussing Lesson 10-6, have each student point out the bird they chose on the bulletin board and present the class with information about their bird such as where it lives, what it eats, and any unique nesting or mating habits it has.

Answers to Challenges (p. 195)

Apply

8. Gills; the flexible backbone of a fish also is an adaptation for life in water.
9. the backbone
10. Answers may include any two of the following: a notochord or a backbone, gill slits, and a hollow nerve cord at some stage of development.

Skill Builder: Applying Definitions

Endo- means inner or inside; *meso-* means middle; *ecto-* means outer or outside. Students should identify the inner layer (B) as the endoderm, the outer layer (C) as the ectoderm, and the middle layer (A) as the mesoderm.

Teaching Tips for Career in Life Service
Animal Technician

EXTENSION You may wish to tell students about other careers that involve working with animals, such as animal center management and animal husbandry. Information about these careers also can be obtained by writing to the American Veterinary Medical Association.

Questions

1. INFER What kinds of science courses might be helpful to an animal technician? (Answers will vary. Accept all logical responses.)
2. APPLY A parasite is an organism that lives on or inside another organism and causes it harm. Many worms are parasites of dogs and cats. Why would an animal technician need to know about these parasites? (Answers will vary. Accept all logical responses.)

LESSON 10-1
What are chordates? (p. 194)

Teaching Strategies

PREVIEW Before beginning this lesson, have students copy the section titles into their notebooks using an outline format. As students read each section, have them write the topic sentence for each paragraph in the section into their notebooks beneath the appropriate section head. Encourage students to use their outlines as study guides.

DISCUSSION Describe the phylum *Chordata*, which includes the animals students are most familiar with. Emphasize that all chordates have three features at some time during their development: a notochord, a hollow nerve cord, and gill slits. Point out that these features distinguish chordates from all other animals.

REINFORCEMENT Be sure students understand that two subphyla of chordates do not have backbones.

CLASS ACTIVITY List the names of the five classes of vertebrates on the chalkboard. Ask students to provide you with the names of several animals that are included in each class. Write the names of each animal on the chalkboard under the appropriate head. Tell students to copy the lists into their notebooks.

REINFORCEMENT Direct students' attention to the picture of the lancelet on p. 194. As you review the characteristics of chordates, have students locate each characteristic on the diagram.

LESSON 10-2
What are fishes? (p. 196)

Teaching Strategies

PREVIEW Before students begin this lesson, have them scan the lesson for the science process skill symbols. Have students identify each skill used in the lesson. Students should then review the definition given for each skill on page 16 of their text.

DISCUSSION Describe the characteristics of fishes. Emphasize to students that in most vertebrates the gill slits disappear at some stage of development, but that in fishes, these structures become gills.

CLASS ACTIVITY If possible, set up an aquarium in the classroom and have students observe different examples of bony fishes. Tell students to note the scales, which cover and protect the skin, and the fins, which are used for steering and balance.

RETEACHING OPTION Write the following head on the chalkboard: *Fishes*. From this head, draw arrows to each of the following heads: *Jawless Fishes, Cartilaginous Fishes, Bony Fishes*. Under *Jawless Fishes*, list lampreys and hagfish. Under *Cartilaginous Fishes* list sharks, rays, and skates. Under *Bony Fishes* list tuna, salmon, bass, and flounder. Have students copy the chart in their notebooks.

CLASS ACTIVITY Have students touch the tips of their noses and their outer ears to feel cartilage. Point out that cartilage is a tough, flexible tissue which makes up some parts of the human body, and the entire skeletons of cartilaginous fishes.

REINFORCEMENT Be sure students recognize that only a few kinds of fishes are classified as either jawless fishes or cartilaginous fishes. Stress that most fishes with which students are familiar are bony fishes.

Answers to Challenges (p. 197)

Check

1. animal whose body temperature changes with the temperature of its surroundings
2. organs that absorb dissolved oxygen from water
3. 2
4. lampreys and hagfish
5. skeleton made up of cartilage
6. for steering and balance

Apply

7. 5
8. **a.** bony fish **b.** bony fish **c.** jawless fish **d.** cartilaginous fish **e.** jawless fish **f.** cartilaginous fish **g.** bony fish **h.** cartilaginous fish

Skill Builder: Inferring

The coloring of a flounder helps it blend in with its surroundings so that it can remain unseen by both its predators and prey. Having both eyes on top of its head allows a flounder to see fishes and other organisms that swim above it.

Teaching Tips for Science Connection

Unusual Fishes

EXTENSION Have interested students research other unusual fishes such as the lantern fish, the walking catfish, the halibut, and the blowfish. Tell students to write their findings in a report. Tell students to be sure to discuss how each fish's unusual adaptation helps it survive.

LESSON 10-3
What are amphibians? (p. 198)

Teaching Strategies

PREVIEW Before students begin this lesson, have them read the TechTerm and its definition and review the Lesson Summary.

DISCUSSION Write the term *Amphibian* on the chalkboard. Tell students that the word *amphibian* comes from the Greek word meaning double life. Then ask the students how they think double life applies to amphibians. Discuss all student responses. Elicit from students that most amphibians spend part of their life in water and part of their life on land.

REINFORCEMENT Be sure students understand that although adult amphibians live on land, all amphibians must reproduce in water.

DISCUSSION Refer students to the photographs of amphibians on p. 198. Describe the three different orders of amphibians. Have students identify the representative organism shown.

EXTENSION Have interested students research the estivation behavior of toads and frogs. Tell students to present their findings in oral reports.

COOPERATIVE/COLLABORATIVE LEARNING Have a volunteer describe the main characteristics of amphibians.

Answers to Challenges (p. 199)

Check

1. double life
2. fishes
3. moist, bumpy skin
4. tailless amphibian
5. so that oxygen and carbon dioxide can be exchanged through the skin

Apply

6. A salamander has a tail at all stages of development; a frog does not have a tail at all stages of development.
7. Amphibians have webbed feet to help them move quickly through water.
8. Accept any six of the following: amphibians spend part of their lives in water and part on land; have smooth, moist skin; are coldblooded; have webbed feet; breathe through gills, lungs, and their skin; do not lay eggs with shells; lay their eggs in water; have a closed circulatory system; have a three-chambered heart.

InfoSearch

You may wish to review students' questions and answers as a class.

Teaching Tips for Technology and Society

Computer Dissections

DEMONSTRATION If possible, run a frog dissection simulation disk. Show students the different organs and organ systems of a frog on the computer screen.

Questions

1. What do you think about live dissection? (Answers will vary. Accept all logical responses.)
2. DEFINE What is a simulation? (a moving model)

LESSON 10-4
How do frogs develop? (p. 200)

Teaching Strategies

PREVIEW Before students begin this lesson, have them copy the lesson objective into their notebooks. As students read the lesson, have them write the sentences that meet the objective.

REINFORCEMENT Before beginning this lesson, students may benefit from a review of insect metamorphosis. Remind students that there are two kinds of metamorphosis, complete and incomplete. Point out that the development of the frog is an example of complete metamorphosis.

DISCUSSION Trace the development of a frog from egg to adult. Refer students to the diagram showing metamorphosis on p. 200 to illustrate your description.

CLASS ACTIVITY Divide the class into small groups. Tell students in each group to draw pictures of frog eggs, tadpoles, young frogs, and adult frogs. Have students cut out their pictures and arrange them in sequence to show metamorphosis. Tell students to use the diagram or p. 200 as a guide.

COOPERATIVE/COLLABORATIVE LEARNING Have students work in pairs to answer the Check and Apply questions.

Answers to Challenges (p. 201)

Apply

7. b, d, c, e, a

8. Check students' flow charts for logic and accuracy. Students' flow charts should indicate the following stages: Eggs are laid, tadpoles hatch from the eggs, legs begin to develop, the tail grows shorter and then disappears, lungs develop and gills disappear, a young frog suited to life on land has developed.

9. Students should recognize that laying a large number of eggs helps to ensure that some amphibians will develop into adults. Accept all logical responses.

10. Amphibian eggs are not protected by a shell. Laying eggs in water helps to prevent the eggs from drying out.

Health and Safety Tip

Warts are caused by viruses. The appearance of a wart in some ways resembles the bumps on a toad's skin. This similarity in appearance is responsible for the misconception that toads cause warts.

Teaching Tips for Activity
Sequencing Tadpole Development

Skills: *sequencing, analyzing*

COOPERATIVE/COLLABORATIVE LEARNING   Answer the questions as a class.

Questions

1. The tadpole develops gills and a tail. The young frog has a tail, four legs, gills, and lungs. The frog loses its tail and gills.

2. The tadpole lives in water. It has a tail to help it swim and gills.

3. The frog lives on land. It has four feet and lungs.

LESSON 10-5
What are reptiles? (p. 202)

Teaching Strategies

PREVIEW   Before students begin this lesson, have them read the objectives and review the Lesson Summary.

DISCUSSION   You may wish to introduce this lesson by having students read the feature about dinosaurs on p. 203. Students often are very interested in dinosaurs, so this feature can serve as a motivational exercise. After students read the feature, discuss the many characteristics of dinosaurs and why some scientists think dinosaurs became extinct.

DISCUSSION   Describe the characteristics of reptiles. Present the reptiles as animals that are well adapted to living on land. Point out that reptiles lay eggs with a tough leathery shell. Then compare the skin of reptiles and amphibians. Elicit from students the advantages of a hard, dry, scaly skin.

REINFORCEMENT   Students often confuse amphibians and reptiles. As you discuss reptiles, you may wish to create a table that compares the major characteristics of amphibians and reptiles. Tell students to copy the table in their notebooks. Have students use their tables to identify characteristics that the two groups of animals share and to identify differences between amphibians and reptiles.

EXTENSION   Tell students that in many areas, alligators are a protected species. Have interested students research why alligators are in danger of becoming extinct and what efforts

are being made to save alligators. Have students present their findings in oral reports.

CLASS ACTIVITY   If possible, take your class to the reptile house of the local zoo to observe the different orders of reptiles.

Answers to Challenges (p. 203)

Check

1. in eggs
2. They have many features of ancient reptiles.
3. Snakes do not have legs.
4. on land
5. by looking at their heads

Apply

6. Snakes do not have legs.
7. Answers may include that the dinosaurs shown have two pairs of legs and clawed feet; the dinosaurs have skin covered with scales. Accept all logical responses.

InfoSearch

You may wish to discuss students' questions and answers as a class.

Teaching Tips for Looking Back in Science
The Age of Dinosaurs

EXTENSION   If possible, take students to a museum of natural history where models of dinosaurs are on display.

Questions

1. Why is the Mesozoic Era sometimes called the Age of Reptiles? (Dinosaurs were the dominant animals during the Mesozoic Era.)
2. HYPOTHESIZE   Why do you think dinosaurs became extinct? (Answers will vary. Accept all logical responses)

LESSON 10-6
What are birds? (p. 204)

Teaching Strategies

PREVIEW   Before students begin this lesson, have them review the TechTerm and its definition and read the Lesson Summary.

DISCUSSION   List the features of birds on the chalkboard in an outline format. Discuss each feature. Emphasize that birds are the only animals with feathers.

DISCUSSION   Describe the five groups of birds: birds of prey, perching birds, wading birds, swimming birds, and nonperching land birds. Discuss how the birds are classified by the shapes of their beaks and feet. Refer students to Figure 1 on p. 204 to illustrate your descriptions.

CLASS ACTIVITY   Take the class on a field trip to observe birds. Bring along a field guide on birds and ask students to try to identify some of the birds they observe.

ITERDISCIPLINARY CONNECTION   Have interested students research the life and work of Audubon. Encourage students to study some of the artwork produced by Audubon and to write a brief biography of his life. As an extension to this activity you may wish to have students research the role of the Audubon Society. Encourage interested students to write to the Audubon Society to find out what the goals of this organization are. Have students share their findings with the class.

RETEACHING OPTION   To introduce this lesson, ask if any students have down jackets or coats. Point out that down clothing is lightweight and very warm. Tell students that down feathers are small fluffy feathers that are close to a bird's skin. Elicit from students that down feathers help to keep a bird warm.

Answers to Challenges (p. 205)

Apply

7. **a.** bird of prey   **b.** swimming bird   **c.** perching bird   **d.** nonperching land bird   **e.** wading bird   **f.** bird of prey
8. Sea gulls have webbed feet and beaks suited to capturing and eating small sea animals such as fish.
9. The upper chambers of the human heart are the atria. The lower chambers are the ventricles.
10. the presence of feathers

Health and Safety Tip

Symptoms of *salmonella* poisoning include stomach cramps, fever, diarrhea, and vomiting. One way to avoid *salmonella* poisoning is to not eat raw eggs or undercooked poultry products. Another way to avoid *salmonella* poisoning is to not use the same cooking utensils and cutting boards for raw poultry as are used for other foods.

Teaching Tips for Activity

Observing a Bird Egg

Skills: *observing, modeling, hypothesizing*

COOPERATIVE/COLLABORATIVE LEARNING   Have students work in pairs.

DISCUSSION   You may wish to tell students that the chicken eggs they purchase at supermarkets are unfertilized eggs. Farmers are able to determine which eggs have been fertilized and which eggs have not been fertilized by holding the eggs up to light.

Questions

1. **a.** white or brown   **b.** slightly bumpy
2. **a.** colorless   **b.** yellow
3. the egg white and the yolk
4. **a.** to protect the developing embryo   **b.** to provide food for the developing embryo
5. to help protect the eggs from damage by the environment or predators; Accept all logical responses.

LESSON 10-7
What are mammals? (p. 206)

Teaching Strategies

PREVIEW   Before students begin this lesson, have them write the lesson objective in their notebooks. As students read the lesson, have them write the sentences from the lesson that provide the information needed in the objective.

DISCUSSION   On the chalkboard, outline the main characteristics of mammals: body hair, a four-chambered heart, warm-blooded, highly developed brain and nervous system, nursing of young from mammary glands. Tell students how each of these characteristics has helped mammals become one of the most successful groups of animals on the earth.

CLASS ACTIVITY   Take the class on a field trip to a local zoo or natural history museum to observe different kinds of mammals.

RETEACHING OPTION   Write the following head on the chalkboard: *Mammals*. From this head, draw arrows to each of the following heads: *Egg Laying, Pouched, Placental*. Under *Egg Laying*, list the duckbill platypus and the spiny anteater. Under *Pouched*, list kangaroos, opossums, and koala bears. Under *Placental*, list dogs, cats, cattle, seals, whales, bats, and humans. Tell students to copy the chart in their notebooks. Point out that the largest group of mammals is the placentals.

EXTENSION   You may wish to tell students that egg-laying mammal are called monotremes and pouched mammals are called marsupials.

REINFORCEMENT   Be sure students understand that seals, whales, and bats are mammals. Students often confuse the classification of these animals. They tend to classify seals and whales as fishes and bats as birds.

Answers to Challenges (p. 207)

Apply

8. Spiny anteaters and duckbill platypuses are warmblooded, have a body covering of hair, and other mammalian characteristics. Accept all logical responses.
9. The way in which their young develop.

Skill Builder: Classifying

Check students' posters for logic and accuracy.

Teaching Tips for Leisure Activity

Pets

DISCUSSION   Ask students to describe their pets. Discuss the kinds of animals people keep as pets and the care and handling that are required for each kind of animal.

Question

What is a pet's main role? (to be its owner's friend)

LESSON 10-8
How do animal embryos develop? (p. 208)

Teaching Strategies

PREVIEW   Before students begin this lesson, have them read the TechTerms and their definitions and review the Lesson Summary.

DISCUSSION   Provide motivation for this lesson by displaying a variety of animal eggs. Depending upon availability, frog, fish, snake, turtle, or bird eggs could be displayed. Then develop the concepts of internal and external fertilization. Guide students to understand that internal fertilization takes place in most land animals. Refer to the fertilization of reptiles, birds, and mammals as internal fertilization. Point out that fish and amphibians have external fertilization.

REINFORCEMENT   Be sure students understand that some organisms have internal fertilization, but external embryonic development. Emphasize that mammals are the only organisms in which embryos develop within the mother's body.

COOPERATIVE/COLLABORATIVE LEARNING   Have students work in pairs to answer the Check and Apply questions.

Answers to Challenges (p. 209)

Check

1. female sex cell

2. male sex cell

3. union of a male sex cell and a female sex cell

4. a developing organism

5. the yolk

6. from the mother

7. inside the mother's body

8. in a hard shell

Apply

9. The development of the embryo of most animals takes place outside the body of the mother. The development of most mammal embryos takes place inside the mother's body.

10. the placenta

Skill Builder: Researching

The gestation periods for the mammals listed are elephant: 20-22 months; mouse: 20 days; dog: 63 days; cat: about 9 weeks; humans: 9 months; guinea pigs: about 28 days; horse: 11 months; cow: 40 weeks. Check students' graphs for logic and accuracy.

Teaching Tips for Activity

Comparing Gestation Time and Animal Size

Skills: *calculating, sequencing, graphing*

COOPERATIVE/COLLABORATIVE LEARNING   Answer the questions as a class.

Questions

1. hamster, rabbit, dog, sheep, human, gorilla, cow, elephant.

2. Check students' tables for logic and accuracy.

3. As a rule, larger animals take longer to develop and have longer gestation periods than do smaller animals.

Answers to Unit Challenges (pp. 210-212)

Understanding the Features: Reading Critically

1. high school diploma; two-year animal technology program

2. to protect it from other animals

3. Answers will vary. Accept all logical responses.

4. Mesozoic Era

5. Answers will vary. Accept all logical responses.

Critical Thinking

1. The body temperature of a coldblooded animal changes with the temperature of its environment. A warmblooded animal's body temperature remains the same. Humans are warmblooded.

2. coldblooded; moist skin; webbed feet; use gills, lungs, and their skin to exchange oxygen and carbon dioxide; eggs do not have shells; live part of their life on land and part in water

3. Answers will vary. Accept all logical responses.

4. to crack the seeds without breaking their beaks

5. Answers will vary. Accept all logical responses.

Interpreting a Diagram

1. eye

2. gill cover

3. the gills

4. A and F

5. mouth

6. to take in food and water

NUTRITION AND DIGESTION (p. 213)

Previewing the Unit

Read the titles of the lessons in this unit aloud. Identify terms in the titles with which students are unfamiliar. Write these terms on the chalkboard. Using the Glossary of the text or a dictionary, define the terms as a class. Have students write the terms and their definitions in their notebooks.

Bulletin Board Suggestions

1. Assemble a bulletin board illustrating the four basic food groups. Divide the bulletin board into four sections. Label each section with one of the following heads: *Dairy Group, Meat Group, Vegetable-Fruit Group, Bread-Cereal Group.* Attach pictures of representative foods under each heading.
2. Assemble a bulletin board showing the human digestive system. Attach a large picture of the digestive system to the bulletin board. Label each organ and gland. Add arrows to show the path of food through the digestive tract.

LESSON 11-1
What are nutrients? (p. 214)

Teaching Strategies

PREVIEW   Have students write the lesson title and objective in their notebooks. As students read the lesson, tell them to write down the sentence or sentences that provide the information needed in the objective.

DISCUSSION   To introduce this lesson, ask students what fuel provides the energy a car needs to run. (gasoline) Then compare the human body to a car. Point out that the body also needs fuel to run. Elicit from students that food is the body's fuel. Define nutrients as the chemical substances in food that are needed for growth and energy.

CLASS ACTIVITY   Randomly read out the names of the foods shown on p. 214. Have students identify the nutrients each food supplies the body with.

CLASS ACTIVITY   Have each student bring in three food labels from different foods. Tell students to circle all the nutrients on the labels and their amounts. Then review the labels as a class. Have students determine which foods are high in nutrients and which foods are low in nutrients.

RETEACHING OPTION   Write the following head on the chalkboard: *Nutrients.* From this head, draw arrows to each of the following heads: *Carbohydrates, Fats, Proteins, Vitamins, Minerals.* From *Carbohydrates,* draw arrows to each of the following heads: *Simple, Complex.* Under *Simple,* list sugars. Under *Complex,* list starches. Have students copy the chart in their notebooks.

Answers to Challenges (p. 215)
Apply

6. Starches give the body energy over long periods of time.
7. Simple carbohydrates only give the body short, quick bursts of energy.

InfoSearch

You may wish to discuss students' questions and answers as a class.

Teaching Tips for Activity
Testing For Fats

Skills: *observing, summarizing*

COOPERATIVE/COLLABORATIVE LEARNING   Answer the questions as a class.

Questions

1. by rubbing the foods on paper
2. Answers will vary.
3. Answers will vary. Accept all logical responses.
4. Answers will vary. Accept all logical responses.

LESSON 11-2
Why are proteins important?
(p. 216)

Teaching Strategies

PREVIEW   Before beginning this lesson, have students scan the lesson for the science process skill symbols. Have students identify each skill used in the lesson. Students should then review the definition given for each skill on page 16 of their text.

DISCUSSION   Discuss the structure and importance of proteins. As the building blocks of living material, the importance of proteins cannot be overemphasized. When discussing the structure of proteins, be sure students understand that although there are only 20 amino acids, they can be put together in many different ways to form thousands of proteins. Make an analogy between amino acids and proteins and the 26 letters of the alphabet and words.

EXTENSION   You may wish to point out that under normal circumstances the body does not use proteins as a source of energy. However, if deprived of other nutrients, the body will break down proteins for energy. Point out that the breakdown of proteins is one reason starvation diets are unhealthy and cause the loss of muscle tissue.

CLASS ACTIVITY   Cut out twenty different shapes from sheets of construction paper. Label each shape with the name of a different amino acid. To illustrate that amino acids can be combined to form thousands of proteins, have students take turns putting the shapes in different sequences.

REINFORCEMENT   Be sure students understand that proteins are broken down into amino acids in the body. The amino acids are then used by body cells to make new proteins. Many students have difficulty understanding this concept.

Answers to Challenges (p. 217)
Apply

6. Proteins are needed for growth and repair.
7. To ensure that they take in all eight of the amino acids needed by the body.
8. Check students' models.

Skill Builder: Researching

A low-protein diet is characterized by a swollen stomach and thin limbs.

Teaching Tips for Activity
Modeling Protein Molecules
Skill: *modeling*

SAFETY TIP   Caution students to be careful when using sharp objects.

COOPERATIVE/COLLABORATIVE LEARNING   Have students compare their models.

Questions
1. amino acids
2. **a.** Answers will vary.   **b.** Answers will vary.
3. **a.** 20   **b.** It combines the amino acids in different ways.
4. The number of possible proteins increases.

LESSON 11-3
Why are vitamins important?
(p. 218)

Teaching Strategies

PREVIEW   Have students read the lesson feature before beginning the lesson. Discuss the concepts presented in the feature. Ask students how they think this information relates to topics they have already studied or to the lesson they are about to study.

DISCUSSION   Bring in a bottle of vitamins and display it in front of the classroom. Point to the bottle and ask students if they know why vitamins are important. Discuss all student responses. Point out that vitamins are needed for the body to function properly. Then outline some of the specific functions of vitamins on the chalkboard.

REINFORCEMENT   Be sure students understand that vitamins do not supply the body with energy. Students often mistakenly think of vitamins as energy sources.

CLASS ACTIVITY   Randomly read out the names of the vitamins listed in Table 1 on p. 218. Have students state each vitamin's use in the body and the good sources of each vitamin. Then read out the deficiency diseases listed in Table 1 and have students state the vitamin that is lacking.

EXTENSION   You may wish to tell students that the body uses ultraviolet rays from the sun to make vitamin D. Vitamin K is made in the large intestine with the help of bacteria that inhabit the intestine.

COOPERATIVE/COLLABORATIVE LEARNING   Have students quiz each other on the material in this lesson.

Answers to Challenges (p. 219)
Apply
4. K
5. B_1, B_2, B_3
6. C
7. riboflavin
8. night blindness

Skill Builder: Organizing
Check students' tables. The signs and symptoms of each deficiency disease are: night blindness: difficulty seeing in dark; beriberi: tiredness, loss of appetite, muscle cramps, paralysis; pellagra: rough skin, diarrhea; scurvy: sore gums; rickets: soft bones and teeth.

Health and Safety Tip
To make the skin and peels of fruits and vegetables safe to eat, they should be scrubbed in water.

Teaching Tips for Looking Back in Science
Scurvy

DISCUSSION   You may wish to use this feature to point out that cures for certain disorders and diseases have been discovered before their causes.

Questions
1. **RELATE**   Why did many sailors at sea get scurvy? (They did not eat foods containing vitamin C.)
2. What are the symptoms of scurvy? (sore, bleeding gums; fatigue; slow healing)

LESSON 11-4
Why are minerals important?
(p. 220)

Teaching Strategies

PREVIEW   Before beginning this lesson, have students scan the lesson looking for words with which they are unfamiliar. Have students work in pairs to define each of the words on their lists.

INTRASCIENCE CONNECTION   Point out that the minerals organisms need to grow come from the earth. Minerals are natural solids formed from elements or compounds in the earth's crust.

DEMONSTRATION   To provide motivation for this lesson, bring in specimens of some of the minerals needed by living things, such as iron, calcium, sodium, and phosphorus. Show each mineral sample to the class. Have students describe each mineral's properties. Then describe the importance and use of each mineral in the human body.

REINFORCEMENT   Bring in a variety of pictures showing the foods listed in Table 1 on p. 220. Point to each food in the pictures. Have students use Table 1 to identify the mineral or minerals each food supplies.

EXTENSION   You may wish to point out that iron-deficiency anemia is very common in teen-age girls because of poor eating habits and the loss of some iron during menstruation. Emphasize the importance of eating foods with a lot of iron.

Answers to Challenges (p. 221)
Skill Builder: Organizing
Check students' tables. Answers will vary.

Teaching Tips for Career in Life Science
Nutritionist

EXTENSION   If possible, have a nutritionist or the school dietician visit your class. Ask the nutritionist to discuss the relationship between diet and health with your students.

Questions
1. **DESCRIBE**   What do nutritionists do in industry? (help to research, develop, and test new food products)
2. What is the educational requirement for a nutritionist? (college degree with a major in nutrition)

LESSON 11-5
What is a balanced diet? (p. 222)

Teaching Strategies

PREVIEW Before beginning this lesson, write the title of each section in the lesson on the chalkboard. Have students copy these titles in their notebooks using an outline format. As students read each section, they should write the topic sentence for each paragraph in the section in their notebooks.

DISCUSSION Discuss the meaning of a balanced diet. Point out that a balanced diet contains the proper amounts of nutrients. Emphasize that a balanced diet is essential for good health. Tell students that they should use the Food Guide Pyramid as a guide to good eating.

CLASS ACTIVITY Distribute an index card to each student. Tell students to write down the name of one food on the index card. Then collect all the cards and have students classify all the foods into the proper food groups as a class.

EXTENSION Have students plan a balanced diet for a whole day.

Answers to Challenges (p. 223)
InfoSearch

You may wish to discuss students' questions and answers as a class.

Teaching Tips for Activity
Planning a Balanced Diet

Skills: *classifying, analyzing*

COOPERATIVE/COLLABORATIVE LEARNING Have volunteers show their menus to the rest of the class.

Questions

1. bran flakes, bread
2. margarine
3. Answers will vary. Accept all logical responses.
4. Answers will vary. Accept all logical responses.

LESSON 11-6
How do living things get energy? (p. 224)

Teaching strategies

PREVIEW Before beginning this lesson, have students review the TechTerms and their definitions and read the Lesson Summary.

DISCUSSION Introduce this lesson by reviewing the things organisms need to live. Ask students to name the things they need to survive. (Answers will most likely include food, water, oxygen, and shelter.) Then develop an understanding of why people need food and oxygen. Discuss the term *oxidation.* Point out that oxidation is the process by which sugar is broken down and energy released.

CLASS ACTIVITY Bring a hand mirror to class. Ask a volunteer to breathe on the mirror. Have students observe that water collects on the mirror. Use this activity to show students that water is a waste product of oxidation.

REINFORCEMENT You may wish to tell students that the oxidation of foods in the body is cellular respiration. Write the chemical and word equations for cellular respiration on the chalkboard to help students identify the reactants and products of this process:
$$C_6H_{12}O_6 + O_2 \rightarrow H_2O + CO_2 + energy$$
glucose + oxygen → water + carbon dioxide + energy

DISCUSSION All students probably are familiar with the term *Calorie.* Many students probably associate the term solely with dieting. Point out that a Calorie is a unit used to measure the amount of energy given off by food.

EXTENSION Some students may wonder why the term *Calorie* is capitalized. You may wish to tell them that a *calorie* (small letter) is equal to the amount of energy needed to raise the temperature of one gram of water 1 °C. A *Calorie* is equal to a kilocalorie, or 1000 calories. Be sure that students understand that on food labels the number of Calories is listed.

Answers to Challenges (p. 225)
Check

1. oxidation
2. water, carbon dioxide
3. no
4. Calorie
5. from food
6. fat

Apply

7. 45 Calories
8. Fats give off more energy than carbohydrates.
9. You would gain weight.

Skill Builder: Calculating

A: 85; **B:** 128; **C:** 49; **D:** 99; **E:** 102

Skill Builder: Comparing

Answers will vary. Accept all logical responses.

Teaching Tips for Science Connection
Chemosynthesis

REINFORCEMENT Before students read this feature, read the term *chemosynthesis* aloud so students can hear its pronunciation.

Questions

1. RELATE Why is photosynthesis not possible on the ocean floor? (No sunlight can reach the ocean floor.)
2. DEFINE What is chemosynthesis? (process of making food from chemicals)

LESSON 11-7
What is the digestive system? (p. 226)

Teaching Strategies

PREVIEW Before beginning this lesson, read the list of TechTerms aloud so students can hear their pronunciations.

DISCUSSION Refer students to Figure 1 on p. 226. Have students locate each organ of the digestive system as you describe the path of food through the digestive tract. Be sure students understand the difference between the digestive tract and the digestive system. Point out that the liver, pancreas, and gall bladder are part of the digestive system but not of the digestive tract.

DEMONSTRATION Demonstrate peristalsis with a piece of rubber tubing and a marble. (The rubber tubing should not be wider than the marble.) Place the marble in the rubber tubing. Then move the marble through the tubing by squeezing behind it.

Answers to Challenges (p. 227)

Apply

6. Check students' flowcharts. Their charts should show the following sequence: mouth, esophagus, stomach, small intestine, large intestine.
7. in order to be swallowed without harming the body or choking

Health and Safety Tip

A person who is choking, but is able to cough should not be interfered with. However, if a person's windpipe is completely obstructed, the Heimlich maneuver should be performed.

Teaching Tips for Science Connection

Vestigial Organs

EXTENSION Have interested students research the symptoms of appendicitis. Tell students to present their findings in an oral report.

Questions

1. DEFINE What is a vestigial organ? (small part of the body that seems to have no use)
2. Why do scientists think some snakes evolved from animals with hips? (The snakes have vestigial hip bones.)

LESSON 11-8
What is digestion? (p. 228)

Teaching Strategies

PREVIEW Have students read the lesson feature before beginning the lesson. Discuss the concepts presented in the feature. Ask students how they think this information relates to topics they have already studied or to the lesson that they are about to study.

DEMONSTRATION Show students simple examples of physical and chemical changes. To demonstrate a physical change, tear up a piece of paper or break up a cracker. To show students a chemical change, burn a match. Then describe mechanical and chemical digestion. Ask students whether mechanical digestion is a physical or chemical change. (physical)

DISCUSSION Describe the parts of the mouth that are involved in the breakdown of foods. Be sure students understand that the teeth and tongue aid in mechanical digestion, and saliva begins the chemical digestion of foods.

REINFORCEMENT Be sure students understand that enzymes control chemical reactions in all parts of the body, not just in

the digestive system. Remind students that enzymes are proteins.

DEMONSTRATION To demonstrate how mechanical digestion increases surface area, hold two sugar cubes together. Ask students how many sides are exposed. (6) Then pull the sugar cubes apart. Again, ask how many sides are exposed. (12)

RETEACHING OPTION Write the following head on the chalkboard: *Digestion*. From this head, draw arrows to each of the following heads: *Mechanical Digestion, Chemical Digestion*. Define these two types of digestion. Have students copy the charts and.definitions in their notebooks.

Answers to Challenges (p. 229)

Apply

6. to avoid choking
7. starches and sugars

InfoSearch

You may wish to discuss students' questions and answers as a class.

Teaching Tips for Career in Life Science

Dental Hygienist

EXTENSION Invite a dental hygienist to talk to your classroom about the proper care of teeth. Have students prepare questions they would like to ask beforehand.

Questions

1. INFER Why must dental hygienists be skillful in working with their hands? (Answers will vary. Accept all logical responses.)
2. What are two things a dental hygienist may do on the job? (Students should restate two of the things given in the feature.)

LESSON 11-9
What happens to food in the stomach? (p. 230)

Teaching Strategies

PREVIEW Have students write the lesson title and objective in their notebooks. As students read the lesson, tell them to write down the sentence or sentences that provide the information needed in the objective.

DISCUSSION Introduce this lesson by asking students if they know what causes their stomachs to "growl." Discuss all student responses. Point out that stomach growling is the result of contractions of stomach muscles. Then discuss the mechanical and chemical digestion that occurs in the stomach. Guide students to understand that contractions of the stomach muscles aid in mechanical digestion.

RETEACHING OPTION Hold up an antacid in front of the class. Ask students what antacids are used to treat. (Many students will know that antacids are used to treat an upset stomach caused by excess stomach acids.) Use students' knowledge of antacids as a springboard for a discussion of chemical digestion in the stomach. Tell students that hydrochloric acid is the acid found in the stomach and that pepsin can only work in an acidic environment.

COOPERATIVE/COLLABORATIVE LEARNING Have one student describe mechanical digestion in the stomach. Have another student describe chemical digestion in the stomach.

Answers to Challenges (p. 231)

Check

1. protects the stomach lining from hydrochloric acid and pepsin.
2. Stomach muscles tighten and squeeze the food.
3. pepsin
4. thick liquid
5. The stomach is a J-shaped, baglike organ.

Apply

6. It carries out both mechanical and chemical digestion.
7. Pepsin could not work.
8. The protein was digested.
9. Food is broken down mechanically and chemically. It enters the small intestine as a thick liquid. The digestion of starches and proteins has started.

Skill Builder: Researching

Check students' tables. How and why ulcers occur is not completely understood. However, stress is known to be a contributing factor. Symptoms include pain in the stomach, especially after eating. Most ulcers are treated with medication.

Teaching Tips for Looking Back in Science

William Beaumont

EXTENSION Dr. William Beaumont experimented with gastric juice and its effect on various foods. Thus, he was able to demonstrate and explain how gastric juice changes foods.

Question

Why was the ability to view a functioning body system extraordinary in the early 1800s? (The use of X rays had not yet been discovered. Most information about body systems was obtained by examining the remains of the deceased.)

LESSON 11-10
What happens to food in the small intestine? (p. 232)

Teaching Strategies

PREVIEW Before beginning this lesson, read the list of TechTerms aloud so students can hear their pronunciations.

DISCUSSION Copy Table 1 on p. 232 onto the chalkboard. Have students note where the digestion of different nutrients begins and ends. Emphasize that all digestion is completed in the small intestine.

DEMONSTRATION Using a meterstick, measure off 6.5 m in the classroom. Tell students that this is the length of the small intestine.

REINFORCEMENT Display a wall chart showing the liver, gall bladder, stomach, pancreas, and small intestine. Point to each accessory organ and describe its digestive function. Point out that the liver is the largest and one of the most important organs in the body.

DEMONSTRATION Place some water and vegetable oil in a jar. Students will observe that the substances do not mix. Then add a detergent to the jar and shake the jar. Ask students to describe what happens. (The detergent causes the oil layer to break up.) Relate this demonstration to the action of bile on fats.

Answers to Challenges (p. 233)

Apply

7. mouth
8. stomach
9. fat

InfoSearch

You may wish to discuss students' questions and answers as a class.

Teaching Tips for Activity

Investigating Fat Digestion

Skills: *observing, comparing*

COOPERATIVE/COLLABORATIVE LEARNING Have students work in pairs.

Questions

1. The oil and water did not mix.
2. The oil layer was broken up.
3. test tube without baking soda
4. test tube with baking soda
5. Baking soda breaks down fats.

LESSON 11-11
How is food absorbed by the body? (p. 234)

Teaching Strategies

PREVIEW Before beginning this section, have students scan the lesson looking for words with which they are unfamiliar. Have students work in pairs or small groups to define each of the words on their list.

DISCUSSION Remind students that organisms need food for growth, repair, and energy. Have students recall that nutrients are needed by body cells. Elicit from students that if nutrients remained in the small intestine, they would do the body no good. Emphasize the importance of absorption.

REINFORCEMENT After students have completed this lesson, review the digestive system and the entire digestive process. Refer students back to the diagram of the digestive system on p. 226. Trace the path of food through the digestive tract. Describe the digestive processes that occur in each organ. Stress the roles of the pancreas, liver, and gall bladder in digestion. Describe absorption in the small intestine. Finally, discuss what occurs in the large intestine.

COOPERATIVE/COLLABORATIVE LEARNING Have students quiz each other on the material in this lesson.

Answers to Challenges (p. 235)

Apply

7. so it can be carried to all body cells

8. Curved lines have a greater surface area than straight lines.

9. It may burst.

Ideas in Action

Answers will vary. Accept all logical responses.

Health and Safety Tips

Check students' reports. Bran foods and vegetables are high in fiber.

Teaching Tips for Activity

Calculating Surface Area

Skills: *measuring, analyzing, calculating*

COOPERATIVE/COLLABORATIVE LEARNING Answer the questions as a class.

Questions

1. 8 cm

2. about 18 cm

3. curved string

4. They increase the surface area.

Answers to Unit Challenges (pp. 236-238)

Understanding the Feature: Reading Critically

1. sore, bleeding gums; fatigue; slow healing

2. hospital, industry, private practice

3. process of using chemicals to make food

4. appendix, third eyelid, muscles in the outer ear, tailbone

5. Answers will vary. Accept all logical responses.

6. his studies of the stomach

7. Answers will vary. Accept all logical responses.

Critical Thinking

1. mechanical; Bile breaks fats into small droplets.

2. The large surface area increases the amount of absorption that takes place.

3. Nutrients must be carried by the blood to all body cells.

4. Answers will vary. Accept all logical responses.

5. Answers will vary. Accept all logical responses.

Interpreting the Diagram

1. to carry food from the throat to the stomach

2. E

3. I

4. to produce digestive enzymes, which are released into the small intestine

5. C

6. small intestine

UNIT 12
SUPPORT AND
MOVEMENT (p. 239)

Previewing the Unit

Read the titles of the lessons in this unit aloud. Identify terms in the titles with which students are unfamiliar. Write these terms on the chalkboard. Using the Glossary of the text or a dictionary, define the terms as a class. Have students write the terms and their definitions in their notebooks. Then, have students work in small groups to carry out the task in the Study Hint.

Bulletin Board Suggestions

1. Assemble a bulletin board that highlights the skeletal system. Attach a diagram of the skeleton to the bulletin board. Label some of the major bones with both their scientific and common names. Use the diagram on p. 240 as a guide. Circle the different types of joints on the skeleton and label each type. Use the bulletin board to help students identify different bones and the places where different types of joints are found.
2. Assemble a bulletin board illustrating the different kinds of muscle tissue in the body. Attach pictures of skeletal muscle, smooth muscle, and cardiac muscle to the bulletin board. Label each different kind of muscle tissue. Use the bulletin board when teaching Lesson 12-5.

LESSON 12-1
What is the skeletal system?
(p. 240)

Teaching Strategies

PREVIEW Have students read the lesson feature before beginning the lesson. Discuss the concepts presented in the feature. Ask students how they think this information relates to topics they have already studied or to the lesson they are about to study.

DISCUSSION To introduce this lesson, ask students if they have ever seen a house or skyscraper being built. Point out that a house has a wooden framework and a skyscraper has an iron girder frame. Ask students what the frame of a building does. (Many students probably will know that the frame supports a building.) Then introduce the skeletal system as the frame of the body. Ask students what they think is one job of the skeletal system. (support)

REINFORCEMENT Remind students that animals are divided into two large groups, vertebrates and invertebrates. Explain that some invertebrates have soft bodies and others have exoskeletons. Have students recall that vertebrates have an endoskeleton.

CLASS ACTIVITY Tell students to feel and describe their knee bones and the bridges of their noses. Elicit the response that bones are very hard. Then, tell students to touch the tips of their noses and their outer ears. Ask students to describe these structures. Explain that the tip of the nose and the outer ear are made up of cartilage. Define cartilage as a tough, flexible connective tissue.

Answers to Challenges (p. 241)

CLASS ACTIVITY Divide the class into small groups. Challenge each group to construct a model of the arm muscles using cardboard, rubber bands, and balloons. When all groups are finished, display the models in the classroom.

REINFORCEMENT Muscle action is a difficult concept for students to understand. Use as many models and diagrams as possible to demonstrate how muscles move bones.

Apply

5. endoskeleton: fish; exoskeleton: grasshopper

Skill Builder: Relating Roots and Word Parts

Answers will vary. Accept all logical responses.

Teaching Tips for Technology and Society
Arthroscopic Surgery

CLASS ACTIVITY Have students look up the meaning of the prefix *arthro-* in a dictionary. (*arthro-*: of the joints) Tell students to write in their own words how the meaning of *arthro-* is related to its use in the term arthroscopic surgery.

Questions

1. IDENTIFY   On what body part is arthroscopic surgery most often performed? (knee)
2. LIST   What are the advantages of arthroscopic surgery? (a person stays awake and thus recovers faster; less tissue is damaged; only a very small scar is left)

LESSON 12-2
What are bones? (p. 242)

Teaching Strategies

PREVIEW Before beginning this lesson, have students review the TechTerms and their definitions and read the Lesson Summary.

DEMONSTRATION If possible, point out the bones of the body on a skeleton. Point out some small bones, such as the finger bones, and some large bones, such as the femur. Have students note that bones come in all shapes and sizes.

REINFORCEMENT Stress that although bones have many different shapes and sizes, all bones have a similar structure.

DISCUSSION Describe the structure of bones. Refer students to the diagram of a bone on p. 242 to illustrate your description. Be sure students understand that bones are made up of both living and nonliving material. To help students remember that calcium is the nonliving material that makes bones hard, discuss the relationship between "drinking milk and healthy bones." Point out that milk and other diary products are good sources of calcium.

CLASS ACTIVITY Obtain prepared slides showing a cross section of bone from a biological supply company. Have students view the slides under a microscope and identify as many parts of bone as they can.

DEMONSTRATION Obtain a bone from a butcher shop. Cut the bone lengthwise. Point out the different parts of the bone.

EXTENSION Have interested students find out about osteoporosis. Tell students to write their findings in a report.

T53

Answers to Challenges (p. 243)

InfoSearch

You may wish to discuss students' questions and answers as a class.

Teaching Tips for Technology and Society

Bone Marrow Transplants

EXTENSION Before students read this feature, you may wish to tell them that leukemia is a disease in which the body produces millions of abnormal immature white blood cells and anemia is a blood disorder in which the blood cannot carry normal amounts of oxygen to body cells.

Questions

1. What are two disorders treated with bone marrow transplants? (anemia, leukemia)
2. HYPOTHESIZE Why do you think a patient's body may reject new bone marrow? (The new marrow is a foreign substance to the body.)

LESSON 12-3
How do joints work? (p. 244)

Teaching Strategies

PREVIEW Before beginning this section, have students scan the lesson looking for words with which they are unfamiliar. Have students work in pairs or small groups to define each of the words on their lists.

DISCUSSION To introduce this lesson, ask students if they have ever broken a bone. Have any students who have broken bones describe how the bones were treated and set for the rest of the class. Then point out that broken bones illustrate that bones do not bend. Explain that movement only can occur where bones meet. Define a joint as the place where two or more bones meet. Describe the three main kinds of joints and give students examples of each.

CLASS ACTIVITY As students read about the four kinds of movable joints on p. 244, have them locate the joints on their bodies.

RETEACHING OPTION Write the following head on the chalkboard: *Joints.* From this head, draw arrows to each of the following heads: *Fixed, Partly Moveable, Movable.* From the head *Movable,* draw arrows to each of the following heads: *Ball-and-socket joints, Gliding joints, Hinge joints, Pivotal joints.* Have students copy the chart in their notebooks. Then give students examples of each type of joint. Tell students to list the examples under the proper heads.

EXTENSION Have interested students find out the differences among compound, simple, and greenstick fractures. Tell students to share their findings in an oral report.

COOPERATIVE/COLLABORATIVE LEARNING Have students quiz each other on the material in this lesson.

Answers to Challenges (p. 245)

Apply

5. Answers may vary, but should include that movement in the shoulder and arm would be limited.
6. to allow the rib cage to move during breathing

InfoSearch

You may wish to discuss students' questions and answers as a class.

Teaching Tips for Activity

Observing Joint Movements

Skill: *observing*

SAFETY TIP Caution students that they should not force movements at their joints.

COOPERATIVE/COLLABORATIVE LEARNING Answer the questions as a class.

LESSON 12-4
What is the muscular system? (p. 246)

Teaching Strategies

PREVIEW Before beginning this lesson, write the title of each section in the lesson on the chalkboard. Have students copy these titles in their notebooks using an outline format. As students read each section, they should write the topic sentence for each paragraph in the section in their notebooks.

DISCUSSION Tell students to "flex their arm muscles." Most students will know that you are asking them to bend their arms. Use students' knowledge as a springboard for a discussion of the muscular system. Point out that muscles that bend joints are called flexors and muscles that straighten joints are called extensors. Describe how flexors and extensors work together to move the body. Emphasize that muscles can only pull bones.

DEMONSTRATION Show students the cartilage on the end of a chicken bone.

RETEACHING OPTION Write the functions of the skeletal system on the chalkboard in an outline format. Then refer students to the diagram of the skeleton on p. 240. Read out the names of some of the major bones of the body. Have students locate each bone on the diagram.

Answers to Challenges (p. 247)

Check

1. A tendon is a strong elastic band of tissue.
2. contracted

Skill Builder: Researching

You may wish to discuss students' exercise programs as a class. Mode refers to the kind of exercise, duration refers to how long an exercise lasts, intensity refers to the level of exercise, and frequency refers to how often an exercise is performed.

Skill Builder: Researching

Sprains and strains are caused by small tears in muscles. Charley horses are caused by bruises and tears in muscle. A muscle cramp occurs when a muscle contracts suddenly and strongly. Tendonitis is caused by an inflammation of tendons.

Teaching Tips for Science Connection

Anabolic Steroids

REINFORCEMENT Taking steroids to increase the size of muscles has become increasingly popular among teenage boys. Emphasize the dangerous side effects of taking steroids.

Questions

1. DEFINE What are hormones? (chemicals that regulate body functions)
2. What is the only way to increase muscle mass and strength? (weight training exercise)

LESSON 12-5
What are the kinds of muscles? (p. 248)

Teaching Strategies

PREVIEW Before beginning this lesson, read the list of TechTerms aloud so students can hear their pronunciations.

DISCUSSION Describe the three kinds of muscle tissue. Emphasize that many internal organs are made up of muscle. Students may tend to think of muscle tissue only in terms of skeletal muscle.

CLASS ACTIVITY Have students observe prepared slides under a microscope showing the three kinds of muscle tissue in the body. Tell students to sketch and label each kind of muscle in their notebooks. Have students note that both skeletal muscle and cardiac muscle are striated.

RETEACHING OPTION To introduce this lesson, tell students to move their feet and to open and close their fingers. Then tell students to stop their stomach muscles from contracting and to stop their hearts from beating for the next few seconds. Obviously, students will be able to carry out your first two directives and not the last two. Use this activity to point out the difference between voluntary muscles and involuntary muscles. Identify smooth muscle and cardiac muscle as involuntary muscles. Then ask students what kind of muscle they think skeletal muscles are. (voluntary)

Answers to Challenges (p. 249)
Skill Builder: Classifying

voluntary: c, f, g; involuntary: a, b, d, e

Teaching Tips for Career in Life Science
Exercise Specialist

EXTENSION If possible, invite an exercise specialist to give a lecture to your class about the benefits of regular exercise.

Questions

1. INFER Why must an exercise specialist enjoy working with people? (The job of an exercise specialist requires a lot of contact with people.)
2. Why do hospitals employ exercise specialists? (to develop exercise programs for patients)

LESSON 12-6
What is skin? (p. 250)

Teaching Strategies

PREVIEW Before beginning this lesson, have students re-view the TechTerms and their definitions and read the Lesson Summary.

DISCUSSION Discuss the structure and function of the skin. Refer students to the diagram of the skin on p. 250. Have students locate the epidermis, dermis, pores, sweat glands, oil glands, and hair follicles on the diagram as you describe each of these structures.

CLASS ACTIVITY Have students work in small groups to make models of the skin. Tell students to use the diagram on p. 250 as a guide. Allow students to use common materials such as buttons, clay, string, and pipe cleaners to make their models.

REINFORCEMENT To help students remember the definitions of the terms epidermis and dermis, tell students that the terms *derm* and *derma* are from the Greek word for skin. Then ask students to list products whose names contain the terms *derm* or *derma*. (Many face creams, make-ups, and skin moisturizers contain the terms *derm* or *derma*.) Have students note that all of these products are used on the skin.

Answers to Challenges (p. 251)
Check/Apply

6. epidermis is the outer layer; dermis is the inner layer of skin
7. oil gland softens and moistens skin; sweat gland removes liquids from the body in the form of sweat
8. The skin covers and protects the body.
9. to replace cells that have been worn away
10. dermis; tiny blood vessels have been cut
11. wrist; skin is a sense organ for touch

Teaching Tips for Activity
Touch Receptors

Skills: *observing, inferring*

COOPERATIVE/COLLABORATIVE LEARNING Students must work with a partner.

Questions

1. Answers will vary. Accept all logical responses.
2. **a.** Answers will vary. Accept all logical responses. **b.** It is depended upon for touch.

Answers to Unit Challenges (pp. 252-254)
Understanding the Features: Reading Critically

1. People are awake during arthroscopic surgery. The cut made is small.
2. whether the healthy bone marrow produces more healthy bone marrow; rejection of the new marrow
3. an increase in the number of muscles fibers
4. Answers will vary. Accept all logical responses.

Critical Thinking

1. When a skeletal muscle contracts, it pulls on a bone.
2. They keep the vertebrae from rubbing against each other.
3. It stretches.
4. injury
5. Answers will vary. Accept all logical responses.

Interpreting a Diagram

1. ilium, ischium, sacrum
2. two
3. cranium
4. knee
5. phalanges
6. collar bone

Previewing the Unit

Read the titles of the lessons in this unit aloud. Identify terms in the titles with which students are unfamiliar. Write these terms on the chalkboard. Using the Glossary of the text or a dictionary, define the terms as a class. Have students write the terms and their definitions in their notebooks.

Bulletin Board Suggestion

Assemble a bulletin board illustrating the heart and the path of blood through the body. Use the diagram on p. 264 as a guide. Use the bulletin board to show students how blood travels from the heart to the lungs, back to the heart, to all other parts of the body, and then back to the heart.

LESSON 13-1
What are the parts of the heart? (p. 256)

Teaching Strategies

PREVIEW Before beginning this lesson, read the list of TechTerms aloud so students can hear their pronunciations.

DISCUSSION Tell students to make a fist and to place it in the center of their chest. Explain to students that the heart is a muscular organ, about the size of a fist, which is found in the center of the chest. Describe the structure of the heart. Compare the atria to receiving rooms and the ventricles to shipping rooms.

REINFORCEMENT Have students study the diagram of the heart on p. 256. Tell students to locate the right and left atria and ventricles. Be sure students understand that as they look at the diagram, the heart's left side is on their right and vice versa. Have students turn their textbooks around and place the books against their chests. Students will then observe that the left side of the diagram is on the left side of their bodies.

CLASS ACTIVITY Divide the class into small groups. Distribute different colors of clay to each group. Have students work together to make models of the heart using the clay. Tell students to label the different parts of the heart. When all groups have completed their models, display the models in the classroom.

DISCUSSION Describe the function of heart valves. Compare the action of a heart valve to a one-way door.

CLASS ACTIVITY If possible, bring a stethoscope to class so that students can listen to their heartbeats.

RETEACHING OPTION Draw a large square on the chalkboard and divide it into four equal parts. Compare the square to the heart. Identify and label the upper and lower chambers of the heart. Emphasize that blood enters the heart through the atria and leaves the heart by way of the ventricles.

Answers to Challenges (p. 257)

Ideas in Action

Check students' tables.

Teaching Tips for Activity
Comparing Animal Heart Rates

Skills: *analyzing, hypothesizing*

COOPERATIVE/COLLABORATIVE LEARNING Answer the questions as a class.

Questions

1. **a.** mouse **b.** small
2. **a.** elephant **b.** large
3. As size decreases, heart rate increases.
4. **a.** Answers will vary. Accept all logical responses. **b.** by finding out the heart rates of people of varying sizes

LESSON 13-2
What are blood vessels? (p. 258)

Teaching Strategies

PREVIEW Have students write the lesson title and objective in their notebooks. As students read the lesson, tell them to write down the sentence or sentences that provide the information needed in the objective.

DISCUSSION Describe the characteristics of arteries, veins, and capillaries. Emphasize that capillaries are the blood vessels through which the exchange of materials takes place.

REINFORCEMENT To help students remember that arteries carry blood away from the heart, tell them to associate the two words beginning with the letter *a, artery* and *away.*

DEMONSTRATION Demonstrate the flow of blood through arteries. Insert a one-hole stopper in a plastic bottle filled with water. Insert a glass tube through the stopper. Squeeze the bottle. Students will observe that water squirts out of the tube. Compare the heart's pumping action on blood in the arteries to your squeezing of the water in the bottle.

CLASS ACTIVITY Have students take their own pulses. Tell students to place their index and middle fingers on the thumb side of their wrist. Tell students to take readings for one minute. Have students record their pulse rates in their notebooks. Be sure students understand that their pulse rates and heartbeat rates are the same.

COOPERATIVE/COLLABORATIVE LEARNING Have students work in pairs to answer the Check and Apply questions.

Answers to Challenges (p. 259)
Apply

7. Arteries carry blood away from the heart. They have thick muscular walls. Veins carry blood back to the heart. Veins have thinner walls than arteries.
8. Blood travels through the veins under low pressure.

InfoSearch

You may wish to discuss students' questions and answers as a class.

Teaching Tips for Activity
Measuring Pulse Rate

Skills: *measuring, analyzing*

COOPERATIVE/COLLABORATIVE LEARNING Have a volunteer demonstrate this activity for the rest of the class.

Questions

1. The pulse rate increased.
2. It increased.
3. Exercise increases heart rate.

LESSON 13-3
What is blood? (p. 260)

Teaching Strategies

PREVIEW Have students read the lesson feature before beginning the lesson. Discuss the concepts presented in the feature. Ask students how they think this information relates to topics they have already studied or to the lesson they are about to study.

DISCUSSION Discuss the functions of blood. Emphasize that blood is a tissue which is part solid and part liquid. Describe the liquid and solid parts of blood. As you describe each part, list it on the chalkboard.

CLASS ACTIVITY If possible, have students observe prepared slides of blood. Tell students to sketch and label in their notebooks the blood cells they observe.

EXTENSION You may wish to tell students that plasma from which clotting factors have been removed is called serum.

RETEACHING OPTION To introduce this lesson, ask students why they think their blood is red. List student responses on the chalkboard. Point out that blood gets its color from the red blood cells in it. Describe the job of red blood cells. Then discuss the other parts of blood and their functions.

Answers to Challenges (p. 261)
Health and Safety Tip

Emphasize the importance of knowing your blood type.

Teaching Tips for People in Science
Charles Drew

EXTENSION Have interested students find out more about the Red Cross and write their findings in a report. Tell students to include an outline of the organization's functions and goals.

Questions

1. LIST What are two advantages of using plasma in blood transfusions rather than whole blood? (Plasma lasts longer than whole blood. Plasma can be used in a transfusion for any blood type.)
2. Why were Charles Drew's research findings timely? (The blood plasma that was collected by blood banks saved many lives during World War II.)

LESSON 13-4
What is circulation? (p. 262)

Teaching Strategies

PREVIEW Before beginning this lesson, have students scan the lesson for the science process skill symbols. Have students identify each skill used in the lesson. Students should then review the definition given for each skill on page 16 of their text.

DISCUSSION To introduce this lesson, show students pictures of different roads and railroad tracks. Point out that these pathways make up the transport system of the United States. Elicit from students that trucks and trains carry materials along these pathways. Then point out that the circulatory system is the transport system of the body. Make an analogy between the trucks and trains and blood. Compare the goods carried by trucks and trains to the materials carried by the blood, such as oxygen, carbon dioxide, glucose, and wastes. Emphasize that transport is the main function of the circulatory system.

DISCUSSION Many students probably are familiar with the sight of a person's face turning red when the person is hot. Use students' knowledge as a springboard for a discussion of how the circulatory system helps regulate body temperature. Point out that when a person is hot there is an increase in blood flow to the surface of the skin. This allows heat loss from the body.

EXTENSION Problems of the circulatory system are the leading causes of death in the United States. Have interested students write to the American Heart Association to find out the risk factors associated with cardiovascular disease. Tell students to organize the information in a chart.

RETEACHING OPTION Write the functions of the circulatory system on the chalkboard in an outline format. Describe each function. Have students copy the information in their notebooks. When describing the transport of hormones, you may wish to tell students that they will learn more about hormones in Unit 15.

Answers to Challenges (p. 263)
Apply

6. Blood is a liquid tissue that carries the materials that are essential for life.

InfoSearch

You may wish to discuss students' questions and answers as a class.

Teaching Tips for People in Science
William Harvey

EXTENSION In addition to studying the circulation of blood in animals, William Harvey also measured the amount of blood pumped by the heart each day. Based on his measurements, Harvey concluded that it would be impossible for the body to replenish the amount of blood pumped by the heart each day. He concluded that blood must be recycled in the body.

Questions

1. On what did William Harvey base his conclusion about circulation? (careful observations and experiments)
2. What was Harvey's profession? (Harvey was a physician.)

LESSON 13-5
What happens to blood as it circulates? (p. 264)

Teaching Strategies

PREVIEW Before beginning this lesson, write the title of each section in the lesson on the chalkboard. Have students copy these titles in their notebooks using an outline format. As students read each section, they should write the topic sentence for each paragraph in the section in their notebooks.

DISCUSSION Refer students to the diagrams on p. 264. Have students trace the path of blood on the diagrams as you describe systemic and pulmonary circulation. When describing the circulation of blood, tell students to think of the heart as a two-sided pump. Point out that the right side of the heart sends blood to the lungs and the left side of the heart pumps blood to all other parts of the body.

REINFORCEMENT Some students may have the misconception that blood returning to the heart is blue. Emphasize that blood returning to the heart is red. It is never blue. You may wish to tell students that veins appear blue because of the way light passes through the skin.

RETEACHING OPTION Using a wall chart of the circulatory system, trace the flow of blood throughout the body. Distinguish between the aorta and pulmonary arteries, and between arteries and veins in general. Make sure students understand that gases and other materials are exchanged between the blood and the body cells across the capillaries.

Answers to Challenges (p. 265)

Apply

8. Check students' flowcharts.
9. The content of blood changes as blood circulates. Blood returning to the right atrium contains more carbon dioxide and wastes. Blood returning from the lungs to the left side of the heart contains a fresh supply of oxygen.

Skill Builder: Building Vocabulary

carotid artery: neck and head; femoral artery: leg; bronchial artery: arm; renal artery: kidney; coronary artery: heart

Teaching Tips for Leisure Activity

Aerobic Exercise

CLASS ACTIVITY Before students read this feature, ask students to name their favorite sports or types of exercise. List student responses on the chalkboard. Circle any activities that are aerobic exercises.

Question

RELATE How can aerobic exercise lower the risk of heart disease? (Regular exercise lowers the amount of fatty materials in the blood, which keeps them from building up on the walls of the blood vessels.)

Answers to Unit Challenges (pp. 266-268)

Understanding the Features: Reading Critically

1. Plasma lasts longer than whole blood. Plasma can be used in a transfusion for any blood type.
2. research in blood plasma; setting up blood banks
3. that blood moved in a circular path
4. Answers will vary. Accept all logical responses.
5. It strengthens the heart, makes a person feel better, gives a person a better physical shape, and lowers the risk of heart disease.

Critical Thinking

1. Blood leaves the heart from the left ventricle and travels to all parts of the body, except the lungs. Blood returns to the heart via the right atrium. From the right atrium, blood flows into the right ventricle. Blood is pumped from the right ventricle to the lungs. Blood returns from the lungs to the heart through the left atrium. Blood flows from the left atrium to the left ventricle and the cycle begins again.
2. When tissues are injured, chemicals are given off by the blood. These chemicals form tiny, sticky threads. The threads stick together and form a clot.
3. The number of white blood cells increases because it is the job of white blood cells to destroy germs.
4. White blood cells in the blood fight disease and harmful chemicals.

Interpreting a Diagram

1. atria
2. ventricles
3. between the left and right sides of the heart
4. It connects to the left ventricle.
5. to carry blood from the heart to the body
6. left atrium
7. from the atria to the ventricles
8. pulmonary veins
9. more carbon dioxide
10. artery

UNIT 14
RESPIRATION AND EXCRETION (p. 269)

Previewing the Unit

Read the titles of the lessons in this unit aloud. Identify terms in the titles with which students are unfamiliar. Write these terms on the chalkboard. Using the Glossary of the text or a dictionary, define the terms as a class. Have students write the terms and their definitions in their notebooks. Then, have the students work in small groups to carry out the task in the Study Hint.

Bulletin Board Suggestions

1. Assemble a bulletin board illustrating the respiratory system. Attach a large picture of the respiratory system to the bulletin board. Use the diagram on p. 270 as a guide. Add arrows to the picture to show the flow of air through the respiratory system.
2. Assemble a bulletin board illustrating the excretory system. Attach pictures of the lungs, the skin, the kidneys, and the large intestine to the bulletin board. Next to each excretory organ, attach labels of the waste products, each organ excretes from the body.

LESSON 14-1
What is the respiratory system? (p. 270)

Teaching Strategies

PREVIEW Before beginning this lesson, read the list of TechTerms aloud so students can hear their pronunciations.

DISCUSSION Refer students to the diagram of the respiratory system on p. 270. Have students trace the flow of air through the respiratory system as you describe what happens to air in each part.

EXTENSION You may wish to tell students that the bronchi divide into many small tubes called bronchioles.

CLASS ACTIVITY Tell students to place their hands on the front of their necks to feel their windpipes. Point out that the bulge near the top of the trachea is the larynx. Tell students that the larynx contains the vocal cords. Students will be able to feel their vocal cords vibrate if they place their hands on their larynxes while speaking.

RETEACHING OPTION Ask students to name the parts of the body that help them to breathe. Write all correct answers on the chalkboard. Fill in any parts of the respiratory system that students omit. Then describe the path air takes on its journey through the respiratory system.

COOPERATIVE/COLLABORATIVE LEARNING Answer the Check and Apply questions as a class.

Answers to Challenges (p. 271)

Apply

6. b, d, a, c, e, f

7. The bronchi and branches of the bronchi are like the branches of a tree. The windpipe is like a tree's trunk.

InfoSearch

You may wish to discuss students' questions and answers as a class.

Teaching Tips for Career in Life Science
Respiratory Therapist

EXTENSION Have students look in the classified sections of different newspapers to find jobs offered in respiratory therapy. Have students describe the information listed in the classifieds.

Questions

1. DESCRIBE What does a respiratory therapist do on the job? (helps patients with breathing problems)
2. How does a person become a respiratory therapist? (A person must complete a one- or two-year training program and then pass an examination.)

LESSON 14-2
What are breathing and respiration? (p. 272)

Teaching Strategies

PREVIEW Have students write the lesson title and objectives in their notebooks. As students read the lesson, tell them to write down the sentence or sentences that provide the information needed in the objectives.

CLASS ACTIVITY To introduce this lesson, tell students to place their hands on their ribs while breathing. Ask students what happens to their ribs when they breathe in, or inhale (The ribs move out.) and what happens when they breathe out, or exhale. (The ribs move in.) Then describe the process of breathing in terms of movement of the ribs and the diaphragm.

DEMONSTRATION Show students a bell-jar lung model. Tell students that when the volume inside the jar increases, air rushes in and inflates the balloons. When the volume inside the jar decreases, air is forced out of the balloons. Relate this model to what happens to the lungs in the chest cavity during breathing.

INTRASCIENCE CONNECTION The amount of force on a unit of area is called pressure. Air pressure is the force air exerts on the earth's surface. People do not feel air pressing down on them because air pressure is equal in all directions. The air inside the body presses outward in all directions.

REINFORCEMENT Emphasize the interaction of the circulatory system and respiratory system. Remind students of the importance of pulmonary circulation.

RETEACHING OPTION Write the following head on the chalkboard: *Respiration*. From this head, draw arrows to each of the following heads: *External, Internal, Cellular*. Have students copy the chart in their notebooks. Then describe each of the three parts of respiration. Emphasize that respiration is a chemical process. Have students copy the information in their notebooks under the proper heads.

COOPERATIVE/COLLABORATIVE LEARNING Have a volunteer

explain the difference between respiration and breathing to the rest of the class.

Answers to Challenges (p. 273)

Check

1. It moves up.
2. Breathing is the process by which air is taken into the body.
3. no
4. carbon dioxide and water
5. It becomes larger.
6. to breathe in
7. to breathe out

Apply

8. **a.** B **b.** A
9. the lungs
10. the diaphragm
11. the chest cavity

Ideas in Action

Answers will vary. Accept all logical responses.

Teaching Tips for Activity

Exercise and Breathing Rate

Skills: *comparing, analyzing, measuring*

COOPERATIVE/COLLABORATIVE LEARNING Students must work in pairs.

Questions

1. **a.** Answers will vary. **b.** Answers will vary.
c. Answers will vary.
2. Answers will vary.
3. Exercise increases breathing rate.

LESSON 14-3
What happens to air before it reaches the lungs? (p. 274)

Teaching Strategies

PREVIEW Have students read the lesson feature before beginning the lesson. Discuss the concepts presented in the feature. Ask the students how they think this information relates to the topics they have already studied or to the lesson they are about to study.

DISCUSSION Describe what happens to air before it reaches the lungs. Discuss the functions of nasal hairs, mucus, and cilia. Point out that in addition to being filtered before it reaches the lungs, air also is warmed and moistened.

RETEACHING OPTION Introduce this lesson by describing two occurrences that are familiar to everyone, sneezing and coughing. Lead students to understand that sneezing and coughing are ways of removing dirt, dust, and germs from the body. Describe the roles of mucus and cilia in protecting the respiratory system. Relate their actions to sneezing and coughing.

COOPERATIVE/COLLABORATIVE LEARNING Have students work in pairs to answer the Check and Apply questions.

Answers to Challenges (p. 275)

Apply

7. a, b
8. Check students' flow charts.

Health and Safety Tip

Check students' lists. Be sure they include the four different Surgeon General's warnings.

Teaching Tips for Science Connection

Respiratory Diseases

REINFORCEMENT Emphasize the health hazards of smoking. Have students make posters encouraging people not to smoke.

EXTENSION Have interested students research other respiratory diseases such as pneumonia, bronchitis, pleurisy, and tuberculosis. Tell students to write their findings in a report.

Questions

1. **RELATE** Why is asbestos being removed from buildings? (to eliminate the risk of getting lung disease from asbestos)
2. Why is secondhand smoke dangerous? (It can cause health problems in nonsmokers.)

LESSON 14-4
How does oxygen get into the blood? (p. 276)

Teaching Strategies

PREVIEW Before beginning this lesson, have students scan the lesson for the science process skill symbols. Have students identify each skill used in the lesson. Students should then review the definition given for each skill on p. 16 of their text.

DISCUSSION To introduce this lesson, bring a bunch of grapes to class. Compare the grapes to alveoli. Emphasize that the alveoli are the units of structure and function in the lungs.

CLASS ACTIVITY Divide the classroom into small groups. Distribute small balloons and markers to each group. Tell students to use the balloons and markers to make models showing gas exchange in the alveoli. Have students use the diagram on p. 276 as a guide. When all groups have completed their models, have a representative of each group display and describe the group's model to the rest of the class.

DEMONSTRATION To show students that exhaled air contains water, ask a volunteer to breathe on a hand mirror. Students will observe that water vapor forms on the mirror.

COOPERATIVE/COLLABORATIVE LEARNING Have a volunteer explain the content differences between inhaled air and exhaled air.

Answers to Challenges (p. 277)

Check

1. mixture of gases
2. alveoli
3. very tiny blood vessels
4. exhalation
5. oxygen
6. carbon dioxide

Apply

7. 78%
8. a
9. b; Exhaled air has a lower concentration of oxygen and a higher concentration of carbon dioxide.

Skill Builder: Graphing

Check students' graphs.

Teaching Tips for Activity
Analyzing Exhaled Air

Skills: *observing, inferring*

COOPERATIVE/COLLABORATIVE LEARNING Have a volunteer perform this activity in front of the class.

Questions

1. a. water vapor **b.** exhaled air
2. It becomes cloudy because exhaled air contains carbon dioxide.
3. It contains carbon dioxide.

LESSON 14-5
What is excretion? (p. 278)

Teaching Strategies

PREVIEW Before beginning this lesson, write the titles of each section in the lesson on the chalkboard. Have students copy these titles in their notebooks using an outline format. As students read each section, they should write the topic sentence for each paragraph in the section in their notebooks.

DISCUSSION Describe the parts of the excretory system. Some students may tend to think of only the kidneys and urinary system as excretory organs. Emphasize that the skin, the lungs, and the large intestine also get rid of body wastes.

REINFORCEMENT Relate the burning of fuel in a furnace to the "burning," or oxidation, of food by the body. Point out that in a furnace, waste materials are formed and must be removed. Tell students that this also is true of the materials taken into the body. Explain that during cellular respiration, waste products, which must be removed from the body, are formed.

Answers to Challenges (p. 279)

Check

1. carbon dioxide, water
2. process of removing waste products from the body
3. remove waste products from the body
4. It gets rid of liquid wastes and helps you get rid of extra heat.
5. Water is removed from wastes in the large intestine.
6. They are excreted through the anus.

Apply

7. c
8. a
9. g
10. respiratory, excretory

Ideas in Action

Answers will vary. Accept all logical responses.

Teaching Tips for Technology and Society
Using Sound to Break Apart Kidney Stones

DISCUSSION To help students understand this feature, compare the breaking up of kidney stones by sound waves to the breaking of glass by a soprano hitting a high note.

Questions

1. LIST What are three ways that kidney stones are treated? (medication, surgery, sound waves)
2. How do sound waves break apart kidney stones? (Sound waves cause particles in kidney stones to vibrate. The motion of the particles makes the stones break apart.)

LESSON 14-6
How does the skin remove wastes? (p. 280)

Teaching Strategies

PREVIEW Before beginning this lesson, have students review the TechTerms and their definitions and read the Lesson Summary.

DISCUSSION To provide motivation for this lesson, ask students when people tend to perspire a lot. Elicit the response that people perspire when they are hot. Then describe how perspiring helps the body to keep cool, in addition to ridding the body of waste water and salts.

CLASS ACTIVITY Have students work in small groups to make models showing the structure of the skin. Tell students to use common objects such as clay, string, and pipe cleaners. Have students use the diagram on p. 280 as a guide.

INTRASCIENCE CONNECTION Students may wonder why they feel "sticky" on hot, humid days. Humidity is the amount of water vapor in the air. High humidity means there is a lot of water vapor in the air. The air is almost full of water vapor. Therefore, perspiration does not evaporate from the skin.

Answers to Challenges (p. 281)

Apply

6. Shivering warms the body.
7. Salts are lost in perspiration.

Designing an Experiment

You may wish to have volunteers describe their experiments to the rest of the class.

Skill Builder: Building Vocabulary

A deodorant is a substance that prevents or destroys undesired odors. An antiperspirant prevents perspiration.

Teaching Tips for Activity
Evaporation and Cooling

Skills: *observing, comparing*

COOPERATIVE/COLLABORATIVE LEARNING Answer the questions as a class.

Questions

1. The wet finger feels cooler.

2. The finger with alcohol feels cooler.
3. a. step 1 **b.** It compares how the fingers feel without any substance on them to how they feel with a substance on them.

LESSON 14-7
How do the kidneys work?
(p. 282)

Teaching Strategies

PREVIEW Before beginning this lesson, have the students scan the lesson for words with which they are unfamiliar. Have students work in pairs or small groups to define each of the words on their lists.

DISCUSSION Compare the kidneys to an aquarium filter. Tell students that an aquarium filter removes waste products and contaminates from an aquarium. Point out that the kidneys remove liquid wastes from the body. The main job of the kidneys is to filter out wastes from the blood.

REINFORCEMENT Be sure students understand the difference between urea and urine. Point out that urea is a waste product formed by the breakdown of proteins. Urine is made up of water, salts, and urea.

EXTENSION You may wish to tell students that the tiny tubes inside the kidneys are called nephrons. Emphasize that the nephrons are the functional units of the kidneys.

DISCUSSION Refer students to the diagram of the urinary system on p. 282. Have students trace the movement of urine through the urinary system from the kidneys to the outside of the body.

RETEACHING OPTION Filter some clay out of a water suspension. Then describe the kidneys as blood filters and explain how the kidneys work.

Answers to Challenges (p. 283)
Apply

7. kidneys, ureters, urinary bladder, urethra
8. Check students' flow charts.
9. nitrogen

10. They are used by the body.
Ideas in Action

Answers will vary. Accept all logical responses.

Teaching Tips for Technology and Society
Dialysis

EXTENSION If possible, arrange for a trip to a local hospital to have students observe a kidney dialysis machine.

Questions

1. DEFINE · What is biomedical engineering? (a field of study that uses engineering ideas to help design machines the help or replace diseased organs)
2. What does a dialysis machine do? (filters a patient's blood and removes waste materials)

Answers to Unit Challenges (pp. 284-286)
Understanding the Features: Reading Critically

1. to prevent lung diseases
2. a field of study that uses engineering ideas to help design machines that help or replace diseased organs
3. medication, surgery, sound waves
4. asthma, pneumonia

Critical Thinking

1. nose or mouth, throat, windpipe, bronchi, small tubes, lungs
2. Dirt, dust, and germs are trapped by mucus. Cilia push the mucus toward the nose.
3. Breathing is the mechanical process by which air is taken into the body. Respiration is the chemical process by which energy is released.
4. Materials are exchanged between the alveoli and the blood.
5. The evaporation of perspiration from the skin helps keep the body cool.

Interpreting a Diagram

1. windpipe
2. bronchi
3. nose and mouth
4. It has nasal hairs that filter the air and mucus that traps dirt and germs.
5. windpipe

UNIT 15
REGULATION AND BEHAVIOR (p. 287)

Previewing the Unit

Read the titles of the lessons in this unit aloud. Identify terms in the titles with which students are unfamiliar. Write these terms on the chalkboard. Using the Glossary of the text or a dictionary, define the terms as a class. Have students write the terms and their definitions in their notebooks. Then, have students carry out the task in the Study Hint.

Bulletin Board Suggestion

Assemble a bulletin board highlighting the nervous and endocrine systems. Divide the bulletin board in half vertically. Draw an outline of the body on both sides of the bulletin board. In one outline, illustrate the nervous system. Use the diagram on p. 288 as a guide. Label the brain, the spinal cord, and the nerves. In the other outline, draw in the endocrine glands at their approximate locations in the body. Label each gland. Use the bulletin board to emphasize how the nervous and endocrine systems work together to regulate body functions.

LESSON 15-1
What is the nervous system?
(p. 288)

Teaching Strategies

PREVIEW Before beginning this lesson, read the list of TechTerms aloud so students can hear their pronunciations.

DISCUSSION Introduce this lesson with a discussion of a sports team's captain. Ask students what the captain of the team does. Elicit the response that the captain of the team gathers information, makes important decisions, and so on. Then make an analogy between the captain of a sports team and the nervous system. Point out that the nervous system is the captain of the body. Identify the brain and spinal cord as the central nervous system. Have students locate the brain and spinal cord in the diagram on p. 288. Then tell the students to locate the nerves. Point out that the nerves carry information to and from the central nervous system.

DISCUSSION Draw and label a neuron on the chalkboard. Point out the parts of a neuron and describe the function of each part. Emphasize that the neuron is the unit of structure and function in the nervous system.

REINFORCEMENT To help students remember the function of the axon, tell them to associate the words beginning with the letter a, axon, and away.

Answers to Challenges (p. 289)
InfoSearch

You may wish to discuss students' questions and answers as a class.

Teaching Tips for Technology and Society
Seeing Soft Tissues

EXTENSION Have interested students find out more about MRI. Tell students to research the specific use of magnets and sound waves in MRI. Have students write their findings in a report.

Question

EXPLAIN Why is MRI valuable in detecting cancer? (MRI can detect some tumors of organs such as the kidneys, liver, and brain.)

LESSON 15-2
What are the parts of the brain? (p. 290)

Teaching Strategies

PREVIEW Have students write the lesson title and objective in their notebooks. As students read the lesson, tell them to write down the sentence or sentences that provide the information needed in the objective.

DEMONSTRATION If possible, show students a model of the brain. Point out the cerebrum, the cerebellum, and the medulla on the model.

RETEACHING OPTION Write the following head on the chalkboard: The Brain. From this head, draw arrows to each of the following heads: Cerebrum, Cerebellum, Medulla. Have students copy the chart in their notebooks. Then describe the functions of each part of the brain. Tell students to copy the information under the proper heads.

EXTENSION You may wish to tell students that the cerebrum is divided into two halves and that each half controls the opposite side of the body. The left half of the cerebrum is usually dominant over the right, which explains why most people are right-handed. Ask students which half of the cerebrum they think is dominant in people who are left-handed. (right side)

Answers to Challenges (p. 291)
Check

1. cerebrum, cerebellum, medulla

2. cerebrum

3. at the back of the brain

4. at the base of the skull

5. to receive and interpret messages

6. eyes, ears, nose, tongue, and skin

Skill Builder: Inferring

Answers will vary. Accept all logical responses. Students should recognize that damage to the medulla would affect digestion, breathing, heartbeat rate, and the activities of many glands and muscles.

Teaching Tips for Activity
Modeling the Brain

Skills: modeling, observing, relating

COOPERATIVE/COLLABORATIVE LEARNING After students complete this activity, have them display their models in the classroom.

Questions

1. **a.** cerebrum **b.** It is the largest part of the brain.

2. spinal cord

3. spinal cord

LESSON 15-3
What are reflexes? (p. 292)

Teaching Strategies

PREVIEW Have students read the lesson feature before beginning this lesson. Discuss the concepts presented in the feature. Ask the students how they think this information relates to topics they have already studied or to the lesson they are about to study.

DISCUSSION Describe reflexes and give students some examples of reflexes, such as sneezing and blinking. Emphasize the protective nature of reflexes. Guide students to understand that reflexes allow the body to react quickly to painful or dangerous situations.

DEMONSTRATION Demonstrate the knee-jerk reflex by tapping a volunteer's knee with a little rubber mallet.

CLASS ACTIVITY Refer students to the diagram on p. 292. Have students trace the path of a reflex as you describe a reflex arc.

REINFORCEMENT Have students draw a reflex arc showing what would happen if a person stuck his or her finger with a pin. Tell students to use the diagram of a reflex arc on p. 292 as a guide. Be sure students understand that the spinal cord, not the brain, controls reflexes.

Answers to Challenges (p. 293)
Apply

7. **a.** stimulus: stepping on a tack; response: pulling your foot away **b.** stimulus: knock; response: opening the door **c.** stimulus: bright light; response: blinking **d.** stimulus: food; response: coughing

Designing an Experiment

Have volunteers describe their experiments to the rest of the class.

Teaching Tips for Technology and Society
Treating Spinal Injuries with Bionics

EXTENSION Have students find magazine and newspaper articles about current research in the treatment of spinal injuries. Have students report their findings to the class.

Questions

1. **DEFINE** What is bionics? (computerized replacements for injured body parts)

2. How are computers used in bionics work? (Nerve signals go through the computer rather than through the spinal cord. The computer signals nerves to move.)

LESSON 15-4
What are sense organs? (p. 294)

Teaching Strategies

PREVIEW Before beginning this lesson, write the title of each section on the chalkboard. Have students copy these titles in their notebooks using an outline format. As students read each section, they should write the topic sentence for each paragraph in the section in their notebooks.

CLASS ACTIVITY Have students observe their surroundings. Tell students to describe what they see, what they hear, what they smell, what they feel, and what they taste. List students responses on the chalkboard. Then ask students what organs they used to observe their surrounding. (eyes, ears, nose, skin, tongue) Point out that the eyes, ears, nose, skin, and tongue are sense organs. Explain that sense organs help people gather information about their surroundings. Emphasize that the sense organs do not work alone, but rather as an integrated unit.

CLASS ACTIVITY Divide the class into small groups. Tell students in each group to work together to draw pictures illustrating the sense organs and their functions. Tell students to use the pictures on p. 294 as a guide. When all groups are finished, have a representative from each group display and describe the group's pictures.

Answers to Challenges (p. 295)
InfoSearch

You may wish to discuss students' questions and answers as a class.

Teaching Tips for Activity
Locating Taste Receptors

Skills: *modeling, observing, comparing*

COOPERATIVE/COLLABORATIVE LEARNING Have students compare their models with two of their classmates.

Questions

1. sugar-sweet; lemon juice-sour; table salt-salty; tonic water-bitter

2. **a.** Answers will vary. Accept all logical responses. **b.** Answers will vary. Accept all logical responses.

LESSON 15-5
How do you see? (p. 296)

Teaching Strategies

PREVIEW Before beginning the lesson, have students scan the lesson for the science process skill symbols. Have students identify each skill used in the lesson. Students should then review the definition given for each skill on p. 16 of their text.

RETEACHING OPTION This lesson can be most effectively taught with the aid of a wall chart or model showing the parts of the eye. Using the wall chart or model, point out the various parts of the eye and discuss the functions of each part.

INTRASCIENCE CONNECTION The eyes work by sensing light. Light is a form of electromagnetic energy that can be changed into heat, electricity, and other forms of energy. The images formed by the lens of the eye are converted into electrical impulses and carried from the optic nerve to the brain.

CLASS ACTIVITY Have students work in small groups to make models of the eye. Have different colors of clay available for student use. Tell students to label each part of the eye on their models.

CLASS ACTIVITY Have students work in pairs to observe how the pupils respond to light. Tell students to observe their partners' pupils after their eyes have been shut for one minute. Students will observe that the pupils become larger to allow in more light.

Answers to Challenges (p. 297)

Skill Builder: Applying Definitions

lens: a curved material that bends light. The lens of the eye bends light to form an image on the retina.

Skill Builder: Applying Concepts

myopia: eye condition in which light rays from distant objects are focused in front of the retina; astigmatism: an irregularity in the curvature of the lens so that light rays from an object do not meet at a single focal point

Teaching Tips for Activity

Investigating Optical Illusions

Skill: *observing*

COOPERATIVE/COLLABORATIVE LEARNING Answer the questions as a class.

Questions

1. **a.** The line on the right. **b.** both lines are the same length

2. Answers will vary.

3. **a.** The closest post **b.** the farthest post **c.** each post is the same height

4. Answers will vary. Accept all logical responses.

LESSON 15-6
How do you hear? (p. 298)

Teaching Strategies

PREVIEW Before beginning the lesson, have students review the TechTerms and their definitions and read the Lesson Summary.

DISCUSSION Refer students to the diagram of the ear on p. 298. Have students trace the path of sound waves from the outer ear to the cochlea.

DEMONSTRATION If possible, show the students a model of the ear.

EXTENSION You may wish to point out that the ears also function in maintaining balance. Point out that there are three looped tubes in the inner ear called semicircular canals. The tubes are filled with a liquid. Balance is affected by the movement of the liquid in the tubes.

Answers to Challenges (p. 299)

Apply

5. The large outer ears gather sounds.

6. Some sounds are too soft to hear. Others are too high-pitched.

7. The brain interprets signals from the cochlea so a person can understand what the signals mean.

InfoSearch

You may wish to discuss students' questions and answers as a class.

Health and Safety Tip

You may wish to discuss students findings as a class.

Teaching Tips for Technology and Society
Hearing Aids

DISCUSSION You may wish to discuss the two kinds of hearing aids. One kind sends amplified sounds into the ear canal. The other kind sends sound vibrations into the bones of the skull. Discuss with students when they think each kind of hearing aid is used. (The hearing aid that sends amplified sounds into the ear canal is used for people who are hard of hearing. The hearing aid that sends sound vibrations into the bones of the skull is used for people who are partially deaf, or have nerve deafness.)

EXTENSION You may wish to have an otologist visit your classroom. Have the otologist bring in different kinds of hearing aids and describe how they work.

Question

ANALYZE How does a hearing aid work? (makes sounds louder so the damaged part of the ear can vibrate)

LESSON 15-7
What is the endocrine system? (p. 300)

Teaching Strategies

PREVIEW Before beginning this section, have students scan the lesson looking for words with which they are unfamiliar. Have students work in pairs or small groups to define each of the words on their lists

DISCUSSION Introduce this lesson by having students recall what they learned about saliva and perspiration in Units 11 and 14, respectively. Remind students that saliva is produced by salivary glands and perspiration is produced by sweat glands. Define glands as organs that make chemical substances used or released by the body. Point out that sweat glands and salivary glands have ducts. Compare glands with ducts to endocrine glands. Explain that together the endocrine glands make up the endocrine system. Then have students locate the glands that make up the endocrine system in Figure 1 on p. 300.

EXTENSION You may wish to tell students that glands with ducts also are called exocrine glands.

REINFORCEMENT Draw a diagram on the chalkboard illustrating the feedback mechanism of a thermostat and a furnace. Guide students to understand how the endocrine system is regulated by making an analogy between a thermostat and the hypothalamus.

Answers to Challenges (p. 301)

Apply

6. testes

7. at the base of the brain.

8. parathyroid, adrenal, ovaries, testes

Skill Builder: Using Prefixes

Endo- means inner; *exo-* means outer.

Teaching Tips for Technology and Society
Human Growth Hormone

REINFORCEMENT You may wish to tell students that they will learn more about genetic engineering in Unit 18.

Questions

1. What organisms do scientists use to produce large amounts of human growth hormone? (bacteria)

2. What does the amount of human growth hormone released determine? (how tall a child will grow)

LESSON 15-8
What are hormones? (p. 302)

Teaching Strategies

PREVIEW Have students write the lesson title and objectives in their notebooks. As students read the lesson, tell them to write down the sentence or sentences that provide the information needed in the objectives.

DISCUSSION Introduce this lesson by asking students what they think people mean when they say someone's "adrenalin is pumping." (Some students probably will know that adrenalin is related to the body's response to stressful situations.) Use students' knowledge as a springboard for a discussion of hormones. Define hormones as chemical substances that regulate body functions. Then describe the specific functions of some hormones, such as growth hormone, insulin, and adrenalin.

CLASS ACTIVITY Randomly read out the names of the hormones listed in Table 1 on p. 302. Have students identify the endocrine gland that secretes each hormone and each hormone's functions.

RETEACHING OPTION Draw an outline of the human body on the chalkboard. Draw in the endocrine glands at their approximate locations in the body. Next to each organ, write the names of the hormones it produces. Describe the functions of the various hormones.

Answers to Challenges (p. 303)

Check

6. Insulin controls blood sugar levels.

7. Growth hormone controls the growth of bones.

Apply

8. Melatonin, growth hormone, ACTH, thyroxin, parathyroid hormone, thymosin, adrenalin, and insulin are found in both females and males. Testosterone is produced by the testes, which are found in men. Estrogen and progesterone are produced by the ovaries, which are found in women.

9. abnormal bone growth

10. ACTH

11. the thymus

InfoSearch

You may wish to discuss students' questions and answers as a class.

Teaching Tips for Technology and Society
Insulin Pumps and Pens

DISCUSSION Discuss with students the advantages of an insulin pump. One advantage of an insulin pump is that it is more like the pancreas than are the daily injections of insulin. Another advantage is that the insulin pump releases insulin into the body only when the body needs it. This helps make the diet and exercise program of the diabetic less restrictive.

EXTENSION Have any students who have diabetes describe how they are being treated—by diet, medication, or daily injections of insulin.

Questions

1. **IDENTIFY** What is the purpose of the insulin pump? (It puts insulin into the bloodstream; this is a treatment for diabetes.)

2. **INFER** What is the advantage of the insulin pen? (It is easy to carry with you.)

LESSON 15-9
What is behavior? (p. 304)

Teaching Strategies

PREVIEW Before beginning this lesson, have students review the TechTerms and read the Lesson Summary.

DISCUSSION Write the following actions on the chalkboard: coughing, swallowing, sneezing, blinking, reading, talking, playing baseball, writing. Ask students which of the actions involve learning and thought and which of the actions cannot be controlled. Discuss student responses. Guide students to understand that coughing, swallowing, sneezing, and blinking are automatic responses, or reflexes. Point out that reflexes also are called innate behaviors. Explain that behaviors such as reading, talking, playing baseball, and writing require learning and are called learned behaviors.

DEMONSTRATION Bring a tape recorder to class. Insert a tape and play a short song. Then rewind the tape and play the song again. Repeat this procedure a few times. Make an analogy between innate behavior and running the same tape over and over in a tape recorder.

DISCUSSION Ask students how they learned to read, tie their shoes, ride a bicycle, and so on. Discuss all student responses. Guide students to understand that learned behaviors must be practiced.

COOPERATIVE/COLLABORATIVE LEARNING Have a volunteer explain the difference between innate behavior and learned behavior for the rest of the class.

Answers to Challenges (p. 305)

Apply

6. innate

7. Classmates would start being late.

Health and Safety Tip

Emphasize the importance of knowing what to do in case of a fire. Point out that schools have fire drills so that students will know what to do in case of fire in the schools.

Ideas in Action

Answers will vary. Accept all logical responses.

Teaching Tips for People in Science

B. F. Skinner

REINFORCEMENT Be sure students understand that many things besides food can serve as reinforcements. Ask students what other things they think serve as reinforcements. (water, approval, and so on)

Questions

1. In what field did B.F. Skinner specialize? (psychology)

2. How does a teaching machine present difficult material? (in a series of small steps)

LESSON 15-10
How do you learn? (p. 306)

Teaching Strategies

PREVIEW Before beginning this lesson, have students scan the lesson for science process skill symbols. Have students identify each skill used in the lesson. Students should then review the definition given for each skill on p.16 of their text.

DISCUSSION Describe the ways in which people learn. Have students relate examples of how they have learned by trial and error, memorizing, reasoning, and reward and punishment.

DEMONSTRATION Bring a lock and a variety of keys to class, including the key that fits the lock. Try the keys until you find the right one to demonstrate trial and error learning.

COOPERATIVE/COLLABORATIVE LEARNING Have any students who have taught their pets "tricks" describe how they trained the animals. (Students will most likely have used rewards.)

DISCUSSION Ask students what rewards and punishments affect their behavior. Discuss all student responses.

Answers to Challenges (p. 307)

Check

1. kind of learning in which each time a person makes a mistake, the person tries something else

2. Answers will vary. Accept all logical responses.

3. reasoning

Apply

8. Answers will vary. Accept all logical responses.

9. Answers will vary. Accept all logical responses.

Ideas in Action

Answers will vary. Accept all logical responses.

Teaching Tips for Activity

Remembering Information

Skill: *observing*

COOPERATIVE/COLLABORATIVE LEARNING Have a student demonstrate this activity for the rest of the class.

Questions

1. Answers will vary.

2. Answers will vary.

3. Answers will vary.

Answers to Unit Challenges (pp. 308-310)

Understanding the Features: Reading Critically

1. the growth of bones

2. a field of science that uses biological principles in engineering

3. psychology

4. It can be used to detect tumors of soft organs.

5. auxins

6. Answers will vary. Accept all logical responses.

Interpreting a Table

1. the rate of body growth

2. growth hormone, ACTH

3. melatonin

4. pancreas

5. calcium and phosphorus

6. problems related to protection against disease

7. muscle reaction, blood clotting, blood pressure

Critical Thinking

1. They allow organisms to respond quickly to dangerous situations.

2. Both the eye and a camera use light to create images; both have lenses to focus light.

3. Trial and error learning involves trying something new each time you make an error. Reasoning is a way to solve problems by thinking about past experiences.

4. Thirty-one nerves branch out from the spinal cord.

5. They regulate body functions. Answers will vary. Accept all logical responses.

Previewing the Unit

Read the titles of the lessons in this unit aloud. Identify terms in the titles with which the students are unfamiliar. Write these terms on the chalkboard. Using the Glossary of the text or a dictionary, define the terms as a class. Have students write the terms and their definitions in their notebooks. Then, have students work in small groups to carry out the task in the Study Hint.

Bulletin Board Suggestions

1. Assemble a bulletin board highlighting some bacterial and viral diseases. List the names of different bacterial and viral diseases down the left side of the bulletin board. (You may wish to use Table 1 and Table 2 on p.316 as guides.) Across the top of the bulletin board, write the following heads: *Cause, Transmission, Symptoms, Treatment.* Fill in the information for each disease. Use the bulletin board when teaching Lesson 16-3.

2. Assemble a bulletin board showing how alcohol affects the body. Construct a chart on the bulletin board showing blood alcohol concentration and its effects. Use the table on p.329 as a guide. Use the bulletin board to emphasize that alcohol is a depressant. Ask students a variety of questions based on the chart.

LESSON 16-1
How does the body fight disease? (p. 312)

Teaching Strategies

PREVIEW Before beginning this lesson, have students scan the lesson for the science process skill symbols. Have students identify each skill used in the lesson. Students should then review the definition given for each skill on p.16 of their text.

DISCUSSION To introduce this lesson, ask students to describe the function of a country's military. (defense) Have students name different branches of the military. (army, navy, air force, marines, and so on) Explain that the human body is constantly waging a battle against germs. Just as most countries have different military branches for defense, the body has different lines of defense to fight germs. Then describe the defenses of the human body.

REINFORCEMENT Have students recall what they learned about the digestive, circulatory, and respiratory systems in Units 11, 13, and 14, respectively. Remind students that hydrochloric acid in the stomach destroys germs that enter the stomach. Review the function of white blood cells. Have students describe the roles of nasal hairs, cilia, and mucus found in the respiratory system.

EXTENSION When describing antibodies, you may wish to tell students that antibodies are produced when antigens, or foreign substances, are in the body. Each antibody fights off a specific antigen. You can demonstrate the antibody - antigen reaction with two interlocking pieces of a jigsaw puzzle.

RETEACHING OPTION Display a wall chart or model of the skin that details the several layers and structures within the skin. Have students note the arrangement of the epidermal cells to form a protective layer. Point out that healthy, unbroken skin acts like a barrier to prevent organisms and foreign substances from entering the body. Then describe the other defenses of the human body.

Answers to Challenges (p. 313)
Apply

7. to prevent germs from being spread through the air

8. The bandage acts as a barrier to prevent germs from entering the body.

9. People would be prone to many infections.

Health and Safety Tip

Check students' reports. Answers will vary. Accept all logical responses.

Teaching Tips for Science Connection
Preventive Medicine

REINFORCEMENT Emphasize the importance of preventive medicine. Stress that decisions students make today relative to a healthy life-style will affect their futures.

Questions

1. STATE What are two ways you can help prevent disease? (Students should state two of the ways given in the feature.)

2. Why is it important to have regular yearly checkups by a doctor and dentist? (Regular checkups can help detect any health problems early and the earlier a health problem is caught, the easier it is to treat.)

LESSON 16-2
What is immunity? (p. 314)

Teaching Strategies

PREVIEW Have students write the lesson title and objectives in their notebooks. As students read the lesson, tell them to write down the sentence or sentences that provide the information needed in the objectives.

DISCUSSION To introduce this lesson, discuss an occurrence with which all students should be familiar, receiving a vaccine. Ask students how they think vaccines are helpful to people. Discuss all student responses. Point out that vaccines are one way of getting active acquired immunity. Describe immunity as resistance to a specific disease. Then explain the differences among natural immunity and active and passive acquired immunity.

RETEACHING OPTION Write the following heads on the chalkboard: *Natural Immunity, Acquired Immunity.* From the head *Acquired Immunity,* draw arrows to each of the following heads: *Active Immunity, Passive Immunity.* Describe each kind of immunity and give students examples of each. Have students copy the information in their notebooks under the proper heads.

REINFORCEMENT Be sure students understand that natural immunity is an immunity that people are born with, but that a developing baby receiving antibodies from its mother is an example of passive acquired immunity.

COOPERATIVE/COLLABORATIVE LEARNING Have students work in pairs to answer the Check and Apply questions.

Answers to Challenges (p. 315)

Apply

7. They all provide the body with resistance to disease.

8. Acquired; the antibodies were not produced by the baby.

InfoSearch

You may wish to discuss students' questions and answers as a class.

Teaching Tips for Looking Back in Science
Edward Jenner's Discovery of Vaccinations

EXTENSION Have students find out the recommended schedule for immunizations. Tell students to organize their findings in a chart.

Questions

1. NAME   Who developed the first vaccine? (Edward Jenner)

2. RELATE   Why did Edward Jenner inject material from cowpox sores into people? (so they would produce antibodies to destroy the smallpox virus)

LESSON 16-3
What are some bacterial and viral diseases? (p. 316)

Teaching Strategies

PREVIEW Have students read the lesson feature before beginning the lesson. Discuss the concepts presented in the feature. Ask students how they think this information relates to topics they have already studied or to the lesson they are about to study.

REINFORCEMENT Before beginning this lesson, you may wish to review the characteristics of bacteria and viruses, which were covered in Units 5 and 6.

DISCUSSION To provide motivation for this lesson, list the names of the following diseases on the chalkboard: diphtheria, meningitis, strep throat, tetanus, toxic shock syndrome, pneumonia, and scarlet fever. Challenge students to state what all of these diseases have in common. Point out that they are all caused by bacteria. Then discuss the germ theory of disease.

CLASS ACTIVITY Randomly read out the names of the diseases listed in Table 1 and Table 2 on p. 316. Have students state whether each disease is caused by a bacterium or a virus and describe the symptoms of each disease.

EXTENSION You may wish to tell the students that most disease-causing bacteria are harmful to the body because they produce toxins, or poisons. The poisons damage a cell's life processes.

EXTENSION Have interested students find out how each disease listed in Tables 1 and 2 on p. 316 is spread and how it is treated. Tell students to organize their findings in a table.

Answers to Challenges (p. 317)

Apply

6. Viruses can be seen only with an electron microscope.

7. diphtheria, strep throat

8. mumps

9. fever, low blood pressure

InfoSearch

You may wish to discuss students' questions and answers as a class.

Teaching Tips for Looking Back in Science
Koch's Postulates

REINFORCEMENT After students read this feature, write the four steps of Koch's postulates on the chalkboard. Have students copy the steps in their notebooks.

Questions

1. DEFINE   What is a bacteriologist? (a scientist who studies bacteria)

2. What is the first step of Koch's postulates? (to remove disease-causing bacteria from a diseased animal)

LESSON 16-4
What are antibiotics? (p. 318)

Teaching Strategies

PREVIEW Before beginning this lesson, have students scan the lesson looking for words with which they are unfamiliar. Have students work in pairs or small groups to define each of the words on their lists.

CLASS ACTIVITY Have students look up the meanings of the prefix *anti-* and the term *biotic* in a dictionary. (*anti-*: against; *biotic*: pertaining to life) Then relate the meanings of these words to the definition of antibiotic. Point out that antibiotics are substances that destroy bacteria.

DEMONSTRATION If possible, show students a sample of *Penicillium notatum*, which is the mold most commonly used in penicillin production.

REINFORCEMENT Be sure students understand that some antibiotics are produced by some types of bacteria and used to destroy other bacteria, and that antibiotics do not work against viruses.

RETEACHING OPTION Ask students if they have ever taken penicillin, streptomycin, or tetracyclene. Point out that these three widely used medicines are antibiotics. Define an antibiotic as a chemical substance that kills bacteria. Identify molds as the major sources of antibiotics, but tell students that some bacteria, plants, and animals also produce antibiotics. Then describe the selectivity of antibiotics. Explain that each antibiotic can be used against only certain kinds of organisms.

Answers to Challenges (p. 319)

Check

1. in a part of the dish where some mold had formed

2. penicillin

3. chemical substances that kill bacteria

4. No.

5. They make people sick.

6. molds

7. Alexander Fleming

Apply

8. Yes; the person could become infected with a virus or bacteria against which penicillin has no effect.

9. No.

Skill Builder: Building Vocabulary

Check students' definitions.

Health and Safety Tip

Emphasize the importance of medical ID bracelets.

Teaching Tips for People in Science

Joseph Lister

EXTENSION You may wish to tell students that the development of sterilization techniques also greatly reduced the mortality rate of women after childbirth. Joseph Lister discovered that mortality rates of women could be reduced almost tenfold if midwives washed their hands between patients.

Questions

1. What did Joseph Lister hypothesize about the infections patients got after surgery? (that they were caused by bacteria)

2. **INFER** Why do you think surgeons wear masks over their noses and mouths during surgery? (to prevent germs they may breathe out from infecting patients)

LESSON 16-5
What is heart disease? (p. 320)

Teaching Strategies

PREVIEW Before beginning the lesson, read the list of TechTerms aloud so that students can hear their pronunciations.

CLASS ACTIVITY To introduce this lesson, write the factors contributing to heart disease on the chalkboard: age, family history, gender, smoking, high blood pressure, obesity, physical inactivity, and high cholesterol levels. Then ask a volunteer to go up to the chalkboard and circle any of the risk factors that can be controlled. Discuss the student's selections. Guide students to understand that there are ways they can prevent heart disease. Point out that age, family history,

and gender are the only risk factors for heart disease that cannot be controlled.

DISCUSSION Describe atherosclerosis. Refer students to the picture on p. 320 to illustrate your description.

REINFORCEMENT Be sure that students understand the relationship among high cholesterol levels, atherosclerosis, and heart attacks. Stress that the heart has its own system of blood vessels.

REINFORCEMENT Be sure students understand that the term *heart disease* does not only refer to actual diseases of the heart, but of the blood vessels as well.

Answers to Challenges (p. 321)

Apply

6. The width of the artery stays the same but the size of the opening inside the artery generally decreases with age due to fat buildup.

7. reduce the amount of fatty substances in the diet

8. smoking, high blood pressure, obesity, physical inactivity, high cholesterol levels

9. Answers will vary. Accept all logical responses.

InfoSearch

You may wish to discuss students' questions and answers as a class.

Teaching Tips for Science Connection

Cholesterol

DISCUSSION Ask student what they know about cholesterol. Have students describe advertisements that mention this term. Then discuss the importance of a low cholesterol diet.

Questions

1. How can a person cut back on cholesterol? (by limiting the amount of red meat, eggs, and whole milk dairy products in the diet)

2. **COMPARE** What is the incidence of heart disease in people who eat more fish than red meat compared with people who eat red meat more often? (It is lower.)

LESSON 16-6
What is cancer? (p. 322)

Teaching Strategies

PREVIEW Before beginning this lesson, write the title of each section in the lesson on the chalkboard. Have students copy these titles in their notebooks using an outline format. As students read each section, they should write the topic sentence for each paragraph in the section in their notebooks.

DISCUSSION It is unlikely that any of your students have not heard or used the term *cancer*. Ask students what they think when they hear the word *cancer*. Discuss student responses. Emphasize that cancer is a group of diseases, not a single disorder.

REINFORCEMENT Review the process of mitosis, which is covered in Unit 4. Point out that normal cells usually divide in an orderly manner, while cancerous cells divide in a rapid, uncontrolled way.

DISCUSSION Describe how cancer spreads and some of its causes. Then refer students to Table 1 on p. 322 and discuss the warning signs of cancer.

COOPERATIVE/COLLABORATIVE LEARNING Have a volunteer explain the difference between a benign tumor and a malignant tumor for the rest of the class.

Answers to Challenges (p. 323)

Apply

8. More women are smoking.

Skill Builder: Building Vocabulary

Benign and malignant are antonyms. Answers will vary. Accept all logical responses.

Health and Safety Tip

Emphasize the importance of practicing self-examination on a monthly basis.

Teaching Tips for Technology and Society

Cancer Detection and Treatment

DISCUSSION Describe the various methods used to treat cancer. Some students may be confused by the use of radiation to treat cancer since radiation also can cause cancer. Point out that carefully controlled dosages are used in radiation therapy.

Questions

1. LIST What are four ways to treat cancer? (surgery, radiation, lasers, drugs)

2. What is a problem of using drugs to fight cancer? (The drugs affect normal cells as well as cancerous cells.)

LESSON 16-7
What is AIDS? (p. 324)

Teaching Strategies

PREVIEW Before beginning the lesson, have students review the TechTerms and their definitions and read the Lesson Summary.

CLASS ACTIVITY Have students look up the meaning of each word of the acronym AIDS: acquired; immune; deficiency; syndrome. Tell students to use the meanings of each word to write a brief description of AIDS in their own words.

DISCUSSION Write the term *AIDS* on the chalkboard. Explain the cause, symptoms, and transmission of this fatal disease. Point out that, at this time, there is neither a cure nor a vaccine for AIDS.

CLASS ACTIVITY Have students find and collect recent newspaper and magazine articles about AIDS. Read and discuss the articles as a class.

Answers to Challenges (p. 325)

Check

5. No.

6. No.

Apply

9. to slow down the spread of AIDS among intravenous drug users

10. It prevents infections from overtaking the body.

InfoSearch

You may wish to discuss students' questions and answers as a class.

Teaching Tips for Activity
Investigating the Spread of AIDS

Skills: *calculating, analyzing*

COOPERATIVE/COLLABORATIVE LEARNING Answer the questions as a class.

Questions

1. a. New York **b.** Maryland

2. 394,021

3. Answers will vary. Accept all logical responses.

LESSON 16-8
How do some drugs affect the body? (p. 326)

Teaching Strategies

PREVIEW Before beginning this lesson, read the list of TechTerms aloud so students can hear their pronunciation.

DISCUSSION Most students are aware that drug abuse is a major problem in the United States. Ask students what they think of when they hear the word *drug*. Elicit from students whether they think drugs are "good" or "bad." Then discuss some of the beneficial uses of drugs, as well as the problem of drug abuse. Emphasize the devastating effect drug abuse has on a person's life.

CLASS ACTIVITY Explain the difference between over-the-counter drugs and prescription drugs. Have students name as many over-the-counter drugs as they can. List student responses on the chalkboard. Then classify each drug named as a painkiller, decongestant, antacid, and so on.

EXTENSION Arrange for a speaker from a drug rehabilitation program to talk to your class. An ex-abuser's discussion of his or her own personal experience may have a dramatic effect on young people's attitudes toward drugs.

RETEACHING OPTION Write the following head on the chalkboard: *Commonly Used Drugs*. From this head, draw arrows to each of the following heads: *Depressants, Stimulants, Hallucinogens*. Under *Depressants*, list barbiturates and narcotics. Under *Stimulants*, list cocaine and crack. Under *Hallucinogens*, list LSD and marijuana. Have students copy the chart in their notebooks. Be sure students recognize that crack is a form of cocaine.

Apply

7. Coffee speeds up the action of the central nervous system.

Health and Safety Tip

Emphasize that a person should work with certain products, such as paint thinners, only in well-ventilated areas.

Skill Builder: Classifying

stimulants: amphetamines, nicotine; depressants: heroin, morphine, tranquilizers; hallucinogens: PCP

Teaching Tips for Activity

Reading Drug Labels

Skills: *observing, hypothesizing*

COOPERATIVE/COLLABORATIVE LEARNING Have students work in pairs.

Questions

1. when the drug should no longer be used because it is ineffective

2. how much and how often the drugs should be taken

3. A child weighs less than an adult.

4. Keep this and all drugs out of the reach of children.

3. They think and react more slowly.

4. It harms the body.

5. an alcoholic

Apply

6. Answers will vary. Accept all logical responses.

Health and Safety Tip

Emphasize the danger of mixing alcohol and other drugs.

Skill Builder: Researching

Check students' reports.

Teaching Tips for Activity

Comparing Blood Alcohol Concentration

Skills: *observing, analyzing*

COOPERATIVE/COLLABORATIVE LEARNING Answer the questions as a class.

Questions

1. 0.08–0.09

2. 0.05–0.06

3. Yes; if a person drinks too much too quickly, unconsciousness, coma, and death may occur.

LESSON 16-9

How does alcohol affect the body? (p. 328)

Teaching Strategies

PREVIEW Before beginning this lesson, have students review the TechTerms and read the Lesson Summary.

DISCUSSION Remind students that alcohol is a depressant. Point out that although many people think alcohol is a stimulant, it actually slows down the action of the central nervous system. Ask students to recall the name of the control center of the brain. (the cerebrum) Explain to students that alcohol greatly affects the cerebrum. When alcohol enters the cerebrum, coordination and judgement are impaired and reaction time is slowed.

REINFORCEMENT Emphasize the dangers of drinking and driving. Alcohol-related car accidents are the leading cause of death of young people.

EXTENSION You may wish to tell students that in addition to harming the liver, heavy drinking also can damage the linings of the esophagus, stomach, and small intestine, as well as the heart and the kidneys.

COOPERATIVE/COLLABORATIVE LEARNING Have students quiz each other on the materials in this lesson.

Answers to Challenges (p. 329)

Check

1. ethyl alcohol

2. It slows them down.

LESSON 16-10

How does tobacco affect the body? (p. 330)

Teaching Strategies

PREVIEW Have students write the lesson title and objective in their notebooks. As students read the lesson, tell them to write down the sentence or sentences that provide the information needed in the objective.

REINFORCEMENT Before beginning this lesson, review the functions of the cilia and air sacs found in the respiratory system.

DISCUSSION Bring in a tube of toothpaste specifically made for smokers. Ask students why there is a need for a special toothpaste for smokers. (Tobacco stains the teeth.) Then describe how substances in tobacco also "stain" the lungs. Point out that smokers have a higher death rate from lung diseases than do nonsmokers. Refer students to the picture on 330 showing a healthy lung and a smoker's lung. Tell students to note the destruction of lung tissue in the smoker's lung. Point out that smokers also have a higher risk of heart disease.

DISCUSSION Discuss the reasons people smoke. Ask students how they think peer pressure is involved in the decisions of young people to start smoking. Encourage students to respond to each other's comments.

CLASS ACTIVITY Have students work in groups to create anti-smoking commercials. Then have each group perform its commercial for the rest of the class.

Answers to Challenges (p. 331)

Apply

5. It would reduce a person's ability to exercise.

6. The body is dependent on nicotine.

InfoSearch

You may wish to discuss students' questions and answers as a class.

Teaching Tips for Activity

Classifying Cigarette Advertisements

Skill: *analyzing*

COOPERATIVE/COLLABORATIVE LEARNING Have students work in pairs.

Questions

1. Answers will vary.

2. Answers will vary.

3. a. tobacco companies **b.** American Lung Association; American Heart Association

Answers to Unit Challenges (pp. 332-334)

Understanding the Features: Reading Critically

1. eat a balanced diet, get the proper amount of rest, exercise regularly, keep clean

2. Vaccines enable people to produce antibodies against certain diseases.

3. remove disease-causing bacteria from a diseased animal; isolate and grow the bacteria; inject the bacteria into a healthy animal; remove and compare bacteria when the animal gets sick

4. The use of antiseptics and sterilization reduces the number of post-operative infections.

5. chicken and fish; Accept all logical responses.

6. surgery, radiation, lasers, drugs

Interpreting a Table

1. 0.08–0.09

2. feeling of relaxation

3. 0.50

4. 28 ounces

5. reaction time is slowed; lack of judgement

6. slight loss of coordination

7. 0.40

8. blood alcohol concentration

Critical Thinking

1. They can get AIDS and hepatitis.

2. Answers will vary. Accept all logical responses.

3. Answers will vary. Accept all logical responses.

4. to prevent their germs from spreading

5. Answers will vary. Accept all logical responses.

REPRODUCTION AND DEVELOPMENT (p. 335)

Previewing the Unit

Before beginning this unit, read the titles of the lessons in this unit aloud. As a class, define any terms in the titles with which students are unfamiliar. Then, have students write the lesson titles in their notebooks. As you proceed through the unit, remind students to carry out the task in the Study Hint.

Bulletin Board Suggestions

1. Assemble a bulletin board illustrating human embryonic development. Attach pictures to the bulletin board showing development during each trimester. Label each picture and attach the pictures to the bulletin board in sequence.

2. Assemble a bulletin board illustrating the five stages of the human life cycle. Have students find and collect pictures representing infancy, childhood, adolescence, adulthood, and old age. Attach all the pictures to the bulletin board to make a collage.

LESSON 17-1
What is meiosis? (p. 336)

Teaching Strategies

PREVIEW   Before beginning this lesson, have students scan through the lesson looking for words with which they are unfamiliar. Have students use the Glossary of the text or a dictionary to define each of the terms they have identified.

DISCUSSION   Introduce the term *gametes*. Define gametes as reproductive cells. Tell students that during the formation of gametes, the number of chromosomes is cut in half. Identify this process as meiosis. Guide students to understand that meiosis is a special kind of cell division that takes place only in the formation of gametes. Develop the idea that during fertilization gametes combine. Point out that since each gamete contains half the number of chromosomes present in body cells, the original number of chromosomes is restored in the zygote.

DEMONSTRATION   Using common objects such as pennies, model meiosis for the class.

RETEACHING OPTION   Draw the stages of meiosis on the chalkboard. Use the diagram on p. 336 as a guide. Review each stage of meiosis to help students understand this complex process. Be sure students understand that the diagram begins with a cell that has already undergone chromosome replication.

Answers to Challenges (p. 337)

State the Problem

Students should recognize that the gamete has an extra chromosome.

Skill Builder: Organizing Information

Check students' lists for logic and accuracy.

Teaching Tips for Science Connection
Nondisjunction

CLASS ACTIVITY   After students finish reading this feature have them study the photograph on p. 337 and locate the extra chromosome in the 21st pair.

REINFORCEMENT   Refer students back to the State the Problem exercise. Elicit from students that the gamete shows evidence of nondisjunction.

Questions

1. In what field did B.F. Skinner specialize? (psychology)

2. How does a teaching machine present difficult material? (in a series of small steps)

LESSON 17-2
What are the parts of the female reproductive system?

(p. 338)

Teaching Strategies

PREVIEW   Before beginning this lesson, read the list of TechTerms aloud so students can hear their pronunciations.

DISCUSSION   Refer students to the diagram of the female reproductive system on p. 338. Have students locate each part of the female reproductive system on the diagram as you describe their structures and functions.

REINFORCEMENT   Emphasize that the ovaries are the main organs of the female reproductive system. Point out that the ovaries produce both hormones and egg cells. Remind students that estrogen and progesterone are the two hormones produced by the ovaries.

CLASS ACTIVITY   If possible, have students observe prepared slides of an egg cell under a microscope. Tell students to sketch their observations.

COOPERATIVE/COLLABORATIVE LEARNING   Have students work in pairs to answer the Check and Apply questions.

Answers to Challenges (p. 339)
Skill Builder: Making a Diagram

Check students' diagrams for logic and accuracy.

Teaching Tips for Science Connection
Ectopic Pregnancy

REINFORCEMENT   Before students read this feature, briefly review the function of the uterus. Remind students that an embryo normally develops inside the uterus.

EXTENSION   You may wish to point out that the possibility of an ectopic pregnancy is one reason a woman should see a doctor as soon as she thinks she might be pregnant.

Questions

1. DEFINE   What is fertilization? (the joining together of a sperm cell and an egg cell)

2. IDENTIFY   What are two possible causes of a tubule ectopic pregnancy? (swelling of the oviducts; scar tissue)

LESSON 17-3
What are the parts of the male reproductive system? (p. 340)

Teaching Strategies

PREVIEW Before you begin this lesson, have students read the TechTerms and review the Lesson Summary.

DISCUSSION Point out the structures of the male reproductive system in Figure 1 on p.340. Explain the function of each structure. Point out that the testes are contained in a pocket of skin (the scrotum) that lies outside the body cavity.

EXTENSION As you discuss the role of testosterone in the development of secondary sex characteristics in males, you may wish to point out that in females, secondary sex characteristics are caused by the production of the hormones estrogen and progesterone.

CLASS ACTIVITY If possible, have students observe prepared slides of a sperm cell under a microscope. Tell student to sketch their observations. Have students look for the head and tail of a sperm cell.

REINFORCEMENT Emphasize that in males, the urethra is part of the excretory system and the reproductive system. Point out that both urine and sperm exit the body through the urethra in males. Be sure students understand that in females the urinary and reproductive systems are completely separate.

Answers to Challenges (p. 341)
Skill Builder: Organizing Information

Review students' tables for logic and accuracy.

Teaching Tips for Science Connection
Sexually Transmitted Diseases

EXTENSION Have interested students research the complications that arise if sexually transmitted diseases, such as gonorrhea, syphilis, or chlamydia are left untreated. Tell students to present their findings in an oral report. Have students include a discussion of how sexually transmitted diseases can affect the babies of pregnant women.

Questions

1. LIST What are two sexually transmitted diseases? (gonorrhea and syphilis)

2. HYPOTHESIZE Why is it not possible to get a sexually transmitted disease through casual contact with an infected person? (The pathogens that cause sexually transmitted diseases cannot live outside the body.)

LESSON 17-4
What is menstruation? (p. 342)

Teaching Strategies

PREVIEW Have students write the lesson title and objective in their notebooks. As students read the lesson, tell them to write down the sentence or sentences that provide the information needed in the objective.

DISCUSSION Describe the menstrual cycle. Point out that ovulation and menstruation are the main occurrences of the menstrual cycle.

EXTENSION In order to emphasize the interaction of the endocrine and reproductive systems, you may wish to identify and describe the hormones that regulate the menstrual cycle. A more detailed description also may help students understand the menstrual cycle, although it is not necessary for students to remember the names of the various hormones. At the beginning of the menstrual cycle, the pituitary gland releases follicle stimulating hormone, or FSH. FSH causes an egg to mature. After about 14 days, another hormone produced by the pituitary, luteinizing hormone, or LH, causes ovulation. The ruptured egg follicle forms a corpus luteum, which secretes estrogen and progesterone. These hormones cause the lining of the uterus to thicken. They also stop the release of FSH and LH. After about 10 days, the corpus luteum begins to break apart. Thus, the amount of estrogen and progesterone in the blood decreases. This causes the lining of the uterus to break apart and menstruation to occur. The inhibition of LH and FSH release also stops and the cycle begins again.

REINFORCEMENT Be sure students understand the difference between the menstrual cycle and menstruation. Emphasize that the menstrual cycle is a monthly cycle of change and that menstruation is only one part of the menstrual cycle.

Answers to Challenges (p. 343)
Apply

6. Yes. A female will continue to have a menstrual cycle, regardless of her age, as long as mature eggs are released from her ovaries.

7. In both reproductive systems, hormones trigger the production of sex cells.

8. d, c, b, a

Skill Builder: Diagramming

Check students' diagrams for logic and accuracy.

Teaching Tips for Science Connection
Hormone Therapy

REINFORCEMENT Have students reread the feature on p. 301 about human growth hormone to illustrate how technology has affected hormone therapy.

Questions

1. DEFINE What is a hormone deficiency? (condition in which a person's body does not produce enough of one or more hormones)

2. DEFINE What is hormone therapy? (a way of treating people suffering from a hormone deficiency disease)

LESSON 17-5
How does fertilization take place? (p. 344)

Teaching Strategies

PREVIEW Before beginning this lesson, write the title of each section in the lesson on the chalkboard. Have students copy these titles in their notebooks using an outline format. As students read each section, they should write the topic sentence for each paragraph in the section in their notebooks.

DISCUSSION To provide motivation for this lesson, refer students to the photograph on p. 344 and ask students to describe what they think is shown in the picture. Discuss all student responses. Point out that the photograph shows an egg cell covered with sperm cells. Describe fertilization. Emphasize that only one sperm cell fertilizes an egg cell.

CLASS ACTIVITY Using the diagrams on p. 344 as guides, draw an egg cell and a sperm cell on the chalkboard. Have volunteers come up to the chalkboard and label the parts of each reproductive cell.

COOPERATIVE/COLLABORATIVE LEARNING Have a volunteer explain the difference between ovulation and fertilization for the rest of the class.

Answers to Challenges (p. 345)

Apply

6. Fertilization can occur only during ovulation. Ovulation is the stage of a menstrual cycle during which a mature egg is present in an oviduct.

7. Sperm cells move using their whiplike tails. Egg cells move when the hairs lining the oviduct move them.

8. 23

9. 23

Health and Safety Tip

Answers will vary. Accept all logical responses.

Teaching Tips for Technology and Society

Reproductive Technologies

CLASS ACTIVITY Have students find and collect newspaper and magazine articles pertaining to infertility and methods used by infertile couples, including *in vitro* fertilization. Read and discuss the articles as a class.

Questions

1. Why do you think that babies produced by *in vitro* fertilization sometimes are called "test tube babies"? (Fertilization of these babies occurs in the laboratory.)

2. **HYPOTHESIZE** Why do you think some women are unable to become pregnant? (Answers will vary. Accept all logical responses.)

LESSON 17-6
How does a human embryo develop? (p. 346)

Teaching Strategies

PREVIEW Before beginning this section, have students scan the lesson looking for words with which they are unfamiliar. Have students work in pairs or small groups to define each of the words on their lists.

DISCUSSION Write the following heads on the chalkboard: *Zygote, Embryo, Fetus*. Distinguish between these three stages of embryonic development. Have students copy the information in their notebooks under the appropriate heads.

REINFORCEMENT Emphasize that the blood of a mother and a developing embryo do not mix. Nutrients and wastes are exchanged by the process of diffusion.

ITERDISCIPLINARY CONNECTION Bring a pack of cigarettes to class and read aloud the Surgeon General's warning that smoking by pregnant women may result in fetal injury, premature birth, and low birth weight. Emphasize that everything that enters a pregnant woman, including harmful substances such as drugs, alcohol, and tobacco, cross the placenta and affect the developing embryo.

RETEACHING OPTION Display a variety of pictures showing different stages in an unborn baby's development in front of the classroom. Arrange the pictures in sequence. Have students identify the placenta, the umbilical cord, and the amnion in any pictures in which these structures are evident.

Answers to Challenges (p. 347)

Ideas in Action

You may wish to discuss students' answers.

Teaching Tips for Activity

Graphing Changes in Fetal Development

Skills: *graphing, analyzing*

COOPERATIVE/COLLABORATIVE LEARNING Answer the questions as a class.

LESSON 17-7
What are the stages of human development? (p. 348)

Teaching Strategies

PREVIEW Have students read the lesson feature before beginning the lesson. Discuss the concepts presented in the feature. Ask students how they think this information relates to topics they have already studied or to the lesson they are about to study.

DISCUSSION To introduce the lesson, define the development of an organism as its life cycle. Then ask students to name the stages of the human life cycle. List students' responses on the chalkboard. (Students probably will mention the stages discussed in their textbooks.) Add to the list any of the five stages that students do not mention. Then describe the events that characterize each stage.

REINFORCEMENT Emphasize that many of the traits characterizing old age are lessened by maintaining a healthful lifestyle throughout a person's entire life. Stress to students that decisions they make today will influence their future health. Encourage students to avoid tobacco and alcohol, and to exercise on a regular basis.

COOPERATIVE/COLLABORATIVE LEARNING Have any students with infant siblings describe the learning processes they have observed in their baby brothers and sisters for the rest of the class.

Answers to Challenges (p. 349)

Apply

6. A very young infant does not identify the new person as a stranger. The 9-month old can relate to its environment, and

knows the difference between a stranger and his or her parents.

7. During infancy, muscle development is increasing while during old age, it is declining.

8. childhood

Skill Builder: Organizing Information

Check students' labels for logic and accuracy.

Teaching Tips for Career in Life Science
Day Care Worker

EXTENSION Arrange for a day care worker to visit your class. Have the day care worker describe a typical work day. Tell students to prepare beforehand questions they would like to ask.

Questions

1. What are the educational requirements for a day care worker? (a high school diploma)

2. Why must day care workers be patient and understanding? (They work with young children who are just learning many new skills.)

Answers to Unit Challenges (pp. 350-352)

Understanding the Features: Reading Critically

1. a condition in which chromosome pairs do not separate correctly

2. It can harm the mother if an embryo grows outside the uterus.

3. gonorrhea, syphilis, AIDS

4. Through hormone therapy, a person suffering from Addison's disease can lead a normal life.

5. They might have blocked or missing oviducts.

6. They work with young children.

Interpreting a Diagram

1. 4

2. 2

3. beginning of meiosis

4. One chromosome from each pair is going to the end of the cell.

Critical Thinking

1. They both produce reproductive cells and hormones.

2. These substances will cross the placenta and harm a developing fetus.

3. Answers will vary. Accept all logical responses.

4. The fetus would not be able to get food or oxygen and would die.

5. It happens over and over.

6. Answers will vary. Accept all logical responses.

UNIT 18
HEREDITY AND GENETICS (p. 353)

Previewing the Unit

Read the titles of the lessons in this unit aloud. Identify terms in the titles with which students are unfamiliar. Write these terms on the chalkboard. Using the Glossary of the text or a dictionary, define the terms as a class. Have students write the terms and their definitions in their notebooks.

Bulletin Board Suggestions

1. Assemble a bulletin board showing the use of Punnett squares to predict the inheritance of traits. Draw Punnett squares on the bulletin board and diagram a variety of different crosses. Include at least one cross to show blending, the determination of sex, and the inheritance of sex-linked traits.

2. Assemble a bulletin board illustrating controlled breeding. Divide the bulletin board into three sections. Label each section with one of the following heads: *Mass Selection, Inbreeding, Hybridization.* Have students find and collect pictures of organisms produced by these methods of controlled breeding. Group and attach the pictures under the appropriate heads.

LESSON 18-1
What is heredity? (p. 354)

Teaching Strategies

PREVIEW Have students read the lesson feature before beginning the lesson. Discuss the concepts presented in the feature. Ask students how they think this information relates to topics they have already studied or to the lesson they are about to study.

DISCUSSION Provide motivation for this lesson by asking students if they look like other members of their families. Challenge students to explain their answers. Students probably will refer to characteristics such as eye color, hair color, skin color, and height. List these characteristics on the chalkboard and identify them as inherited traits. Define inherited traits as characteristics that are passed from parents to their offspring.

REINFORCEMENT Have students recall that during fertilization, male and female sex cells join together. Point out that each of the sex cells contains material that determines the inherited traits of the offspring.

COOPERATIVE/COLLABORATIVE LEARNING Have a student explain the difference between heredity and genetics for the rest of the class.

Answers to Challenges (p. 355)
Apply

6. They inherit the traits from the same parents.

7. They are identical twins.

8. Answers will vary. Accept all logical responses.

InfoSearch
You may wish to discuss students' questions and answers as a class.

Teaching Tips for People in Science
Gregor Mendel

CLASS ACTIVITY Bring a variety of pea pods to class to demonstrate some of the traits studied by Mendel. For example, bring in smooth and wrinkled seeds, and green and yellow pods. Have students observe each seed and pod and record their observations.

Questions

1. Why was Mendel able to observe many generations of pea plants? (Pea plants grow and reproduce quickly.)

2. IDENTIFY What was Mendel's original hypothesis? (Traits are passed from parents to offspring.)

LESSON 18-2
What are genes and chromosomes? (p. 356)

Teaching Strategies

PREVIEW Before beginning this lesson, have students review the TechTerms and their definitions and read the Lesson Summary.

REINFORCEMENT Before beginning this lesson, review the processes of cell division and meiosis. Remind students that during cell division, each chromosome makes a copy of itself. Have students recall that meiosis is the special process by which gametes are formed. Ask students to compare the number of chromosomes in gametes and in body cells. (Gametes have only half the number of chromosomes as body cells.) Point out that during fertilization, two gametes combine and the original number of chromosomes is restored in the zygote. Emphasize that since chromosomes control heredity, the zygote receives traits from both parents.

CLASS ACTIVITY Have students look up the meanings of the word parts *chromo-* and *-some* in a dictionary. (*chromo-*: colored; *-some*: body) Ask students how the meanings of these word parts are related to the term *chromosomes*. (Chromosomes are dark-colored structures, or bodies, in the nucleus.)

EXTENSION You may wish to tell students that the German biologist Walther Fleming coined the term *chromosomes* to describe the dark, threadlike particles he observed in the nucleus using a microscope. Fleming made his observations in 1882.

Answers to Challenges (p. 357)
Check

1. in the nucleus of cells

2. its parents

3. along each chromosome

4. genes

5. inherited

Apply

6. One produced by asexual reproduction because it would receive all its chromosomes from one parent cell.

7. Daughter cells would have only half the number of chromosomes as their parent cells.

Ideas in Action

Answers will vary. Accept all logical responses.

Teaching Tips for People in Science

Barbara McClintock

EXTENSION   The term "jumping" genes actually refers to the ability of chromosomes to break apart and join together differently during the formation of eggs or sperm. This process allows each egg and sperm cell to contain a different combination of genes.

Questions

1. INFER   How could Barbara McClintock tell where "jumping" genes occurred? (A "jumping" gene caused changes in the traits controlled by the genes next to the place where it landed.)

2. Why do you think most scientists did not take Barbara McClintock's work seriously in 1951? (Answers will vary. Accept all logical responses.)

LESSON 18-3
How do chromosomes carry traits? (p. 358)

Teaching Strategies

PREVIEW   Before reading this lesson, write the title of each section in the lesson on the chalkboard. Have students copy these titles in their notebooks using an outline format. As students read each section, they should write the topic sentence for each paragraph in the section in their notebooks.

DISCUSSION   Refer students to the diagram on p. 358 showing the structure of a DNA molecule. Compare a DNA molecule to a twisted ladder. Have students locate the sugar molecules and the phosphate groups that make up the sides of the DNA ladder and the nitrogen bases that make up the steps of the ladder. Tell students to note that adenine and thymine, and cytosine and guanine always occur in pairs. Emphasize that the arrangement of nitrogen bases in a DNA molecule determines inherited traits.

CLASS ACTIVITY   Using commercial kits or common items such as styrofoam, toothpicks, pipe cleaners, and so on, have students build models of DNA molecules. Tell students to identify and label each part of a DNA molecule. Display students' models in the classroom.

DEMONSTRATION   Show students a model of DNA replication using a zipper.

REINFORCEMENT   Students may have difficulty understanding the meaning and roles of genes, chromosomes, and DNA. Stress that chromosomes are long strands of DNA. Genes are particular sequences of nitrogen bases in the DNA.

EXTENSION   Students may wonder how the genetic code in DNA controls an organisms traits. You may wish to point out that the traits of all organisms depend on the proteins in their cells. DNA controls the making of proteins. Each particular sequence of nitrogen bases, or gene, codes for a particular amino acid.

Answers to Challenges (p. 359)

Check

1. DNA

2. nitrogen bases

3. cytosine

4. inherited traits

5. by replication

Apply

6. Answers will vary. Accept all logical responses.

7. They will be identical twins.

8. sugar molecules and phosphates

9. No; base C pairs only with base G.

InfoSearch

You may wish to discuss students' questions and answers as a class.

Teaching Tips for Looking Back in Science

Discovering the Structure of DNA

EXTENSION   Have interested students find out about the work of the American biologist Walter Sutton. He developed the chromosome theory, which states that genes are sections of chromosomes. Tell students to write their findings in a report.

Questions

1. LIST   What three scientists discovered the structure of DNA. (Watson, Crick, and Franklin)

2. On what did Rosalind Franklin base her prediction of the shape and composition of a DNA molecule? (X-ray photographs of DNA crystals)

LESSON 18-4
Why can offspring differ from their parents? (p. 360)

Teaching Strategies

PREVIEW   Before beginning this lesson, read the list of TechTerms aloud so students can hear their pronunciations.

DISCUSSION   Provide motivation for this lesson by asking students if they have the same eye color as both of their parents. From the class response, it should become apparent that offspring can have different inherited traits from their parents. Explain how pairs of genes determine an organism's traits.

RETEACHING OPTION   Describe Mendel's work with pea plants. Draw diagrams on the chalkboard to illustrate Mendel's crosses. Introduce and define the terms *pure* and *hybrid*. Follow this with a development of the terms *dominant* and *recessive*.

Answers to Challenges (p. 361)

Apply

6. two tall genes; one tall gene and one short gene

7. No; because the short gene in pea plants is recessive.

8. brown

9. Answers will vary. Accept all logical responses.

Skill Builder: Researching

Check students' posters.

Skill Builder: Defining

The Principle of Dominance: One factor, or gene, for a trait may hide the other gene and prevent it from being expressed in an organism. The Principle of Separation: The two factors for a trait separate, or segregate, during the formation of gametes. The Principle of Independent Assortment: Factors for different traits separate independently of one another during the formation of gametes.

Teaching Tips for Activity

Modeling the Structure of DNA

Skills: *modeling, inferring*

SAFETY TIP Caution students to be careful when using scissors.

COOPERATIVE/COLLABORATIVE LEARNING Have students work in pairs.

Questions

1. a. guanine **b.** adenine

2. a. sugars, phosphates **b.** nitrogen bases

3. No; the sequence of nitrogen bases is not the same in all DNA molecules.

LESSON 18-5

How do genes combine in offspring? (p. 362)

Teaching Strategies

PREVIEW Before beginning the lesson, have students scan the lesson looking for words with which they are unfamiliar. Have students work in pairs or small groups to define each of the words on their lists.

REINFORCEMENT Be sure students understand that the lower case letter of the dominant trait is used to represent a recessive trait. Some students may be tempted to write the first letter of the recessive trait.

DISCUSSION Describe how Punnett squares are used to predict traits. Guide students through the examples shown on p. 362.

CLASS ACTIVITY Have students practice monohybrid crosses using Punnett squares. Have students work in pairs or small groups. Place more able students with students of lesser ability to allow for peer tutoring.

RETEACHING OPTION Draw Punnett squares on the chalkboard and diagram various monohybrid crosses. Identify the dominant trait and the recessive trait for each cross. Have students describe the genetic makeup and appearance of the offspring for each cross.

Answers to Challenges (p. 363)

Apply

6. 2

7. 2

8. Two of the four offspring are hybrids.

InfoSearch

You may wish to discuss students' questions and answers as a class.

Teaching Tips for Activity

Investigating the Effects of Chance on Heredity

Skills: *analyzing, measuring*

COOPERATIVE/COLLABORATIVE LEARNING Answer the questions as a class.

Questions

1. a. unattached ear lobes **b.** attached ear lobes

2. Answers will vary.

LESSON 18-6

How are traits blended? (p. 364)

Teaching Strategies

PREVIEW Before beginning this lesson, have students scan the lesson for the science process skill symbols. Have students identify each skill used in the lesson. Students should then review the definition given for each skill on p.16 of their text.

DEMONSTRATION Put blue food coloring in one cup of water and red food coloring in another. Mix the two cups of water together. The water will turn purple. Relate this activity to blending.

EXTENSION You may wish to tell students that other terms for blending are incomplete dominance and codominance.

REINFORCEMENT Emphasize that blended genes do not disappear. Draw a Punnett square on the chalkboard. Use the Punnett square to show students that blending occurs only in hybrids and that when hybrids are crossed, the pure traits appear again in their offspring.

DEMONSTRATION If possible, bring a white, a red, and a pink four-o'clock flower to class to show students an organism that exhibits blending.

Answers to Challenges (p. 365)

Apply

8. Neither gene is dominant.

9. No blending can occur in organisms that are pure for a certain trait. They have two of the same genes.

Skill Builder: Predicting

Two kittens will have short tails. One kitten will have a long tail and one kitten will not have a tail.

Teaching Tips for Technology and Society
The Human Genome Project

EXTENSION Have interested students contact the National Insititutes of Health (NIH) or the Ethical, Legal, and Social Issues (ELSI) Working Group for more information on social issues concerning the project. Tell students to share their findings with the class.

Questions

1. What are some benefits to mapping the human genome? (treating genetic disorders, preventing genetic disease)

2. What are some ethical issues that a genome map might raise? (random genetic testing and possible discrimination)

LESSON 18-7
How is sex determined? (p. 366)

Teaching Strategies

PREVIEW Have students write the lesson title and objective in their notebooks. As students read the lesson, tell them to write down the sentence or sentences that provide the information needed in the objective.

DISCUSSION Refer students to the photograph of human chromosomes on p. 366. Remind students that humans have 23 pairs of chromosomes. Have students observe pair 23 and describe the difference between the two chromosomes in the pair. Elicit the response that the two chromosomes are not identical. Point out that the chromosome map shown is that of a male. Explain that in humans males have different sex chromosomes called Y. Then describe how chromosomes in a sperm cell determine the sex of offspring. Be sure students understand that the sex chromosomes in females are identical.

REINFORCEMENT Draw a Punnett square on the chalkboard showing the inheritance of sex. Ask students what ratio of offspring will be male (1/2) and what ratio will be female. (1/2)

REINFORCEMENT Be sure students understand that all body cells contain chromosome pair 23. Stress that sex chromosomes are not found only in gametes. Students often have this misconception.

ITERDISCIPLINARY CONNECTION King Henry VIII of England (1491-1541) had some of his wives put to death for failing to bear him sons. His actions had important political and religious ramifications. Point out the irony of Henry VIII blaming his wives for failure to produce sons.

Answers to Challenges (p. 367)
Apply

6. Egg cells, because they all have an X chromosome.

7. 125; The ratio of males produced during fertilization is 1/2.

InfoSearch

You may wish to discuss students' questions and answers as a class.

Teaching Tips for Technology and Society
Amniocentesis

REINFORCEMENT Before students read this feature, read the term *amniocentesis* aloud so that students can hear its pronunciation.

Question

What is amniocentesis? (a test performed during a woman's pregnancy that involves removing amniotic fluid surrounding the fetus to learn about fetal chromosomes and enzyme levels)

LESSON 18-8
What are sex-linked traits?
(p. 368)

Teaching Strategies

PREVIEW Have students read the lesson feature before beginning the lesson. Discuss how they think this information relates to topics they have already studied or to the lesson they are about to study.

DISCUSSION Briefly review the inheritance of sex. Then point out that certain other traits are inherited along with sex. Identify these traits as sex-linked traits. Emphasize that most of the genes for sex-linked traits are found on the X chromosomes.

REINFORCEMENT Using the Punnett square on p. 368, show students how sex-linked disorders are inherited. Stress that because most genes for sex-linked disorders are carried on the X chromosome and are recessive, a woman must be pure recessive to show the trait.

EXTENSION People with normal color vision can sense the three basic colors of red, green, and blue. Colorblind people have reduced ability to see red or green, or both.

COOPERATIVE/COLLABORATIVE LEARNING Have a volunteer show a cross involving a sex-linked disorder to the rest of the class.

Answers to Challenges (p. 369)
Apply

6. by inheriting two X chromosomes carrying the recessive gene for hemophilia

7. One gene is normal and one gene is for the sex-linked disorder.

State the Problem

Acquired characteristics are not passed from parents to offspring.

Teaching Tips for Looking Back in Science
Hemophilia in the Royal Family

CLASS ACTIVITY Show students a pedigree chart for the British royal family. Ask students to name the members of the royal family who were carriers for hemophilia, who suffered from the disorder, and who were normal. Write student responses on the chalkboard.

Question

How many of Queen Victoria's offspring inherited the gene for hemophilia? (three)

LESSON 18-9

What are some inherited diseases? (p. 370)

Teaching Strategies

PREVIEW Before beginning the lesson, write the title of each section on the chalkboard. Have students copy these titles in their notebooks using an outline format. As students read each section, they should write the topic sentence for each paragraph in the section in their notebooks.

DISCUSSION Introduce this lesson by having students recall what they learned about diseases in Unit 16. Remind students that some diseases are caused by bacteria and viruses that enter the body. Then compare infectious diseases and inherited diseases. Point out that an inherited disease is caused by an inherited gene. Stress that people are born with inherited diseases. Identify sickle-cell anemia, Tay-Sachs disease, and PKU as three inherited diseases.

REINFORCEMENT Review the normal structure of red blood cells and the size of capillaries. This review will help students understand the effects of sickle-cell anemia.

DEMONSTRATION If possible, show students slides of sickle cells and normal red blood cells.

EXTENSION People who have PKU lack an enzyme that breaks down phenylalanine to thyroxine. Instead, phenylalanine is converted to phenylpyruvic acid. If left untreated, phenylpyruvic acid damages various organs, especially the brain. A baby who tests positive for PKU is fed a diet lacking phenylalanine, which prevents all symptoms of the disease. You may wish to show students the actual warnings for people with PKU that are on some food labels. The warning states that the food contains phenylalanine.

RETEACHING OPTION Write the following head on the chalkboard: *Inherited Diseases.* From this head, draw arrows to each of the following heads: *Sickle-Cell Anemia, Tay-Sachs Disease, PKU.* Describe the symptoms of each inherited disease. Have students copy the information in their notebooks under the proper heads.

Answers to Challenges (p. 371)

Check

1. an inherited gene

2. They are shaped like a sickle or crescent.

3. a person who inherits one recessive gene and one dominant gene

4. Phenylketonuria is an inherited disease.

Apply

9. Both diseases stop an enzyme from being produced.

10. No; neither parent carries a gene for sickle-cell anemia.

InfoSearch

You may wish to discuss students' questions and answers as a class.

Teaching Tips for Activity
Predicting Tay-Sachs Disease

Skills: *analyzing, predicting*

COOPERATIVE/COLLABORATIVE LEARNING Answer the questions as a class.

Questions

1. hybrid

2. Tt

3. one

4. TT

5. 1 out of 4

LESSON 18-10

Can the environment affect inherited traits? (p. 372)

Teaching Strategies

PREVIEW Before beginning this section, have students scan the lesson looking for words with which they are unfamiliar. Have students work in pairs or small groups to define each of the words on their lists.

DEMONSTRATION Provide motivation for this lesson by demonstrating how the environment might affect inherited traits. Show students two plants, one having received the proper amount of sunlight and one that was kept in a darkened place. Encourage students to describe the plants and to suggest how the unhealthy plant may be helped. Elicit the response that the plant should be put in sunlight. Point out that when the environment of a plant is not right, it will not grow and develop properly.

REINFORCEMENT Emphasize that the genes for traits are not affected by the environment. Only the development of the trait is affected.

EXTENSION Have interested students use library references to research the studies that have been done on identical twins to determine how the environment affects inherited traits. Have students present their findings in an oral report.

Answers to Challenges (p. 373)

Apply

7. lack of sunlight; lack of water

8. No.

9. They would not be able to make vitamin D.

Designing an Experiment

Have volunteers describe their experiments to the rest of the class.

Teaching Tips for Science Connection
Plant Fertilizers

DISCUSSION Bring a bottle of plant food to class. Read out the names of the minerals contained in the plant food. Then discuss why plant food is used.

Questions

1. LIST   What nutrients do the most widely used chemical fertilizers contain? (nitrogen, phosphorus, potassium)

2. Why do plants need nutrients from the soil? (to carry on their food making processes)

LESSON 18-11
How is genetics used to improve living things? (p. 374)

Teaching Strategies

PREVIEW   Before beginning this lesson, read the list of TechTerms aloud so students can hear their pronunciations.

DISCUSSION   Provide motivation for this lesson by asking students to imagine that they are corn farmers. Tell them that as they walk through their corn fields, they notice some corn plants that are taller and look healthier than the others. Ask students to explain what they might do to grow more of these tall, healthier-looking plants. Discuss all student responses. Then describe the different methods of controlled breeding, and in particular mass selection.

CLASS ACTIVITY   Bring in pictures showing the many different breeds of dogs. Hold up each picture in front of the class. Have students identify as many breeds as they can. Point out that purebred animals are produced by inbreeding. Define inbreeding as the mating of closely related organisms.

REINFORCEMENT   When explaining hybridization, be sure students do not confuse organisms that are produced by hybridization, such as mules, with organisms that are hybrid for certain traits.

RETEACHING OPTION   Write the following head on the chalkboard: *Controlled Breeding.* From this head, draw arrows to each of the following heads: *Mass Selection, Inbreeding, Hybridization.* Have students copy this chart in their notebooks. As you describe each method of controlled breeding, have students copy the information under the appropriate head.

Answers to Challenges (p. 375)
Check

1. to produce offspring with certain traits

2. mass selection

3. inbreeding

4. the mating of two different kinds of organisms

5. They are very similar.

Apply

6. They are used to produce organisms with certain traits.

7. Yes; inbreeding involves mating closely related organisms. Hybridization involves mating two different species.

8. Undesirable traits also are passed to offspring.

9. Answers will vary. Accept all logical responses.

InfoSearch

You may wish to discuss students' questions and answers as a class.

Teaching Tips for Career in Life Science
Animal Breeder

EXTENSION   If possible, arrange for a professional animal breeder to talk to your class about his or her work.

Questions

1. RELATE   Why should you enjoy working outdoors if you would like to become an animal breeder? (Most animal breeders work directly with animals outdoors.)

2. IDENTIFY   For what trait is a workhorse bred? (strength)

LESSON 18-12
What is genetic engineering?
(p. 376)

Teaching Strategies

PREVIEW   Before beginning this lesson, have students review the TechTerms and their definitions and read the Lesson Summary.

DEMONSTRATION   Show students a model of gene splicing. Cut out a strip of construction paper. Bend the strip into a circle and staple the ends together to make a DNA chain. Then cut the chain open and insert a strip of different colored construction paper by stapling it to the original strip.

REINFORCEMENT   Be sure students understand that gene splicing is carried out by chemical means on large numbers of bacteria. Some students may envision a scientist snipping open a DNA chain and manually inserting genes.

EXTENSION   You may wish to tell students that pieces of DNA that contain DNA from a different organism are called recombinant DNA.

REINFORCEMENT   Be sure students understand the point of genetic engineering. Remind students that genes control inherited traits. Point out that by inserting human genes into bacteria scientists get bacteria to produce human proteins such as insulin.

COOPERATIVE/COLLABORATIVE LEARNING   Have a volunteer describe the three steps of gene splicing for the rest of the class.

Answers to Challenges (p. 377)
Apply

6. Scientists may use bacteria to produce the enzyme that is lacking by inserting the human gene that codes for the enzyme into the DNA of bacteria.

7. Answers will vary. Accept all logical responses.

Skill Builder: Modeling

Check students' models.

Teaching Tips for Technology and Society

Genetic Engineering

EXTENSION Have students interview an agricultural extension agent or plant scientist to find out about other foods that are genetically engineered. Have students find newspaper articles reporting the information.

Question

What are three proteins that genetically-engineered farm animals can produce in their milk? (an enzyme that fights emphysema, an enzyme that dissolves blood clots, and lactoferin, which fights bacteria)

Answers to Unit Challenges

Understanding the Features: Reading Critically

1. Mendel's hypothesis about inherited traits forms the basis of modern genetics

2. She discovered jumping genes.

3. The two scientists who discoverd the structure of DNA.

4. map all of the human genes; sequence all the base pairs

5. Amniocentesis is performed to obtain fetal cells for doctors to study

6. Queen Victoria's grandchildren married members of other royal families.

7. fertilizer

8. Answers will vary. Accept all logical responses.

9. Genetic engineering can produce tomatoes that taste better.

Critical Thinking

1. Answers will vary. Accept all logical responses.

2. Answers will vary. Accept all logical responses.

3. Sequences of DNA, or genes, code for specific proteins.

4. They show the expected results of various crosses.

5. Answers will vary. Accept all logical responses.

Interpreting a Diagram

1. adenine

2. cytosine

3. thymine

4. guanine

5. Adenine pairs with thymine. Guanine pairs with cytosine.

6. Chromosomes make copies of themselves.

Previewing the Unit

Read the titles of the lessons in this unit aloud. Identify terms in the titles with which the students are unfamiliar. Write these terms on the chalkboard. Using the Glossary of the text or a dictionary, define the terms as a class. Have students write the terms and their definitions in their notebooks.

Bulletin Board Suggestions

1. Assemble a bulletin board illustrating the different kinds of fossils that scientists study to learn about evolution. Attach pictures showing imprints, bones, shells, animals preserved in ice, and so on. Use the bulletin board to point out each type of fossil.

2. Assemble a bulletin board showing the geologic time scale. Draw the geologic time scale on the bulletin board. Fill in the dates for each era, period, and epoch. Attach pictures showing the dominant life forms of each time span.

LESSON 19-1
How are fossils formed? (p. 382)

Teaching Strategies

PREVIEW Have students write the lesson title and objective in their notebooks. As students read the lesson, tell them to write down the sentence or sentences that provide the information needed in the objective.

DISCUSSION Show students pictures or actual samples of fossils. Point out that fossils are the remains, or traces, of organisms that lived long ago. Identify each type of fossil you display and describe how it was formed.

CLASS ACTIVITY If possible, arrange for your class to visit a natural history museum. Have students observe the different types of fossils on display in the museum.

DEMONSTRATION Bring in an ice cube in which you have frozen a small leaf. Point out that freezing is one way extinct organisms have been preserved.

DEMONSTRATION Demonstrate sedimentation. Mix some mud and sand in a jar of water. Allow the jar to stand. Have students observe and describe what happens. (The mud and sand settle in layers.) Point out that the sand and mud are sediments. Relate this demonstration to the formation of sedimentary rocks.

INTRASCIENCE CONNECTION Obtain samples of the sedimentary rocks coquina and shell limestone. Allow students to examine the two types of sedimentary rock. Have students look for shells and fossils in the coquina.

Answers to Challenges (p. 383)
Apply

5. The fossils were buried under sediments before they turned to rock.

6. Answers will vary. Accept all logical responses.

InfoSearch

You may wish to discuss students' questions and answers as a class.

Teaching Tips for Activity
Making Fossils

Skills: *modeling, observing*

COOPERATIVE/COLLABORATIVE LEARNING Have students work in pairs.

Questions

1. Answers will vary. Accept all logical responses.

2. The fossil made with petroleum jelly is the mold. The fossil made without petroleum jelly is the cast.

LESSON 19-2
What is geologic time? (p. 384)

Teaching Strategies

PREVIEW Before beginning the lesson, write the title of each section in the lesson on the chalkboard. Have students copy these titles in their notebooks using an outline format. As students read each section, they should write the topic sentence for each paragraph in the section in their notebooks.

CLASS ACTIVITY To help students understand what is meant by the relative age of rocks, find out the relative height of students. Have all of the students stand. Have one student state how tall he or she is. Then have each student state whether he or she is taller or shorter than the previous student. Point out that students are not stating their exact heights. They are describing their heights relative to other students.

CLASS ACTIVITY Have students work in small groups to make models of sedimentary rock beds. Tell students to use different colors of clay to represent each rock layer. After all groups are finished making their models, have a representative from each group describe the relative ages of the rock layers. Have the student point out which layer is the oldest, which is the youngest, and so on.

DISCUSSION Have students observe the geologic time scale on p. 384. Point out the major divisions on the scale. Read out the names of the eras, periods, and epochs so students can hear their pronunciations. Tell students to note the dominant life forms of each era.

Answers to Challenges (p. 385)
Apply

6. Sediments build up layer by layer.

7. Mesozoic

8. Cenozoic

Skill Builder: Sequencing

F, E, D, C, B, A; Fossil B is younger than fossil D.

Teaching Tips for Science Connection
Radioactive Dating

EXTENSION   You may wish to point out that the carbon-14 radioactive dating method is used only for fossils less than 50,000 years old. Other radioactive dating methods are used for older fossils.

Questions

1. CALCULATE   If you had a 20-gram sample of C-14 today, how much would be left in 5730 years? (10 grams)

2. DEFINE   What is a half-life? (the unit used to measure the rate of decay of a radioactive element)

LESSON 19-3
What is evolution? (p. 386)

Teaching Strategies

PREVIEW   Have students read the lesson feature before beginning the lesson. Discuss the concepts presented in the feature. Ask students how they think this information relates to topics they have already studied or to the lesson they are about to study.

DISCUSSION   Define evolution as the process by which organisms change over time. Be sure students understand that evolution can occur only when there is a change in the gene pool of the population. Remind students that genes control inherited traits. Identify mutation as one way the gene pool of a population can change.

CLASS ACTIVITY   Tell each student to carefully observe four different organisms and list as many different adaptations as they can for each of the organisms they observe. Review students' lists as a class. Have students explain how each organism's adaptations enable the organism to survive in its environment.

COOPERATIVE/COLLABORATIVE LEARNING   Have students work in pairs to answer the Check and Apply questions.

Answers to Challenges (p. 387)
Apply

6. Some mutations cause organisms to die before they reproduce.

Skill Builder: Designing an Experiment

Have volunteers describe their experiments to the rest of the class.

Teaching Tips for Looking Back in Science
The Voyage of the *Beagle*

REINFORCEMENT   Have students trace the path of the *HMS Beagle's* voyage and locate the Galapagos Islands on a world map.

INTRASCIENCE CONNECTION   During his voyage on the *Beagle*, Darwin also observed how earthquakes and other geologic processes could change the land. These observations influenced Darwin's ideas about evolution. He began to think that organisms would have to adapt to such changes in their environment.

Questions

1. What was the purpose of the voyage of the *HMS Beagle?* (to prepare maps and to observe and collect specimens of various plants and animals)

2. What did Darwin infer about the 13 species of finches in the Galapagos Islands? (They had evolved from a common ancestor.)

LESSON 19-4
What is natural selection? (p. 388)

Teaching Strategies

PREVIEW   Before beginning this lesson, have students scan the lesson for the science process skill symbols. Have students identify each skill used in the lesson. Students should then review the definition given for each skill on p.16 of their text.

DISCUSSION   Describe the four main ideas of Darwin's theory of evolution: overproduction, competition, variation, and survival of the fittest. Be sure students understand the evolution of a new species occurs over a long period of time.

CLASS ACTIVITY   Bring in a variety of pictures showing members of the same species. Hold up each picture in front of the class. Tell students to observe how variations occur among members of the same species. Ask students to describe how the organisms shown in each picture are alike and how they are different.

REINFORCEMENT   Darwin's theory of evolution is often difficult for students to understand. Be sure students understand that the environment does not cause evolution. The environment only determines which variations will be selected.

EXTENSION   Have students research the work of Alfred Russell Wallace. Wallace was a British scientist who influenced Darwin's theory of evolution. Tell students to write their findings in a report.

Answers to Challenges (p. 389)
Apply

4. a. Variation   **b.** Struggle   **c.** Survival

Skill Builder: Researching

Check students' reports. Lamarck's theory of evolution was based upon acquired characteristics being passed on from parents to offspring.

Teaching Tips for Activity
Modeling Natural Selection

Skills: *modeling, hypothesizing*

SAFETY TIP   Caution students to be careful when using scissors.

COOPERATIVE/COLLABORATIVE LEARNING Have students work in pairs.

What evidence supports evolution? (p. 390)

Teaching Strategies

PREVIEW Before beginning this lesson, have students scan the lesson looking for words with which they are unfamiliar. Have students work in pairs or small groups to define each of the words on their lists.

DISCUSSION Have students study the diagrams on p. 390 showing the evolutionary history of the horse. Emphasize that the fossil record of the horse is very complete. Compare the earliest horse to the modern horse. Point out the ways horses have changed over time. Tell students to note that the size of horses has changed. Ask students to describe other ways horses have changed. (The number of toes and the structure of the legs have changed.)

EXTENSION You may wish to tell students that in addition to the fossil record, the study of living things also has revealed important evidence of evolution. There is evidence of evolution from anatomy, embryology, and biochemistry.

EXTENSION Have each student research one species of dinosaurs. Tell students to write their findings in reports. Encourage students to include pictures in their reports.

Answers to Challenges (p. 391)

Check

1. The most complete fossil record of evolutionary change is that of the horse.

2. that changes have taken place throughout the earth's history

3. Nobody knows for sure.

4. about 400 different species

5. about the size of a small dog

Apply

6. Answers will vary. Accept all logical responses.

7. It has become bigger.

Skill Builder: Measuring and Calculating

1 mm = 100 mm

Teaching Tips for Looking Back in Science

The Moths of Manchester

REINFORCEMENT Be sure students understand that the example of the moths of Manchester illustrates natural selection, not evolution.

Question

EXPLAIN Why did the population of the black moths increase after coal-burning factories were built? (Soot given off by the factories changed the color of the tree trunks from gray to black. This enabled the black moths to blend in with the tree trunks, and thus, fewer black moths were eaten by birds.)

How have humans changed through time? (p. 392)

Teaching Strategies

PREVIEW Before beginning this lesson, have students review the TechTerm and its definition and read the Lesson Summary.

DISCUSSION Refer students to the pictures of hominid skulls on p. 392. Have students compare the size of the skulls as you describe human evolution. Emphasize the trend toward increasing brain size.

REINFORCEMENT Draw a time line on the chalkboard highlighting human evolution.

EXTENSION Have interested students find out about one of the following hominid species: *Australopithecus afarensis*, *Australopithecus africanus*, *Homo habilis*, *Homo erectus*. Tell students to describe the characteristics of the species they choose in oral reports. Be sure students identify where, when, and by whom the species was discovered.

INTRASCIENCE CONNECTION Neanderthals lived during the Ice Age in Europe. They lived in caves and used fire to keep warm.

COOPERATIVE/COLLABORATIVE LEARNING Have one student describe the characteristics of Neanderthals for the rest of the class. Have another student describe Cro-magnons.

Answers to Challenges (p. 393)

Check/Apply

6–7. Answers will vary. Accept all logical responses.

Skill Builder: Building Vocabulary

Anthropo- means human. It comes from the Greek word *anthropos* meaning man. *-Logy* means study of. It comes from the Greek word *logia*.

Ideas in Action

Answers will vary. Accept all logical responses.

Teaching Tips for People in Science

The Leakeys

CLASS ACTIVITY Have students find and collect articles written by the Leakeys in *National Geographic*. Read and discuss the articles as a class.

Questions

1. IDENTIFY What is the goal of most anthropologists? (to trace the evolutionary development of humans.)

2. Where was "Upright Human" discovered? (Kenya, Africa)

Answers to Unit Challenges (p. 394-396)

Understanding the Features: Reading Critically

1. to prepare maps and observe and collect specimens of various plants and animals

2. Answers will vary. Accept all logical responses.

3. Anthropologists use carbon-14 to date fossils.

4. Mary Leakey and Richard Leakey both discovered "Handy Man." Richard Leakey also discovered "Upright Human."

Critical Thinking

1. All the carbon-14 would be changed to nitrogen.

2. A variation is a difference in a trait among individuals of the same species. A mutation is a change in a gene.

3. The long-necked giraffes were able to reach the leaves of trees. They were better able to compete and survive in the environment. Thus, they reproduced and passed on the trait of being long-necked to their offspring.

4. Answers will vary. Accept all logical responses.

5. Answers will vary. Accept all logical responses.

Interpreting a Table

1. eras, periods, epochs

2. Cenozoic

3. 225 million years

4. a scale showing the living things dominating each era in the earth's history

5. Paleocene

6. Cretaceous

7. primitive apes
8. Cenozoic, Mesozoic, Paleozoic, Precambrian

9. 0.025 million years ago

Internet Addresses and Other Resources for
CAREERS IN LIFE SCIENCE

The Student Edition of *Concepts and Challenges* introduces students to many exciting careers in life science. Following are both street and Internet addresses of organizations to which your students can write for more information on the careers highlighted in this book. Encourage students to pursue information about careers that interest them.

UNIT 1
Lesson 1-1
Career in Life Science: Wildlife Biologist (p. 15)

CONTACT
U.S. Department of the Interior
Fish and Wildlife Service
18th and C Street, NW
Washington, DC 20210

ON THE INTERNET
http://www.fws.gov/

UNIT 3
Lesson 3-1
Career in Life Science: Air Pollution Technician (p. 53)

CONTACT
Air and Waste Management Association
1 Gateway Center, Third Floor
Pittsburgh, PA 15222

ON THE INTERNET
http://www.awma.org/

UNIT 4
Lesson 4-8
Technology and Society: Cornea Transplants (p. 93)

CONTACT
Eye-Bank for Sight Restoration, Inc.
210 East 64th Street
New York, NY 10021

UNIT 5
Lesson 5-5
Career in Life Science: Florist (p. 109)

CONTACT
Society of American Florists
1601 Duke Street
Alexandria, VA 22314

ON THE INTERNET
http://www.safnow.org/

UNIT 10
Lesson 10-1
Career in Life Science: Animal Technician (p. 195)

CONTACT
American Veterinary Medical Association
1931 North Meacham Road
Schaumburg, IL 60173

ON THE INTERNET
http://www.avma.org/

UNIT 11
Lesson 11-4
Career in Life Science: Nutritionist (p. 221)

CONTACT
American Dietetic Association
216 W. Jackson Boulevard, Suite 800
Chicago, IL 60606-6995

ON THE INTERNET
http://www.eatright.org/

UNIT 12
Lesson 12-5
Career in Life Science: Exercise Specialist (p. 249)

CONTACT
The American Alliance for Health,
Physical Education, Recreation and Dance
1900 Association Drive
Reston, VA 20191

ON THE INTERNET
http://www.aahperd.org/

UNIT 18
Lesson 18-6
Technology and Society: Human Genome Project (p. 365)

CONTACT
National Human Genome Research Institute (NHGRI)
9000 Rockville, 31 Center Drive
Bethesda, MD 20892

ON THE INTERNET
http://www.nhgri.nih.gov/

TEACHER NOTES